Agency, Freedom, and Responsibility in the Early Heidegger

New Heidegger Research

Series Editors:

Gregory Fried, Professor of Philosophy, Boston College, USA

Richard Polt, Professor of Philosophy, Xavier University, USA

The New Heidegger Research series promotes informed and critical dialogue that breaks new philosophical ground by taking into account the full range of Heidegger's thought, as well as the enduring questions raised by his work.

Titles in the Series:

After Heidegger?
Edited by Gregory Fried and Richard Polt

Correspondence 1949–1975
Martin Heidegger, Ernst Jünger, translated by Timothy Quinn

Existential Medicine
Edited by Kevin Aho

Heidegger and Jewish Thought
Edited by Micha Brumlik and Elad Lapidot

Heidegger and the Environment
Casey Rentmeester

Heidegger and the Global Age
Edited by Antonio Cerella and Louiza Odysseos

Heidegger Becoming Phenomenological: Preferring Dilthey to Husserl, 1916–25
Robert C. Schaff

Heidegger in Russia and Eastern Europe
Edited by Jeff Love

Heidegger's Gods: An Ecofeminist Perspective
Susanne Claxton

Making Sense of Heidegger
Thomas Sheehan

Proto-Phenomenology and the Nature of Language
Lawrence J. Hatab

Heidegger in the Islamicate World
Edited by Kata Moser, Urs Gösken and Josh Michael Hayes

Time and Trauma: Thinking Through Heidegger in the Thirties
Richard Polt

Contexts of Suffering: A Heideggerian Approach to Psychopathology
Kevin Aho

Heidegger's Phenomenology of Perception: An Introduction, Volume I
David Kleinberg-Levin

Confronting Heidegger: A Critical Dialogue on Politics and Philosophy
Edited by Gregory Fried

Proto-Phenomenology, Language Acquisition, Orality and Literacy: Dwelling in Speech II
Lawrence J. Hatab

Transcending Reason: Heidegger's Transformation of Phenomenology
Edited by Matthew Burch and Irene McMullin

The Fate of Phenomenology: Heidegger's Legacy
William McNeill

Agency, Freedom, and Responsibility in the Early Heidegger
Hans Pedersen

Agency, Freedom, and Responsibility in the Early Heidegger

Hans Pedersen

ROWMAN & LITTLEFIELD
Lanham • Boulder • New York • London

Published by Rowman & Littlefield
An imprint of The Rowman & Littlefield Publishing Group, Inc.
4501 Forbes Boulevard, Suite 200, Lanham, Maryland 20706
www.rowman.com

6 Tinworth Street, London SE11 5AL, United Kingdom

Copyright © 2020 by Hans Pedersen

All rights reserved. No part of this book may be reproduced in any form or by any electronic or mechanical means, including information storage and retrieval systems, without written permission from the publisher, except by a reviewer who may quote passages in a review.

British Library Cataloguing in Publication Information Available

Library of Congress Cataloging-in-Publication Data

Library of Congress Control Number: 2020942903

ISBN: 978-1-78661-255-7 (cloth : alk. paper)
ISBN: 978-1-5381-4832-7 (pbk : alk. paper)
ISBN: 978-1-78661-256-4 (electronic)

∞™ The paper used in this publication meets the minimum requirements of American National Standard for Information Sciences—Permanence of Paper for Printed Library Materials, ANSI/NISO Z39.48-1992.

Contents

Acknowledgments		ix
List of Abbreviations for Heidegger's Works		xi
Introduction		xiii
1	A Heideggerian Theory of Motivation	1
2	The Heideggerian Argument against Causal Theories of Action	31
3	The Role of Deliberation in Heideggerian Agency	59
4	Heideggerian Freedom and the Free Will Debate	83
5	Heideggerian Responsibility—Responsibility as Responsiveness	113
6	Concluding Thoughts	147
Bibliography		159
Index		163

Acknowledgments

This project has had a long gestation period, and many more people have provided me with insight, encouragement, and help along the way than I can list here. I do, though, want to acknowledge some of those people here. During my graduate studies, I was fortunate enough to be taught by three excellent Heidegger scholars—Michael Gelven, Theodore Kisiel, and Charles Guignon—all of whom contributed to shaping the way that I understand Heidegger, specifically, and philosophy, more generally. Charles, especially, as my *Doktorvater*, provided voluminous feedback on my work and greatly influenced my approach to writing about Heidegger.

My colleagues in the philosophy department at Indiana University of Pennsylvania have been very accommodating over the course of the last year, as each of them has taken on some extra work to spare me from the most onerous teaching and service obligations. I am especially grateful for the comments that Mary MacLeod and Brad Rives provided on the first two chapters of this work. I am also grateful to my students over the years, who have always forced me to consider how I can do better in making convoluted philosophical terminology more tractable and connected to their lived experience.

On a personal level, my parents were always incredibly supportive of my decision to pursue philosophy, first, as a student and, then, as a professor. They likewise encouraged and nurtured in me a general intellectual curiosity and openness from a very young age. My mother, Rebecca, deserves special mention for her assistance with proofreading the draft of this book. Finally, I would like to thank my wife, Faye, for putting up with me during this process, helping with the formatting of the final draft, and being my most ardent "publicist."

List of Abbreviations for Heidegger's Works

The following texts are cited parenthetically in this book. Other texts are cited in notes and listed in the Bibliography.

SZ: Martin Heidegger, *Sein und Zeit* (Tübingen: Niemeyer, 1953). The pagination of this edition is included in GA 2; in *Being and Time*, tr. John Macquarrie and Edward Robinson (New York: Harper & Row, 1962); and in *Being and Time*, tr. Joan Stambaugh, rev. Dennis J. Schmidt (Albany: State University of New York Press, 2010). I will note in the parenthetical citation when I modify the translation; otherwise, translations are those of the Macquarrie and Robinson translation.

GA: Martin Heidegger, *Gesamtausgabe* (Frankfurt am Main: Vittorio Klostermann, 1975). Cited in the following format: (GA volume number: German page/translation page). I will note in the parenthetical citation when I modify the translation; otherwise, translations are those of the listed translators.

GA 9. *Wegmarken* (1919–1961). Ed. Friedrich-Wilhelm von Herrmann, 1976, 1996 (rev. ed.)./*Pathmarks*. Ed. William McNeill. Cambridge: Cambridge University Press, 1998.

GA 18. *Grundbegriffe der aristotelischen Philosophie* (1924). Ed. Mark Michalski, 2002./*Basic Concepts of Aristotelian Philosophy*. Tr. Robert D. Metcalf and Mark Basil Tanzer. Bloomington: Indiana University Press, 2009.

GA 19. *Platon: Sophistes* (1924–25). Ed. Ingeborg Schüßler, 1992./*Plato's "Sophist."* Tr. Richard Rojcewicz and André Schuwer. Bloomington: Indiana University Press, 1997.

GA 22. *Die Grundbegriffe der antiken Philosophie*. Ed. Franz-Karl Blust. 1993, 2004 (1926)./*Basic Concepts of Ancient Philosophy*. Tr. Richard Rojcewicz. Bloomington: Indiana University Press, 1997.

GA 26. *Metaphysische Anfangsgründe der Logik im Ausgang von Leibniz* (1928). Ed. Klaus Held, 1978, 1990 (2nd rev. ed.), 2007 (3d rev. ed.)./*The Metaphysical Foundations of Logic*. Tr. Michael Heim. Bloomington: Indiana University Press, 1984.

GA 29/30. *Die Grundbegriffe der Metaphysik. Welt—Endlichkeit—Einsamkeit* (1929–30). Ed. Friedrich-Wilhelm von Herrmann, 1983./*The Fundamental Concepts of Metaphysics: World, Finitude, Solitude*. Tr. William McNeill and Nicholas Walker. Bloomington: Indiana University Press, 1995.

GA 31. *Vom Wesen der menschlichen Freiheit. Einleitung in die Philosophie* (1930). Ed. Hartmut Tietjen, 1982, 1994 (rev. ed.)./*The Essence of Human Freedom: An Introduction to Philosophy*. Tr. Ted Sadler. London: Continuum, 2002.

GA 61. *Phänomenologische Interpretationen zu Aristoteles. Einführung in die phänomenologische Forschung* (1921–22). Ed. Walter Bröcker und Käte Bröcker-Oltmanns, 1985, 1994 (rev. ed.)./*Phenomenological Interpretations of Aristotle: Initiation into Phenomenological Research*. Tr. Richard Rojcewicz. Bloomington: Indiana University Press, 2008.

Introduction

At the most general level, when we develop a philosophical account of action, we aim to analyze what exactly is going on when we "do stuff" in the broadest sense of the term. What is happening when I go get a drink from the kitchen? What is happening when I am writing a paper? The most common way of analyzing our actions in philosophical work on action theory in the past several decades is through reference to various mental states and their causal efficacy. If someone asks why I am going to the kitchen to get a drink, I might very well reply that I am thirsty and that I think there are drinks in the kitchen. Thinking through this answer more carefully and trying to say something clearer about the process that brings the action about, one might say that I have a desire for something to drink (another way of saying that I am thirsty) and that I have a belief that I can find something to drink in the kitchen. It is then the combination of this desire and this belief that causes my action of going to the kitchen. Though it often gets much more complicated and sophisticated, this is in essence the account of action found in much contemporary philosophy of action—some combination of discrete mental states causes our actions.

This common understanding of action then often serves as the presupposition for the long-running and interconnected debates over the existence of free will and moral responsibility.[1] If we understand our actions as being caused by certain mental states, it naturally follows to wonder whether these mental states have prior causes. If there is a long causal chain leading up to the immediate causes of our actions, a causal chain that extends well beyond ourselves as agents, then it begins to seem quite likely that there are problems with our normal assumptions about our ability to control our own lives and actions. This leads to the worry that we are not in fact free. Instead, all of our actions are causally determined. Going a step further, if we begin to have doubts on our ability to freely perform actions, then it seems like there will also be doubts about the degree to which we are responsible for our actions. This leads to the roughly tripartite division of positions in the contemporary free will debate. One can be a libertarian and argue that there are at least some cases where our actions are not causally determined, in which case we act with free will and can be responsible for our actions. At the other end of the spectrum, one could argue that all of our actions are causally determined, and this fact eliminates the possibility of any meaningful sense of free will or responsibility. Compatibilists take the middle path of arguing that our actions could very well be causally determined, but this fact does not rule out the possibility of having meaningful senses of freedom or responsibility. Again, of course, this oversimplifies the issues, as there has been an enormous amount of philosophical and general intellectual effort expended trying to think through the nature and truth of causal determinism and its implications for human action and moral responsibility, but I think this description captures the essence of the problem in its most general form and the array of responses to it. This, in very simplified, succinct form, is what I take to be the understanding of agency, freedom, and responsibility found in much mainstream philosophical work on these topics.

In this work, I will try to use Heidegger's early thought, by which I mean roughly his work in the 1920s and early 1930s, to develop an alternative account of the three central concepts of agency, freedom, and responsibility and the connections between them. Before going further into the actual substance of this volume, I want to offer some reflections on the methodological approach I take here. I am taking the approach to Heidegger scholarship arguably pioneered by Hubert Dreyfus and taken up by his students and those influenced by them, which attempts to develop a sort of rational reconstruction of Heidegger's views that can be put into conversation with mainstream, Anglo-American, or "Analytic," philosophical accounts of the same concepts and can be seen as a plausible alternative to such accounts.

I do, of course, recognize that there are potential downsides to taking this approach. From the perspective of Heidegger scholars, I suspect there are several potential issues. First, my interpretation of Heidegger does not take into consideration all of Heidegger's work over the course of his whole life or even all of his early work from the 1920s and 1930s. Rather, as indicated above, I am seeking to use Heidegger's thought to develop accounts of agency, freedom, and responsibility that can provide plausible and interesting alternatives to the accounts of these ideas found in much mainstream philosophical discussion of these topics. This means that I do neglect certain areas of Heidegger's work that might not fit with the main thrust of the account I am developing. Second, Heidegger very explicitly tries to reformulate various central philosophical issues so that we are not bound to think about them using the linguistic and conceptual framework of mainstream philosophy. This, I believe, is the reason for many of his difficult neologisms and convoluted forms of expressions. So, while there might be some benefit to my attempts here to clarify what Heidegger is saying so that it can be understood by those less well-versed in his thought, this also runs the risk of undoing his attempts to break out of the conceptual constraints and presuppositions of the mainstream philosophical tradition. Third, there is sometimes a tendency to criticize this approach to interpreting Heidegger as overly "ontic" as opposed to properly ontological, to use his terminology. As the reader will see as this volume progresses, I try to regularly use examples of concrete actions and what brings them about to make sense of what Heidegger is saying, and there is a worry that by doing so, I am reducing Heidegger's thought to a sort of philosophical anthropology or psychology that seeks to understand human existence from consideration of specific behaviors and mental phenomena instead of getting at the more fundamental issue of the ontological structure of human existence as such, which is Heidegger's real aim.

There is another potential issue with my methodological approach that presents itself from the other direction. Philosophers working in the mainstream tradition might still find the Heideggerian position I present too opaque and the arguments underdeveloped. I do not claim to give thorough accounts of the state of the literature with regard to philosophy of action or the free will debate. Instead, with the possible exception of chapter 3, which deals with the role of deliberation in action, I will begin every chapter with a brief synopsis of some prominent views in the mainstream philosophical debate that I feel can be fruitfully contrasted with the Heideggerian view I develop. I also do not claim to present thorough, definitive arguments against the mainstream views of action, free will, and responsibility. I do probably go beyond what Heidegger explicitly states at times to make his views more plausible, and I do try to provide Heideggerian responses to potential criticisms of the interpretation I develop. However, I have tried to walk that difficult line of staying more or less true to his thought while making it as plausible as possible to scholars with little background in Heidegger and more familiarity with the mainstream work on these subjects. There are certainly places where Heidegger's texts provide scant resources for fleshing out particular positions or responding to objections, so I recognize that there are some holes or at least weak spots in the account I develop if one is looking for a generally defensible philosophical account of these issues.

So, one might very well ask why I should take this particular approach if I recognize that it is unlikely to satisfy a large number of Heidegger scholars, and it is unlikely to satisfy philosophers working in the mainstream of research on agency, free will, and responsibility. My rather optimistic hope is that readers from both camps can find something of interest here. Heidegger scholars can perhaps see new avenues through which to extend Heidegger's thought and argue for its continued relevance, and Analytic philosophers might see a different approach to considering some of these fundamental issues that, while still underdeveloped, bears promise. From the perspective of Heidegger scholars, I think it is important to try to demonstrate what is interesting and relevant about Heidegger's thought to the general, contemporary philosophical discourse. It is now approximately a century since Heidegger began as a lecturer at Freiburg and started delivering what we now recognize as his influential early lecture courses that put him on the path to *Being and Time* and philosophical "stardom." At this temporal remove from the beginning of his career, it cannot be taken for granted that Heidegger will have anything like a central place in the philosophical canon going forward, especially given his notorious and reprehensible political views and his extremely difficult writing style. Anecdotally, I have had discussions with many students and colleagues who express some variation of this sentiment: "Well, Heidegger's thought sounds somewhat interesting, but his work is almost impossible to read, and he was a Nazi, so I think I will forego any serious engagement with him." If Heidegger scholars are interested in keeping Heidegger scholarship alive in the larger discipline of philosophy, which is itself under attack in the current intellectual milieu, we must engage in this project of making the case for Heidegger's continued relevance. I do take the views I develop here to be more or less consistent with Heidegger's own views and to make sense of at least certain passages and works in his early thought, and I do think that the work presented here highlights various themes running through many of Heidegger's early lecture courses and provides something like a coherent interpretation of the first decade or so of Heidegger's thought from the particular perspective of what he has to say about agency, freedom, and responsibility. In this sense, I consider this to be a work of Heidegger scholarship, which I hope helps to clarify and unify some aspects of his early work. I do not pretend that I am unique in taking this approach, as I am clearly following many other Heidegger scholars who frame their work similarly, but I do think it is worthwhile to clearly lay out the rationale for this approach to Heidegger scholarship and make something of a case for its appeal.

With regard to those philosophers working in the mainstream of philosophy of action, free will, and responsibility, I hope they can see in this work at least some interesting, even if underdeveloped, alternatives to the presuppositions that drive the debate over free will and responsibility. It is my view that the current state of the free will debate is one of stalemate. Different philosophers have meticulously staked out the variety of arguments that are logically possible within the available conceptual framework and have dug in for trench warfare. Almost all philosophers are libertarians, compatibilists, or hard determinists—the three main views on free will available once it is accepted that our actions are to be fundamentally understood in causal terms. The movement that there is in the debate largely seems to be with regard to the fairly small details of these possible stances on free will. As we will see as this work unfolds, I attempt to develop an account of agency that is not understood in causal terms at a fundamental level. Once the presupposition of a causal understanding of action is removed, that opens up the possibility of a very different way of understanding freedom, and in turn, a different way of understanding responsibility. One of the things that I have always greatly appreciated about Heidegger's philosophical approach is that he does not rush into trying to develop solutions for whatever is considered a "pressing philosophical problem." Instead, he first tries to dig out the ontological presuppositions that give rise to the problem in the first place and then proposes an alternative ontological framework out of which the problem does not arise. So, even if those scholars engaged in the mainstream debates on these issues disagree with the particulars of the Heideggerian view I put forward or find parts of it to be underdeveloped, I hope my work here can spur some reflection on the ontological framework that makes the free will debate possible in its current form and perhaps even further scholarship that aims not so much at staking out and defending a position within the structure of the current debate but instead seeks ways to dissolve the debate altogether.

Before moving on to providing an outline of the structure of the work to follow, I also wanted to situate the substance and method of my work within the context of existing work on Heidegger's views on agency, freedom, and responsibility. There are scholars, who, contra the Dreyfusian approach, have taken a purely more historical approach, according to which the aim is to trace the development of Heidegger's thought on agency from his early work to his later. In particular, there are two book-length works of exemplary scholarship that I have in mind: Reiner Schürmann's *Heidegger on Being and Acting: From Principles to Anarchy* and Bret Davis's *Heidegger and the Will: On the Way to Gelassenheit*.[2] Both works aim to show how Heidegger, in his early thought, begins with an understanding of agency that is still similar to traditional philosophical accounts, even if Heidegger does introduce important variations, and then as Heidegger's thought evolves, his conception of agency becomes radically different from that found in the mainstream tradition. For Schürmann, the focus for Heidegger's early understanding of agency, as exemplified by *Being and Time*, is the idea of making one's actions one's own by explicitly choosing the principles on which one acts. Though with obvious differences, this account of agency fits reasonably well in the Kantian tradition that is concerned with the autonomy of the individual. Schürmann makes the case that as his thought evolves, Heidegger shifts to an anarchic account of agency, according to which action should neither strive to proceed from a firm ground or principle (from an *archē*, generally speaking) nor strive to aim at some fixed goal or *telos*. Davis's work on Heidegger follows a similar trajectory, though Davis uses the language of the will and willing to chart its course. Davis shows how in his early work, coming to a head in his 1930 lecture, *The Essence of Human Freedom*, Heidegger is still following that Kantian and Nietzschean tradition that focuses on the autonomy of the will and willful self-creation. In his later work, Heidegger moves toward the ideal of *Gelassenheit*, a sort of letting oneself be moved to act or letting actions happen through oneself, that overturns the traditional focus on the importance of the individual will.

I will not substantially engage with these approaches to Heidegger's account of agency here. I think that the basic interpretation of the evolution of Heidegger's thought on this issue put forward by Schürmann and Davis is essentially right, but pushing so far into Heidegger's later thought, I feel that the possibility for a fruitful confrontation with the mainstream Analytic work on agency, free will, and responsibility is lost to a great extent. In his later works, Heidegger has gone so far beyond the usual framework for thinking about action that it becomes very hard to use his work to raise questions about the mainstream Analytic accounts in the way that I want to do here. Also, I do admit to finding Heidegger's early work, with its careful analysis of everyday human experience and action, more tractable and more compelling than his later work in the sense that the later work seems almost to willfully defy being connected back up with lived experience of the world. Heidegger certainly has his reasons for deconstructing and moving away from the conceptual framework of the philosophical tradition and the application of this framework in understanding our everyday lives, but I always try to abide by what I take to be one of the guiding principles of the early Heidegger—finding concrete phenomenological attestation for the conceptual apparatus one is building. That is, any conceptual framework developed by a philosopher that claims to explain some aspects of human existence should manifest itself in our lived experience, at least if we pay attention in the proper way. I find this search for attestation much easier to do when working with Heidegger's early work, which is more closely connected to traditional phenomenology and its emphasis on detailed description of lived experience, than his later work, though this perhaps is a failing on my part to properly understand the latter.

I would say that there are two scholars in particular who share my methodological approach and, in their works, do give substantive accounts of Heideggerian agency, freedom, responsibility, and the interconnections between them. One is, of course, Dreyfus himself. He establishes the basic parameters for his Heideggerian account of agency in his commentary on *Being and Time* titled, *Being-in-the-World: A Commentary on Heidegger's* Being and Time, *Division 1*.[3] He further develops various aspects of this account of agency in subsequent essays. The other scholar, whom I found myself increasingly citing while working on this volume, is Steven Crowell. I believe that in his volume of collected essays, *Normativity and Phenomenology in Husserl and Heidegger*, there emerges a fairly consistent overarching account of the central concepts of agency, freedom, and responsibility, even if it was not necessarily his explicit intention to work out such an account.[4] While these two scholars have certainly influenced the way that I think about Heidegger's views on these issues, there will, of course, be differences on specific issues between my view and theirs, and I will point out these differences as this volume unfolds. For now, I would like to suggest a general difference between my work here and theirs. I do think that my work is unique insofar as I explicitly try to develop a Heideggerian account of agency, show what Heideggerian freedom would be given that view of agency, and then show what Heideggerian responsibility would be given those views of agency and freedom. So, I think that my work has a bit more cohesion and structural unity than that of Dreyfus or Crowell on these issues, though, again, it should be remembered that neither set themselves the specific task of working out an interconnected theory of all three concepts.

SUMMARIES OF THE CHAPTERS

With those general considerations out of the way, I will now proceed to give summaries of the chapters to give the reader a better sense of where I am headed with things and how all of this is supposed to fit together. The first chapter develops a Heideggerian theory of motivation to serve as the foundation for the chapters that follow it. In the general sense, a theory of motivation attempts to lay out the fundamental aspects of human agency that bring about our actions. This is in essence laying out the ontological structure of agency. I develop a Heideggerian theory of motivation through contrast with the Humean theory of motivation, which is still a fairly common view in much contemporary philosophy of action and moral psychology. According to the Humean theory of motivation, human actions can be analyzed and explained by reference to beliefs and desires that lead to the action. I will focus here on Heidegger's early lecture courses, in which he analyzes and interprets key aspects of Aristotle's practical philosophy on the way to presenting his own "existential analytic" of human existence in *Being and Time*. In these early lecture courses, we can find something like the Humean focus on beliefs and desires as the main components of action, but Heidegger, through his appropriation of Aristotle, expresses this a bit differently. For Heidegger, there is a "conative" component of agency that is responsible for the pull we feel toward performing certain actions that roughly fills the role of desire on the Humean view. Similarly, there is what I call the "orienting" component of agency that directs the conative component toward particular actions. This orienting component roughly fills the role of belief on the Humean view, though I will highlight important differences between the Heideggerian and Humean views as that chapter unfolds. I will then show how these conative and orienting components of action morph into *Sorge* (care) in *Being and Time*. Specifically, Heidegger locates them in the basic existential structures of disposedness (*Befindlichkeit*), the feeling of being pulled toward things in the world that matter to us, and understanding (*Verstehen*), the understanding of ourselves as persons of a certain sort that structures our experience of the world and allows certain actions to stand out as important.

The second chapter will focus on Heidegger's view of the connection of causality to human action. Heidegger departs from causal theories of action by attempting to show that the fundamental ontological features of human existence have a temporal structure that is incompatible with our normal conception of causality. Heidegger claims that we have tended to understand causality in large part in terms of temporal succession.[5] Typically, we think if one event consistently precedes another, then the first event is likely the cause of the second. This conception of causality aligns well with the understanding of time as a series of successive "nows," with each present "now" passing out of existence and giving rise to a future "now." However, Heidegger makes the case that human existence is best understood as stretching back into the past and forward into the future and that at any point, the present moment of our existence is made possible only by this temporal stretching out. The future and past interact reciprocally to give rise to the present, a temporal movement that is more circular than the linear temporal progression assumed by common conceptions of causality. The conative component of agency, disposedness in *Being and Time*, is the "past-directed" aspect of human existence, while the orienting component is the "future-directed" aspect of human existence. If this is right, then human agency, which arises through the interaction of the conative and orienting components, cannot be causal at the fundamental level. I will argue, however, that Heidegger does not think that causality has no role at all to play in our actions. I make the case that events do have a causal influence on our actions, but this causal influence is itself made possible by the underlying, noncausal interaction of the conative and orienting components.

The third chapter deals with the role of deliberation in action. The structure of this chapter will be somewhat different, since as far as I can tell, there is no consensus position on the role and nature of deliberation in action in mainstream philosophy of action scholarship. Instead, I put forward my account of Heideggerian deliberation in contrast to the competing interpretation developed by Dreyfus and adopted by many Heidegger scholars following him.

Dreyfus argues that explicit deliberation is absent in our activity, except in cases of breakdown, where our normal, nondeliberative activity fails, and we must explicitly think through how to proceed. I will argue that there is a more expansive role for deliberation in Heidegger's conception of agency than Dreyfus allows. Specifically, I will aim to show that deliberation is an extension of the orienting component of agency, and thus, built into the fundamental structure of agency, not something that occurs only when our normal process of acting fails. The basic idea is that orienting articulates the world around us in such a way that certain actions stand out as meaningful, and deliberation is the more fine-grained articulation of the situation of action. In other words, when we deliberate, we are further refining the general articulation of the situation of action provided by our broader self-understandings so that certain courses of action stand out as meaningful.

In the fourth and fifth chapters of the volume, I develop Heideggerian accounts of freedom and responsibility that build upon the account of action developed in the earlier chapters. As has already become clear, the Heideggerian accounts of these concepts will have to differ quite a bit from the mainstream accounts of freedom or responsibility that rely on a causal analysis of human action. I do think, though, that Heidegger shares a key concern with the traditional approaches to these problems, namely, the concern over whether or not we can be the basis or ground of our actions, even if Heidegger's approach to this issue will be noncausal. This concern perhaps most obviously manifests itself in Division II of *Being and Time* in Heidegger's discussion of authentic existence, but the exploration of freedom and responsibility is also a recurring theme in his lecture courses throughout the late 1920s into the early 1930s.

Chapter 4 attempts to work out a Heideggerian account of freedom built around two of the main concerns of the contemporary free will debate—the abovementioned concern about being the ground of our actions and the necessity of being able to pursue alternative courses of action. In our normal, everyday thinking, it is common to think that for there to be free will, we must as agents be the ground of our actions, and we must have the ability to choose between different courses of action. The three basic positions in the contemporary free will debate can be characterized in terms of their views on these two basic questions. Libertarians would agree that both conditions are necessary for free will and that both conditions actually hold for us as agents, at least in some circumstances. Hard determinists would agree that both conditions are necessary for free will but would deny that either condition holds. Compatibilists often argue that the ability to choose alternative courses of action is not necessary for free will but that there still is some sense in which we can be the ground for our actions that can serve as the basis for free will and being responsible for our actions.

My first step in developing a Heideggerian stance on these two basic issues is to try to get clear on what Heidegger means by freedom in his early thought. There are two plausible interpretations of Heideggerian freedom from this period. One is the sort of existential freedom that is most associated with the account of authenticity in Division II of *Being and Time* and focuses on the resolute choice of the individual agent to adopt particular self-understandings. The second interpretation of freedom, which I focus on, is derived mainly from his lecture courses in this period, where he frequently discusses freedom in terms of "freeing up" entities encountered in the environment to be what they are. This way of thinking about freedom seems to make it a much more general ontological characteristic of human existence as opposed to something primarily associated with the realm of human action. While acknowledging that Heidegger himself probably does want freedom to have this broader ontological connotation, I will make the case that there is still a way to connect freedom as "freeing up" to the sort of more mundane actions considered in the first part of the book. For Heidegger, we free entities to be what they are insofar as we open up a clearing in which entities can come to presence. I will argue that the general account of agency developed in the first part allows for the connection of this sense of freedom to our normal actions in that it is our capacity to take on various self-understandings that opens the space in which things, people, and events can provide the motivation for us to act. That is, freedom in the narrower domain of human action is a subspecies of this broader, ontological freedom. So, I will make the claim that all human beings are free in that we all open, through our capacity to project ourselves toward some specific self-understanding, a space in which there can be things that motivate us to act. In this way, we are the ground for our actions, which provides the Heidegger response to the first concern of the mainstream free will debate. I then consider what is meant by Heidegger's frequent claim that this sense of freedom has a certain "binding" character. I ultimately argue that Heidegger's view aligns to some extent with mainstream compatibilists in that he does think we are the ground of our actions, but it is not necessary that we have the ability to pursue alternative courses of action to be free. The difference, of course, between the Heideggerian view and mainstream compatibilism is that the Heideggerian view is noncausal, while mainstream compatibilists still understand agency, freedom, and responsibility in causal terms.

The fifth chapter develops a Heideggerian conception of responsibility that is built upon the preceding accounts of agency and freedom. As with freedom, responsibility, on the Heideggerian view, cannot be understood fundamentally in terms of causality, as is often the case in the mainstream philosophical debate. Instead of understanding responsibility in terms of causality, we can use Heidegger's thought to develop a conception of responsibility as responsiveness. This conception of responsibility focuses on the root word "respond" (the German equivalent would be *Verantwortlichkeit* and *antworten*, "answer") and interprets Heidegger as endorsing responsiveness, not being the cause of one's own actions, as the key aspect of responsibility. I want to start fleshing out this general idea by first considering to what exactly a responsible agent is responsive. I will posit two different modes of responsibility, each of which is characterized by a different form of responsiveness. I will call the sort of responsibility that is potentially exhibited in our everyday actions first-order responsibility. If an agent exhibits this sort of responsibility, that means that they are responsive to the pull to perform the actions necessary to enact their operative self-understandings, those self-understandings that orient their everyday actions. I will make the case that second-order responsibility is to be understood in terms of the main aspects of authentic existence as laid out in *Being and Time*. The responsiveness in second-order responsibility is not the responsiveness to the pull to perform a certain action or even to take on a particular self-understanding. Instead, second-order responsibility is constituted by being responsive to enacting a different mode of existence or agency—authentic agency. This is why I decided to use the "first-order" and "second-order" designations. First-order responsibility has to do with everyday actions and the ways we can fail or succeed at enacting specific self-understandings, while second-order responsibility, as we will see, has to do with the second-order issue of enacting a different stance toward one's being as an agent altogether.

NOTES

1. Robert Kane briefly touches on the connection between causal theories of action and the free will debate in chapter 6 of his *A Contemporary Introduction to Free Will* (Oxford: Oxford University Press, 2005).

2. See Reiner Schürmann, *Heidegger on Being and Acting: From Principles to Anarchy* (Bloomington, IN: Indiana University Press, 1987) and Bret Davis, *Heidegger and the Will: On the Way to Gelassenheit* (Evanston, IL: Northwestern University Press, 2007).

3. Hubert Dreyfus, *Being-in-the-World: A Commentary on Heidegger's* Being and Time, *Division 1* (Cambridge, MA: MIT Press, 1991).

4. Steven Crowell, *Normativity and Phenomenology in Husserl and Heidegger* (Cambridge: Cambridge University Press, 2013).

5. I will briefly consider whether Heidegger is overly simplistic and reductive in his understanding of causality in chapter 6.

Chapter 1

A Heideggerian Theory of Motivation

It is somewhat difficult to pick a starting point from which to develop a Heideggerian account of action, as Heidegger never explicitly attempts to develop a well-defined "theory of action" of the sort that one finds in contemporary philosophy of action literature. Heidegger does, though, spend considerable time describing and analyzing everyday, practical human existence and the ontological structures underlying it, especially in his early work on Aristotle in his lecture courses leading up to the publication of *Being and Time*. So, to try to get an initial handle on what a Heideggerian account of action would look like, I will start by considering what a Heideggerian theory of motivation would look like. Generally speaking, when philosophers of action use the phrase "theory of motivation," they mean a theory that attempts to give an account of the process that brings about our actions. Considering a theory of motivation, then, perhaps gets at the most basic question of human agency. Taking a cue from the root of the word "motivation," a theory of motivation attempts to say what it is that moves us to act.

In this chapter, then, I intend to develop a Heideggerian theory of motivation through a juxtaposition with what has often been called the Humean theory of motivation. Although it is not clear that Hume himself actually endorsed this view, it is based on interpretations of and extrapolations from Hume's famous claim: "Reason is, and ought only to be, the slave of the passions, and can never pretend to any other office than to serve and obey them."[1] Put very succinctly, according to the Humean theory of motivation developed from this passage, human actions can be analyzed and explained by reference to the beliefs and desires that lead to the action. We have desires for certain things, and on the basis of the beliefs we have about how to satisfy those desires, we undertake various actions. For instance, my action of walking to the kitchen can be explained in terms of the combination of my desire to eat something and my belief that I will find something to eat in the kitchen. Though far from the consensus view in current philosophy of action scholarship, the Humean theory has held and continues to hold a prominent place in much contemporary philosophy of action and moral psychology. Donald Davidson emphasizes the role of desires and beliefs in explaining action in his influential work "Actions, Reasons, and Causes."[2] Robert Audi, in his article "Intending," does much the same thing but uses the term "want" in place of "desire."[3] Michael Smith provides a defense of the Humean theory of motivation in his "The Humean Theory of Motivation."[4] Most recently, Neil Sinhababu has defended the Humean theory, first in several articles and then in his book titled, *Humean Nature: How Desire Explains Thought, Action, and Feeling*.[5] As is made apparent by Audi's use of "want" instead of "desire," we need not be exclusively focused on the term "desire" here. Davidson too makes this clear by saying that he is talking about what he calls "pro-attitudes" of all sorts, inclusive of "desires, wantings, urges, promptings, and a great variety of moral views, aesthetic principles, economic prejudices, [and] social conventions," whatever "can be interpreted as attitudes of an agent directed toward actions of a certain kind."[6] What is important is that on all variations of this view, actions are brought about by the combination of two components: some pro-attitude that provides the push to act and some doxastic state that provides direction with regard to how to accomplish what is desired.

By comparing the Humean theory of motivation with the Heideggerian account that I develop, I can show how the Heideggerian account has some similarities to mainstream contemporary philosophy of action and also how his thought differs in important and interesting ways. Specifically, I will make the case that the Heideggerian theory of motivation shares with the Humean theory the general idea that actions occur through the combination of a conative component and an orienting component, which serves to direct the impetus to act provided by the conative component. As will become clear, I do not want to claim that Heidegger thinks that we have beliefs in the normal usage of the term "operative" in our actions, but he does maintain that there has to be something which orients desire and channels it toward a specific end.

OUTLINE OF A HEIDEGGERIAN THEORY OF MOTIVATION

Life as Movement

In several lecture courses in the early- to mid-1920s, Heidegger devotes considerable time to analyzing Aristotle's definition of life. The essential feature of life for Aristotle is movement. In his early lecture course, *Phenomenological Interpretations of Aristotle*, in the winter of 1921–1922, he claims,

"Elsewhere, people speak of process, stream, the flowing character of life. This latter way of speaking is motivated by and follows a fundamental aspect in which we encounter life, and we take it as a directive towards the ensemble of the basic structures of life as movement, motility" (GA 61, 113–115/85). Two years later, toward the very beginning of his 1924 lecture course, *Basic Concepts of Aristotelian Philosophy*, Heidegger emphasizes that, for Aristotle, the basic aspects of the soul (*psuchē*), that which makes living beings alive, are "*krīnein* and *kineīn*—the 'setting apart and determining' and the 'moving-itself' in the world, the moving about in the world" (GA 18, 44–45/32). Going forward another two years, at the end of the 1926 lecture course *Basic Concepts of Ancient Philosophy*, Heidegger briefly discusses Aristotle's conception of life (*zoē*) in *De Anima*.[7] There, he gives the following general definition of a living being: "We say something is living where we find that: it moves in an oriented way, i.e., in a way oriented by perception; it moves itself and can stop itself; it was young and ages; it takes in nourishment and grows; etc."[8] The basic determination operative in the movement of living beings is the determination of whether something is beneficial or harmful. Indeed, the "world in natural being-there is not a fact that I take notice of; it is not an actuality or reality. Rather, *the world is there for the most part in the mode of the beneficial and the harmful, of that which uplifts or upsets being-there*" (GA 18, 47–48/34). As we will see, he thinks that human activity is more complicated, but it is built from this basic foundation.

In the *Basic Concepts of Aristotelian Philosophy* lecture course, Heidegger broadens the claim that animals experience the world in terms of the harmful and beneficial by stating that the "world is there in living in such a way that living, being-in-itself, always *matters* to it in some way" (GA 18, 50–51/36). In the later 1926 lecture course, Heidegger repeats this language when he goes on to further clarify what is meant by moving in an oriented way, as he says that the motion of living beings is "different than the change of place to which lifeless things are subject . . . to move oneself toward something which matters to life in one way or another; an oriented motion in the respective surrounding world."[9] It is now not just that living beings are oriented in their movement by what is harmful or beneficial but rather they are oriented by this broader notion of things that matter. Here the key determination of life is oriented motion understood as motion toward something that matters. The self-orienting ability possessed by animals, *krīnein* in the Greek, or the capacity for distinguishing, is *aīsthesis* (perception). "The *aīsthesis* of animals," Heidegger states, "is not a theoretical capacity; on the contrary, it exists in a context of pursuit and flight."[10] Again, he is making it clear that animals immediately perceive the environment around them in terms of what matters—what is beneficial to them or what harms them. Perception is this fundamental capacity to distinguish things from one another in the environment that allows for oriented movement.

The Role of *ōrexis* in the Action of Animals

Now up to this point in this section, I have not said anything about the Humean theory of motivation or how a Heideggerian theory of motivation might contrast with it. Indeed, Heidegger does not spend much time discussing the key concepts of the Humean theory: desires and beliefs. However, I think the basis for this comparison starts to take shape when we consider his interpretation of Aristotle's conception of *ōrexis* (commonly translated as desire) and show how this becomes a key term, not only in his reading of Aristotle but also as a key for understanding how the Aristotelian framework of his early lectures serves as the basis for Heidegger's more familiar analysis of human agency in *Being and Time*.[11] It is here that my reconstruction of Heidegger's views moves beyond the focus on how the world around us is experienced or perceived and starts to get into the structure of human agency as such.

As we have already seen for Heidegger, life is movement. Having established that living beings are characterized by their ability to move themselves toward something that matters to them, Heidegger proceeds to discuss Aristotle's consideration of the basis of motion (*archē kinēseos*). Aristotle states that it is the object of desire (*orektōn*) that is the basis of movement. For Aristotle, it is the object of desire that brings about the motion of a living being.[12] As Aristotle states in *De Anima*, "in every case the mover is the object of desire" (433a27), and the "first mover of all is the object of desire, since it moves us without being moved" (433b12).[13] Suppose a lion sees a gazelle and then proceeds to chase it. According to Aristotle's account, the gazelle is the object of desire. Upon seeing the gazelle, the lion's desire to eat the gazelle is stirred into motion. The desire in turn pulls the lion into motion in pursuit of the gazelle. In this way the gazelle causes movement but is itself unmoved.

What Heidegger chooses to highlight in this seemingly straightforward understanding of the movement of living beings is the specific conception of desire (*ōrexis*) at work here. For Heidegger, one of the important and interesting things about Aristotle's account is that the "point of departure for the motion is not the pure and simple observation of a desirable object" and that "it is not the case that the living being first observes things disinterestedly, merely looks about in a neutral attitude, and then moves toward something; on the contrary, *ōrexis* is fundamental."[14] What this shows is that living beings have a fundamental openness to being affected by the world, which allows things immediately to appear to them as desirable or undesirable. There is found in *ōrexis* not only the urge toward the object of desire but also the capacity to experience things in the world as desirable or as mattering in some way. Heidegger expresses this dual aspect of *ōrexis* when he describes it as "feeling oneself attuned in such and such a way, feeling well and ill, and thus also being on the lookout for" (GA 22, 185–187/156).

Now one may ask why Heidegger emphasizes the importance of distinguishing (*krīnein*) for life, and hence, the motion of living beings. It is apparent that when a living being moves toward an object of desire, the living being has distinguished that particular object as something desirable. The capacity of *ōrexis* to reveal objects as desirable is the capacity to distinguish objects from one another, at least insofar as their desirability is concerned. Remember that for Aristotle the object of desire is the basis of motion. However, living beings can only be moved by the desirable object if they take it as something desirable. Returning to the example of the lion and the gazelle, the gazelle does prompt desire to move the lion, but the gazelle can only do this in the first place because the lion sees the gazelle as something to be eaten.[15] For animals, this distinguishing takes place through perception (*aīsthesis*). Perception here is not to be thought of as a straightforward sensing of things in the world in terms of their objective qualities, but rather "it exists in a context of pursuit and flight."[16] In other words, perception is always already oriented toward seeing things as desirable (worthy of pursuit) or detrimental (worthy of being avoided).

The emerging picture of the structure of animal action is as follows. Desire does provide the conative component of action, but here it is thought of as a pull out toward something encountered in the environment. It is, after all, the object of desire that activates desire and serves as the true basis of the movement. Having a desire, desiring, is thus reconceived as being drawn toward something encountered in the environment rather than an internal state that provides a "push" to initiate movement purely from within the animal. However, desire cannot be activated without some perceptive capacity that allows the animal to encounter the environment in terms of what is harmful and beneficial or, more broadly, important and unimportant. This is what I will call the "orienting" aspect of action. Heidegger conjoins the orienting component with the conative component of action in his early discussions of *ōrexis*, but as I will proceed to show, we can pull apart these two aspects of action and provide deeper analysis of them separately while still acknowledging their fundamentally intertwined nature.

The Conative Aspect of Agency

We see this location of both the conative and orienting aspects of actions in desire carry over into *Being and Time* with Heidegger's choice of care (*Sorge*) as the fundamental characterization of human existence. However, we will now begin to tease apart these dual aspects of action and consider them separately. Throughout his early lecture courses, and really carrying through *The Fundamental Concepts of Metaphysics* lecture course in 1929–1930, Heidegger uses different, but related, terms to try to get at that feeling of being pulled toward certain things and activities, which he finds to be characteristic of the conative component of action. As early as the 1921/1922 lecture, *Phenomenological Interpretations of Aristotle*, Heidegger describes one basic movement of life in terms of *Neigung*, which can be translated as "inclination," saying, "This categorial sense, inclination, is included in the relationality of life itself and imparts to life a peculiar weight, a direction of gravity, a pull toward something" (GA 61, 99–100/75). Here the idea is to capture the basic sense in which the motivational force behind our actions comes from our being pulled out by the things in the world about which we care, by the things that matter to us. In the *Basics Concepts of Aristotelian Philosophy*, Heidegger spends a fair amount of time analyzing the *pāthe*, passions or affects, and what it means to be moved by something. He maintains that the "*pāthe* are not 'psychic experiences,' are not 'in consciousness,' but are a being-taken of human beings in their full being-in-the-world. That is expressed by the fact that the whole, the full occurrence-context, which is found in this happening, in being-taken, belongs to the *pāthe*" (GA 18, 197–198/133). In other words, he is claiming that the passions are not merely psychological states but rather indicate a basic aspect of human existence, this fundamental aspect of "being-taken" by the world in which we find ourselves or inexorably being drawn toward certain things or activities.

It is relatively easy to see how these early Aristotelian formulations of life in terms of inclination and "being taken" are transformed into Heidegger's analysis of Dasein in terms of *Befindlichkeit*, *Geworfenheit*, and *Stimmung* in *Being and Time*. There, Heidegger talks about thrownness (*Geworfenheit*) as the "facticity of [our] being delivered over" (SZ, 135), and he says of disposedness (a reasonably good translation for *Befindlichkeit* here) that it is a "disclosive submission to the world, out of which we can encounter something that matters to us" (SZ, 137). Indeed, in the section in which he discusses moods and disposition, Heidegger drops in what would be a strange reference to Aristotle, stating, "Aristotle investigates the *pāthe* in the second book of his *Rhetoric*. . . . What has escaped notice is that the basic ontological Interpretation of the affective life in general has been able to make scarcely one step forward worthy of mention since Aristotle" (SZ, 138–139). Once we trace Heidegger's focus on this sense of being pulled out toward things that matter to us from his early lectures to *Being and Time*, it makes perfect sense for him to be thinking of Aristotle here.

The Orienting Aspect of Agency

Now we can consider how the orienting aspect of action works in human agency. For humans, action has the same basic structure as that of animals, but humans possess the ability to make distinctions in more sophisticated ways than animals. In the case of human beings, "*krīnein* is not limited to *aīsthesis* but is also found in *noūs*."[17] Heidegger here references the five intellectual virtues discussed by Aristotle in Book VI of the *Nicomachean Ethics* (*tēchne*, *epistēme*, *phrōnesis*, *noūs*, and *sophīa*) as being the five modes of distinguishing specifically available to human beings. It might seem strange that Heidegger here characterizes the intellectual virtues as modes of distinguishing. Heidegger explains this interpretation of the virtues to some extent in his earlier 1924 lecture course titled, *Plato's Sophist*. Heidegger's interpretation of the intellectual virtues in this lecture begins with and is guided by Aristotle's characterization of the intellectual virtues as "five states in which the soul grasps the truth in its affirmations and denials" (1139b15).[18] In Heidegger's words, the intellectual virtues are "five ways human Dasein discloses beings in affirmation and denial" (GA 19, 20–21/15). What Heidegger means by this is that in Aristotle's description of the intellectual virtues, Aristotle is describing the various ways that we as human beings can understand things in the world and ourselves. According to Heidegger, some of the modes of distinguishing (i.e., intellectual virtues) correspond with certain types of movement. For example, the movement of *poīesis* corresponds with the virtue of *tēchne*. The virtue of *tēchne* characterizes the way in which we understand things in the world in terms of their usefulness for our projects. *Poīesis* is the activity (or movement in a broad sense) of making or producing something. Heidegger maintains that the movement of *prāxis*, or properly human action, corresponds to the virtue of *phrōnesis*.[19] For Heidegger, *phrōnesis* is the capacity through which we understand ourselves as certain types of people, and indeed, through which we understand what it is to be human more generally. The sort of actions characterized by *prāxis*, then, are not those that serve in the production of some object but rather those that make us a certain type of person. Heidegger uses Aristotle's example of the doctor to make this point. The doctor might act with the goal of healing the patient's ailment, which is an example of *poīesis*, but this action simultaneously serves to make the doctor who they are, and thus also counts as *prāxis*. With respect to other intellectual virtues, Heidegger claims that no corresponding movement is associated with them. According to Heidegger, there is no movement corresponding to *epistēme*, "since *epistēme* is theory and simply beholds," while the movement associated with the virtue of *noūs* is "not attained by humans; it determines the first mover."[20]

While his early lectures do not deal much with the orienting component of action, Heidegger clearly fleshes this out in *Being and Time* through his analysis of understanding (*Verstehen*).[21] It is ultimately understanding as a fundamental component of human existence that accounts for the creation of distinctions, which in turn allows things encountered in the world to have the pull on us that they do. Though this is a frequently explicated bit of

Heidegger's thought, I do want to recount the basics here to make sure that my interpretation is clear and on firm ground. Building on the analysis of *poīesis* and *tēchne* in the earlier Aristotle lecture courses, Heidegger, in *Being and Time*, describes our everyday existence as one in which we are primarily engaged in various projects and experience entities in the world in terms of their usefulness for these projects. In one of his much referenced examples involving a hammer, Heidegger says:

> With the "towards-which" of serviceability there can again be an involvement: *with* this thing, for instance, which is ready-to-hand, and we accordingly call a "hammer", there is an involvement in hammering; with hammering, there is an involvement in making something fast; with making something fast, there is an involvement in protection against bad weather; and this protection "is" for the sake of providing shelter for Dasein—that is to say, for the sake of a possibility of Dasein's Being. (SZ, 84)

We can be engaged in the project of trying to protect ourselves from the elements, and so would naturally see putting siding on a house as serving this aim. In turn, we would see a hammer as something that can be used in order to "make the siding fast," that is, get it to stay in place on the side of the house. We exist, he claims, in a "totality of involvements," where entities encountered are understood as useful for achieving certain aims, and those aims are useful for achieving others. The hammer, the siding, and even the action of hammering are not completely unrelated objects and events, but rather they exist in an interconnected web of involvement. Heidegger explains the central importance of that overarching for-the-sake-of-which that structures this web of involvements as follows:

> But the totality of involvements itself goes back ultimately to a "towards-which" in which there is *no* further involvement: this "towards-which" is not an entity with the kind of Being that belongs to what is ready-to-hand within a world. . . . This primary "towards-which" is not just another "towards-this" as something in which an involvement is possible. The primary "towards-which" is a "for-the-sake-of-which". But the "for-the-sake-of" always pertains to the Being of Dasein. (SZ, 84)

That for the sake of which we act is ultimately not some completed project or some further action. Instead, Heidegger is claiming that that for the sake of which we act is always a possibility of our being. In his example of putting up siding, he suggests that we are beings who need shelter, and it is this aspect of our being as needing shelter that provides the web of involvements that allows all of the entities and actions to be what they are.

Heidegger goes on to define understanding in terms of this idea of the for-the-sake-of-which. He states that in the "'for-the-sake-of-which', existing

Being-in-the-world is disclosed as such, and this disclosedness we have called 'understanding'. In the understanding of the 'for-the-sake-of-which,' the significance which is grounded therein, is disclosed with it" (SZ, 143). Understanding, for Heidegger, just is that opening up of a web of involvements that allows things and activities to take on significance. He goes on to claim the structure of understanding is "projection," and specifically, "understanding projects Dasein's being both upon its 'for-the-sake-of-which' and upon significance, as the worldhood of its current world" (SZ, 145). The suggestion here is that understanding is not the mere intellectual grasp of a particular aspect of one's being but rather that the sort of existential understanding that Heidegger has in mind involves living toward the enactment of a certain way of being.

Connecting this back to our analysis of Heidegger's earlier lecture courses on Aristotle, we can say that our projection toward certain possible ways of being creates distinctions between different possible actions. It makes some appear beneficial and worthwhile, others detrimental, and others do not even register and remain in the background of insignificance. The various self-understandings we adopt allow the world, as a web of relations of significance, to manifest itself. This is the specifically human mode of *krīnein* as developed in *Being and Time*. He even goes on to say that, in "its projective character, understanding goes to make up existentially what we call Dasein's '*sight*'" (SZ, 146). This clearly echoes his earlier discussion of perception being the distinguishing and therefore orienting capacity that allows animals to act, though, of course, he clarifies things by saying the sort of existential sight of understanding "does not mean just perceiving with the bodily eyes" (SZ, 147). It is, rather, that general way in which we experience things and actions as having significance. Adding to his earlier discussion of Aristotle's intellectual virtues as the main ways of distinguishing that make things appear as desirable, Heidegger makes it clear in *Being and Time* that we are more specifically concerned with accomplishing tasks that matter to us based on the sort of person we take ourselves to be. The activity of *poīesis* (making) is still very much the operative mode of our everyday actions, but Heidegger adds here that the content, that is, what we are concerned with making and accomplishing, comes from the self-understandings toward which we project.

Based on Heidegger's discussion of *das Man*, which is translated as "the they" or "the one," various scholars have attempted to make Heidegger's line of thinking here more concrete by considering the importance of the norms that are constitutive for the various possible ways of existing that we can take on.[22] When describing our everyday activity and considering who is, in fact, the agent, Heidegger states that the "'who' is not this one, not that one, not oneself, not some people, and not the sum of them all. The 'who' is the neuter, *das Man*" (SZ, 126). He goes on to describe this phenomenon more concretely, as he says that we "take pleasure and enjoy ourselves as *they* take pleasure; we read, see, and judge about literature and art as *they* see and judge; likewise we shrink back from the 'great mass' as *they* shrink back; we find shocking what *they* find shocking" (SZ, 126–127). In other words, in any given situation, we do what any other person sharing our self-understandings would do. Even though there appears to be a negative connotation to Heidegger's description of *das Man*, there has been a tendency, inaugurated by Dreyfus, among Heidegger scholars to frame this in a more positive light. On Dreyfus's reading, the "source of intelligibility of the world is the average public practices through which alone there can be any understanding at all."[23] Dreyfus goes on to claim that "Dasein just is a more or less coherent pattern of the comportment required by public 'roles' and activities."[24] The self-understandings that we take on, which structure the world so as to let certain things stand out as meaningful, are constituted by socially defined norms. Heidegger makes essentially the same point, though without the explicit emphasis on norms, in his later lecture, *The Fundamental Concepts of Metaphysics*. There he analyzes the claim that a chalkboard in a classroom is badly placed (GA 29/30, 497–502/343–345). Heidegger maintains that it is objectively correct that the chalkboard is poorly placed, but that the possibility of making such a judgment relies on there being teachers and students with certain expectations. This shows how the language of norms can be helpful. When there are certain norms associated with being a teacher (e.g., communicating information to students from the front of a classroom) and being a student (e.g., dutifully recording the information that your teacher gives you in class), these norms make it possible for a chalkboard to be poorly placed. The commitment to those norms lets the chalkboard be what it is. Heidegger, again, does not explicitly do this, but it is easy to see how one could push this further and say that our commitment to being students and teachers lets the chalkboard be what it is.

It is easy enough to see how norms would not only make entities encountered in the world appear in terms of their significance but our commitment to certain norms would also make certain actions stand out to us as particularly significant or important. To use Heidegger's example of the professor in the classroom again, if I project myself toward the possibility of being a professor, this means that I have committed to certain norms that are constitutive for this particular way of existing. For example, a professor is expected to come to class and deliver a lecture or oversee some other sort of learning activity in the classroom. If I consistently fail to abide by this norm, then I am no longer a professor. It is because I implicitly or explicitly understand this norm to be constitutive for this way of being that I am drawn to performing individual actions that enable me to enact this norm and, thus, this way of being. So, the action of driving to school matters to me insofar as it is necessary for delivering a lecture in class. My commitment to that norm lets this specific action show up as something that should matter to me. With this, we see the connection back to the early Aristotelian considerations. It is my commitment to being a professor and the norms that constitute this way of being that distinguishes between actions that matter, actions that I am drawn to perform and those that do not. *Krīnein*, in human action, takes the form of this commitment to being a certain type of person, adopting a certain self-understanding.

While I am greatly indebted to and largely sympathetic toward these sorts of interpretations that focus on the importance of norms for human action, I do wonder if they are too narrowly focused. I want to suggest that there are also for-the-sake-of-whichs, that is, self-understandings, that are biologically rather than purely socially or culturally defined. If we consider my oft-used example of being a professor, this is a for-the-sake-of-which that is purely socially constituted. That is, the role of being a professor can only exist within specific cultural and historical situations in which entities like universities as we know them exist and people place some value on higher education, and being a professor is defined purely by accumulated social norms. The existence of this way of being and the norms that define it are obviously contingent—societies in which there is no possibility of being a professor have existed in the past, exist currently, and will presumably exist the future.

However, it should be remembered that the closest that Heidegger comes to giving a concrete example of something that would count as a "for-the-sake-of-which" is when he talks about hammering done to make a building safe from bad weather. He seems to be saying here that the way of being that lets the action of hammering matter is something like being a creature who needs shelter. It is not obvious that this way of being is fundamentally defined by the enactment of certain norms the way that, say, being a professor is. If I am hiking and am suddenly caught in a nasty thunderstorm, certain features of the environment around me will stand out in terms of their possibilities for providing shelter (a cave, an abandoned cabin, etc.). They will stand out as such by virtue of my understanding of myself as a being who requires shelter in such circumstances, not primarily by virtue of any socially defined role such as being a hiker or an outdoors enthusiast. Moreover, it seems to me that being a creature who needs shelter is a way of existing that all of us as humans are necessarily thrown into and one which we must enact at all times. This is different from the self-understanding of being a professor, which clearly is not a self-understanding that all humans can or do take on.

I recognize that this claim that there can be primarily biologically based self-understandings might strike some Heideggerians as quite wrongheaded.[25] The worry is that I seem to be suggesting that it is possible to make sense of the world as a human being, for Heidegger, without considering any sort of historical or cultural situatedness and proposing that we can experience the world as meaningful purely through our biological, embodied interaction with it. Typically, it is thought that a large part of what Heidegger is getting at with the concept of thrownness is that we are thrown into a world that already has a structure provided by the culture, the customs, and indeed the language in which we find ourselves immersed, and we could not make sense of ourselves or the world without that background. Indeed, Dreyfus even criticizes Heidegger's selection of a being who needs shelter as his sole example of a for-the-sake-of-which in *Being and Time*, saying:

> Making a shelter, however, is an unfortunate example of a for-the-sake-of-which, since it suggests an instinctual necessity built into the organism by nature, rather than a possible way in which Dasein's being is an issue for it. In Heidegger's defense we should note that he speaks of providing a shelter as a possibility of Dasein's being. The idea may be that people are not caused to build houses the way birds are caused by their instincts to build nests.[26]

I think, though, that I can agree with the general thrust of this worry, while still maintaining that there is meaningful and interpretively faithful distinction to be made between for-the-sake-of-whichs that are purely socially constituted and those that have a biological basis. I want to maintain that biological self-understandings are always shaped by and enacted in accordance with the norms of one's historical and cultural situation, but their fundamental existence is not dependent on the agent's historical and cultural situation in the way that being, say, a professor is. Of course, when enacting the for-the-sake-of-which of being a creature who needs shelter, the society in which one finds oneself will have various norms that dictate what is an "acceptable" form of shelter. Most people currently living in the United States would not find a cave suitable as a long-term shelter, though it fulfills most basic biological requirements, while people enacting this self-understanding in other cultures or other epochs might very well be quite content with living in a cave. It is still the case, though, that every one in every culture must enact the self-understanding of being a creature who needs shelter.

Furthermore, I am not sure that Heidegger himself is as opposed to the notion of biological for-the-sake-of-whichs as some current scholars of his work are. There is the previously mentioned solitary example of a for-the-sake-of-which in *Being and Time*. There are also Heidegger's discussions of animality and biological life in other early works, some of which we considered in this chapter. In his early work on Aristotle, while he clearly thinks that there are important and unbridgeable differences between animal and human existence, he also has a pattern of considering life more generally as the basis for the discussion of particularly human existence.[27] This same pattern plays out in his later lecture course, *The Fundamental Concepts of Metaphysics*, as well. In that work, he engages in a lengthy analysis of animals' behavior and interaction with their environment before proceeding to consider what he takes to be the fundamental aspects of human action that make us different. It is in this work that he makes his oft-cited claim that animals are "poor in world," while humans are "world-forming" (GA 29/30, 397/274). As in his earlier lectures on Aristotle, he returns to the idea that the fundamental difference here is the fact that we have *lōgos*, while animals do not (GA 29/30, 418/288).[28] However, I read him as more Aristotelian in his thought process, meaning that he posits something additional found in human existence that makes it essentially different from that of the animal, while simultaneously acknowledging that our existence shares certain features of animality. In fact, he says explicitly, "our earlier analysis of captivation as the essence of animality provides as it were a suitable background against which the essence of humanity can now be set off" (GA 29/30, 408–410/282).

I hope by this point to have effectively made my case that suggesting the existence of biological self-understandings is not as antithetical to Heidegger's thought as it might initially appear. I want to also explain why I think it important that I make the case for this category of for-the-sake-of-which, even if I can only do so in the broadest of strokes here. When thinking about how the Heideggerian account I am developing can plausibly explain certain actions and even, as I will argue later in chapter 4, a certain notion of freedom, it seemed necessary to make it clear that some self-understandings are not entirely reducible to social norms and historical situatedness, even if the way they are enacted is always shaped by these things. This is an instance where I might be extending Heidegger's thought further than what is customary, but I do so for the sake of the greater plausibility of the general Heideggerian account of agency that I am trying to develop. In other words, I think the Heideggerian account of agency would be weaker, less plausible, and have less explanatory power if it were in fact right that there cannot be biological for-the-sake-of-whichs. Again, though, happily for me, I do think there is some textual basis for including these self-understandings in a Heideggerian account of agency.

Finally, I want to conclude this section with a recap of the basic structure of Heideggerian agency as I have developed it here, as this will be the conceptual foundation for everything that comes afterward in this work. There is a conative component of action—the feeling of being pulled toward performing certain courses of action that stand out as significant or important. There is also an equally fundamental (*gleichursprünglich* in Heidegger's terms) orienting component of action that allows for there to be distinctions between significant actions that matter to us and insignificant actions that do not. The conative component would not work without the orienting component, and the orienting component could not bring about action on its own without the conative component. Heidegger tries to capture the essence of the conative component through the use of terms like "inclination" (*Neigung*) or "disposedness" (*Befindlichkeit*), and he fleshes out the structure of the orienting component in his analysis of understanding (*Verstehen*) as the projection of oneself toward various possible self-understandings (for-the-sake-of-whichs, or *Worumwillen*). These self-understandings can be purely socially constituted, as the self-understanding of being a professor is, but they can also be biologically rooted, as being a creature that needs shelter is, but in either case, the enactment of any possible way of understanding takes place in and through the norms pertaining to that self-understanding made available by one's cultural and historical situatedness.

POTENTIAL CRITICISMS

Now that I have laid out the basic components of the Heideggerian theory of motivation, I want to consider some potential counter-examples, or types of actions that might seem prima facie difficult to explain on this view. I know that this is not necessarily a method used in Heidegger scholarship, and the following section will certainly be one where I push past Heidegger's texts quite a bit. However, the hope is that considering these potential counter-examples will allow me to add some features to the account developed here to make it better able to explain a wider variety of actions and more plausible as a general theory of motivation. These added features will also in some cases allow me to more easily tie in considerations from later chapters to this basic account of the structure of agency.

Mundane Actions

I like to think the Heideggerian view put forward here can plausibly account for a wide array of medium- to high-complexity actions. By this, I mean I think it can account for relatively complex actions like writing a paper, driving to school, reading a book, etc., as these are all actions that would matter to someone who understands themselves as a professor. But what about the very mundane, simple actions that we perform almost constantly? Here I am thinking about things like flipping a light switch or pouring a glass of water. I am bringing up the example of flipping the light switch in particular, because it is one of the examples used by Davidson in his seminal "Actions, Reasons, and Causes," and in general, I would say that the sort of actions taken as paradigmatic in mainstream action theory are simpler actions of this sort.[29] Davidson would explain the action of flipping the switch by saying that the agent had a pro-attitude of wanting there to be light in the room and a belief that flipping the switch would accomplish this. If the Heideggerian account of action is going to hold up as a plausible alternative to mainstream theories of action, and in this chapter, especially as an alternative to Humean theories of motivation, it has to be able to provide an equally satisfying account of these sorts of actions.

It seems like it would be difficult, to say that the action of flipping a light switch on upon entering a dark room matters to me because of a for-the-sake-of-which that is completely defined by social norms. What would even be the plausible candidate for a specific for-the-sake-of-which that is purely socially constituted that would explain why an agent would be drawn to the simple action of flipping a light switch? It seems like the most likely option is to appeal to *das Man* here and say something like, "Well, that is just what one does when one enters a dark room," and explain it by virtue of being acculturated into certain expected practices without specifying a particular for-the-sake-of-which. By doing so, it could be denied that something like flipping a light switch is an "action" in the proper sense of the term, maintaining that it is really just a mere deed and reserve the term "action" for those actions that can be explained by a definite for-the-sake-of-which.[30] This strikes me as an option that lacks explanatory power. If the Heideggerian account of agency is such that for many of our daily actions, the best explanation we can offer is to say that it is merely doing what one does based on the social norms into which one has been enculturated, the Heideggerian account is not a very appealing one, assuming we want a theory that explains the widest possible spectrum of actions.

However, I think the more plausible explanation is to posit a biological for-the-sake-of-which at work here. This is one of the places where I think the importance of broadening the interpretation of Heidegger's conception of understanding beyond the norms-focused one is particularly felt. Like Heidegger's example of hammering mattering because we understand ourselves as beings who need shelter, flipping the light switch when I enter a dark house matters because I understand myself as a being who needs light in order to see and move. For someone who is blind, they would not have this self-understanding and would not be pulled to turn on the lights when entering a room. This need not imply that there is no role being played here by social norms. As someone who lives in the United States in the twenty-first century, I have always been in an environment where the common practice for providing light when it is dark is to have light bulbs that can be turned on through electrical switches placed on walls at a convenient height for an adult of average height. When walking into a dark room, I am drawn to find a source of light and that manifests itself as immediately looking at or feeling along walls to find some sort of switch. In earlier eras or different societies today, the specific way someone enacts the possibility of being a creature who needs light would be quite different. Maybe enacting this possibility would involve lighting a candle or lamp or starting a fire. Maybe in the not-too-distant future, light switches will be obsolete, and we will enact this possible way of being by telling our AI-enabled digital assistants to turn on the lights.

I would argue that this same sort of explanation can be used for a variety of simple, everyday actions. I am drawn toward putting on a coat before going outside on a cold day, because I understand myself as a being that needs protection from the cold, even as social norms dictate what sort of coat I use. I am drawn toward pouring myself a glass of water, because of my understanding of myself as a being who needs fluids to survive, even as social norms might dictate what sort of container I use for the water or whether I insist on filtered water. Again, it seems that disallowing the positing of biological self-understandings in a Heideggerian account of agency would make it hard or impossible to adequately explain a wide array of common actions.

Actions Not Directed toward a Goal

Another type of counter-example to the Heideggerian account would be actions that are seemingly without a goal and not connected with any particular self-understanding. As discussed above, flipping a light switch is a very simple action that might not immediately appear to have been made salient by any particular self-understanding, but at least, it is clear that this action has some goal and, as I argue above, could be explained by appeal to a biological for-the-sake-of-which. Here, I am thinking of activities that appear to lack entirely a goal and a connection with a particular self-understanding, for example, the ubiquitous "messing around" on the Internet or binging a forgettable show on Netflix. Oftentimes, we go online with no specific goal, just clicking through websites which might not even be of great interest to us, or we find ourselves on the couch watching TV for hours without any deep connection to what we are watching or any lasting significance attached to the activity.

There seem to be two potential ways to understand these actions on the Heideggerian account of agency. The first option is almost certainly not one that Heidegger himself would endorse. It might be argued that there is some operative for-the-sake-of-which that allows people to be pulled toward performing these sorts of actions. Maybe at this point at the beginning of the third decade of the twenty-first century, something like being a social media influencer is a way of being that is well-defined enough so as to count as a for-the-sake-of-which in Heidegger's sense. Insofar as I understand myself as this sort of person, then actions such as constantly scrolling through various social media feeds and Internet comment sections might have a pull for me insofar as performing them is constitutive for my self-identity. Taking a slightly different tack, perhaps one could argue that our understanding of being a friend is now such that the norms that define this self-understanding require a constant monitoring of our friends' social media feeds in order to provide timely messages of congratulations or condolences or in order to be aware of upcoming social events. It seems harder to explain Netflix binging, but perhaps, again, we are at a point where something like "consumer of streaming entertainment" is a well-defined self-understanding that can allow certain courses of action to stand out as meaningful.

I believe Heidegger's preferred response to this objection, though, comes from his analysis of inauthentic existence and our tendency to distract ourselves from confronting our understanding of the nature of human existence.[31] There is a goal for these activities, namely, distracting ourselves from the weight of our existence—the need to make choices about our lives, to respond to obligations we have acquired, to define who we are as individuals. In Heidegger's words, "Dasein lets itself be carried along solely by the looks of the world; in this kind of being, it concerns itself with becoming rid of itself as being-in-the-world," and "curiosity is concerned with the constant possibility of distraction" (SZ, 172). We are drawn toward this goal of distraction precisely because it is possible for us to exist in such a way so as to have an authentic understanding of the nature of our existence. This is because we do, at least tacitly, understand ourselves as beings who must, as individuals, take responsibility for our lives and our decisions. Though Heidegger frames this sort of inauthentic distraction of ourselves as an undesirable, even condemnable activity, one need not be so negative in order to preserve the essence of this explanation of these activities. It is almost certainly true that we tend to distract ourselves entirely too much from the burden of existing, and it does not align with the general spirit of Existentialism to mention this, but there is also a growing understanding of the serious issues raised by things like decision fatigue and stress brought on by awareness of one's duties and limited time to devote to them, so maybe there is a more charitable way of seeing these distracting activities, at least when pursued in moderation. In any case, I will provide a fuller discussion of authentic awareness of the nature of our existence and what that implies for our understanding of responsibility in chapter 5.

Weakness of the Will

There is another, perhaps similar, category of action that might initially seem to be hard to explain with the theory of motivation outlined here—cases of weakness of the will. Suppose that I understand myself as a professor, and I see a stack of ungraded student exams. The norms that are constitutive for being a professor make it so that the action of grading the exams should matter to me. The exams sitting on my desk should exert a pull on me, soliciting me to take up the action of grading. However, for some reason I do not do it and decide just to watch TV (or do some other trivial action) instead. In this example, it is not that there is some conflicting action that makes it impossible for me to grade the exams. Rather, I just end up not performing the action that should matter to me and not really doing much at all. Given what I have said so far, it seems hard to explain how this could happen. I should be pulled to perform those actions that matter to me based on the self-understanding I have taken on.

I do think that there is a potential Heideggerian explanation of what is happening in these cases, though it does require stretching some of his ideas. I would propose that in cases of weakness of the will, the self-understanding that is normally operative in our actions, that normally makes actions appear as meaningful and allows them to exert a pull on us, weakens a bit. It is not, in the above example, that I completely stop understanding myself as a professor, but rather the extent to which I identify with that self-understanding lessens so that actions that should exert a pull on me no longer do, even as I recognize that they should. This is similar to, but not as severe as, what Heidegger describes as the experience of anxiety and, later, being-toward-death. He says of the experience of anxiety: "Here the totality of involvements of the ready-to-hand and the present-at-hand discovered within-the-world, is, as such, of no consequence; it collapses into itself; the world has the character of completely lacking significance" (SZ, 186). In this passage, Heidegger is describing a total loss of significance, during which nothing stands out as mattering at all. When authentically confronting our own death, Heidegger claims that we come to realize that in our normal, everyday actions, "one Dasein can be represented by another," and that the

> great multiplicity of ways of Being-in-the-world in which one person can be represented by another, not only extends to the more refined modes of publicly being with one another, but is likewise germane to those possibilities of concern which are restricted within definite ranges, and which are cut to the measure of one's occupation, one's social status, or one's age. (SZ, 239)

Conversely, "dying is something that every Dasein itself must take upon itself at the time" (SZ, 240). In the course of our normal, everyday actions, we, as laid out in this chapter, orient ourselves according to the various self-understandings that we have taken on, self-understandings which are largely defined by social norms. This means that anyone else could, in principle, occupy the same role as myself and perform roughly the same actions, since their self-understandings would be shaped by the same social norms as the ones that I have adopted. The possibility of dying, however, is different, since every individual must face dying alone, unable to be "represented" by anyone else. When we authentically confront the fact of our own mortality, then we recognize that no one particular self-understanding or even cluster of self-understandings exhausts our being, so that we are always able to understand ourselves as existing apart from and beyond any particular self-understanding.

Returning to cases of weakness of the will, they are like the experience of anxiety in that actions that are normally significant for us are not in that moment. The actions no longer exert the pull that they normally would, but it is not a complete collapse of significance. This is due, I am suggesting, to the underlying, often implicit, recognition that we are not ultimately reducible to any one self-understanding, or even any cluster of self-understandings. We exist as individuals unable to completely discharge our being into the roles that we occupy and that guide our normal actions. Every once in a while, that recognition creeps into the course of daily actions, and the usual, almost total identification with certain self-understandings lessens a bit, though, again, not as completely as what Heidegger describes in authentic being-towards-death. When this happens, we experience "weakness of the will" and just are not pulled toward the actions we normally would be and know that we should be.

Conflicting Actions

Here I am thinking about cases where an agent is drawn to two conflicting courses of action and must take one or the other. There could be two variations of this. Suppose that after arriving home from a long day at work, I feel that I should put in some work on my book and also should prepare my lecture for class tomorrow. However, it is already late, and I realize that I cannot do both. On the Heideggerian view of motivation that I lay out here, there does not yet seem to be any mechanism that can explain why I end up choosing one action over the other, since both matter to me based on my understanding of myself as a philosophy professor and what is called for by the norms that are constitutive for that self-understanding. The second variation would be a case in which actions that matter based on two separate self-understandings come into conflict with one another. Shifting the above example slightly, suppose that I come home and feel that I should prepare my lecture for tomorrow based on my understanding of myself as a professor and also that I should take my wife out for dinner based on my understanding of myself as a husband, and again, I realize that I do not have time to do both.

There can, I think, be a Heideggerian explanation of these sorts of cases, but I am not yet in the position to lay out that explanation. I will return to this issue in chapter 3, which deals with the role of deliberation for Heideggerian agency. My general approach will be to say that deliberation serves to provide a more finely grained articulation of the situation in which we find ourselves so that we allow one action or the other from a conflicting pair to emerge as mattering more. This can happen either by deliberating about what is important to being a certain type of person or by deliberating about what self-understanding one finds more important in a given situation.

HIGHLIGHTING THE CONTRASTS BETWEEN MY HEIDEGGERIAN VIEW, THE DREYFUSIAN HEIDEGGERIAN VIEW, AND THE HUMEAN VIEW

Finally, I want to close this chapter by drawing some specific contrasts between my Heideggerian view, Dreyfus's account of Heideggerian agency, and the Humean view. As with the consideration of the potential criticisms of my account, making these contrasts will allow me to add or highlight certain aspects of my account and set up some moves I will make in later chapters.

Direction of Fit

We can further refine the differentiation between the Heideggerian and Humean conceptions of the conative and orienting components at work in action by considering the idea of direction of fit. While there is debate over this idea, it is a common claim of Humean theorists that desires are distinguished from beliefs at least in part because of their "direction of fit."[32] Desires are concerned with how we want the world to be, so desires are directed toward reshaping the world to fit with what we want. Conversely, beliefs are supposed to line up with how the world actually is, so we work to revise our beliefs to fit the world. For the Heideggerian theory of motivation, it might be more appropriate to say that the direction of fit is reversed for the conative and orienting components. As we have seen, desire for Heidegger is about being grabbed by something in the world and being pulled toward it.

Another way of putting this is to say that the Humean theory tends toward an internalist view of desire. That is, desires are seen as purely self-contained mental states that serve as the internal springs that bring about externally manifested actions. In the simplest form, a desire is a mental representation of how the agent wants the world to look that serves as the motivational force behind an action. The motivating force here essentially works from the inside out. The Heideggerian theory presents a more complicated picture. For Heidegger, action is brought about not by internal mental states but, rather, by the complex interaction of the agent with the surrounding environment. To desire something is to be drawn out toward something encountered in the world, not to have an internal mental conception of the object of desire that then pushes one to act.

We can see how the direction of fit is likewise reversed for the orienting component on the Heideggerian theory with the following example. When one walks by a restaurant and feels the pull toward the food being served, this is only possible on the basis of a self-understanding that allows one to find the food on offer desirable. For instance, if one walks by a restaurant and smells hamburgers grilling, the smell might very well exert a pull on someone who strongly identifies themselves as a meat-eater. Conversely, someone who identifies strongly with being a vegetarian or a health food devotee would more likely experience revulsion when confronted with the same smell. In this example, it is not the "belief" that is revised in order to fit with the world but rather a particular self-understanding that allows the various things encountered in the world to show up in the way that they do. Heidegger is clear that we do not "shape" the world in the sense of creating things in the world or their qualities ex nihilo. Instead, our interpretive stance toward the world allows only certain aspects of things to manifest themselves in any given moment. A defender of the Humean theory might still object that I am merely reversing the terminology here by calling the desire to reshape the world the "orienting component" of action. I do not think this quite right, though. For Heidegger, our self-understandings already give us the world to be understood in a certain light; they do not provide us with a template for how we want the world to appear. For instance, if someone understood themselves as homeless, that self-understanding would structure the world for them in such a way that enclosed bus stops, for instance, stand out as available shelter from the wind, and the weekly offering of free meals by local charitable organizations stand out as not-to-be-missed events. It is not as though they are trying to change the world to match up with their understanding of what it is to be homeless, but rather, the ordinary features of the world that those of us fortunate enough to comfortably afford a home and food usually do not notice stand out as very meaningful for those who are homeless.

One could lodge a further objection to this characterization by considering other examples of hunger. There are certainly instances when we walk by a restaurant, smell something appetizing, and then feel hungry and are pulled towards getting food. However, it could be objected that a desire for food often pops up when no clear stimulus like that is present. I could be sitting at my desk working and suddenly, without provocation, desire a burrito and would then, presumably, want to "reshape" the world so that I had a burrito in front of me. This second example seems to support the Humean account. The Heideggerian account, though, can still accommodate this type of situation. When Heidegger discusses thrownness as an essential aspect of human existence, he means both that we are delivered over to the world in which we find ourselves and that we are delivered over to certain possible ways of being. He states that "in every case Dasein, as essentially disposed, has already gotten itself into definite possibilities," and that "Dasein is being-possible which has been delivered over to itself—thrown possibility through and through" (SZ, 144, translation modified). In other words, it is not just things encountered in the world that draw us out towards them, but it is also the case that there are certain possible ways of being human into which we are thrown and to which we are called to respond. These for-the-sake-of-whichs into which we are thrown are part of our facticity, in Heidegger's language, to which we are delivered over. In the specific instance of hunger, we must respond to the fact of being beings that need food to survive. Again, it is not a matter of reshaping the world to fit our desire but, rather, having our desire shaped by immutable aspects of our existence as humans. The Heideggerian response to this potential counter-example also shows once more the importance of allowing for biological for-the-sake-of-whichs. Without this allowance, it would be hard to explain those urges for food, sex, etc. that are not elicited by something encountered in the environment.

This might seem like a tangential, unimportant distinction between the Humean and Heideggerian views. However, I do think it crystalizes what I have implied about the Heideggerian account of agency in this chapter and will set up some important considerations in the following chapters. By maintaining that the Heideggerian view reverses the direction of fit in comparison to the Humean view, I am claiming that there are some antirealist aspects of the Heideggerian position. On the Heideggerian view I am developing, we never encounter a brute natural world that manifests itself completely independently of the way we experience it. We always have things appear to us as useful, important, insignificant, etc. in the course of everyday activities, and this experience of things in the world and possible courses of action is always made possible by our practical concerns and the self-understandings we have adopted that structure those concerns. This will have important implications for how Heidegger understands the role of causality in the explanation of our actions, which will be the focus of chapter 2, with subsequent implications for how he understands freedom and responsibility, topics covered in chapters 4 and 5, respectively.

The Role of Explicit Mental States in Action

As mentioned earlier, Hubert Dreyfus was quite influential in establishing the framework of a particular line of Heidegger of scholarship and, of particular interest here, developed what amounts to a Heideggerian account of agency. I will have more to say about various aspects of Dreyfus's account and what separates it from my own in the next two chapters. Here I want to focus on the contrast between the Heideggerian theory of motivation developed in this chapter and the likely Dreyfusian equivalent. I am not sure if Dreyfus would agree with my analysis of action in terms of conative and orienting components, but he would surely agree on the importance of *Befindlichkeit* and *Verstehen* as the fundamental components of Heideggerian agency. I think that the main point of divergence between the Dreyfusian/Heideggerian theory of motivation and mine lies in the interpretation of the role of mental states (like beliefs and desires) in bringing about action. As I laid out at the beginning of this chapter, the Humean theory of motivation places prime importance on beliefs and desires as explicit, discrete mental states that bring about our actions. Dreyfus long argued that Heidegger's conception of action is best described as a sort of skillful coping, in which explicit mental states (like desires and beliefs) mostly play no role in bringing about our actions.[33] Dreyfus claims that a careful phenomenological analysis of human action (such as Heidegger's) will reveal that explicit, well-defined mental states just are not there during the course of most of our daily activities. Rather, explicit mental states only come to play a role in bringing about our actions when we encounter some sort of stumbling block that interrupts the normally smooth flow of our activities. In Dreyfus's words, "temporary breakdown calls forth deliberate action and thus introduces 'mental content'."[34] When we encounter these "breakdowns," we then have to deliberate about what our next move should be. For Dreyfus, "when I start to deliberate, I do not just notice mental states that were already there; I start to have beliefs and desires."[35] For example, I might more or less automatically get up and go to the kitchen to get something to drink without explicitly deliberating about this action or being aware of any explicit desire to have something to drink or any explicit belief that the kitchen is the place to find something to drink. It seems that Dreyfus is suggesting with his phrase "start to have beliefs and desires" that if I were to get to the kitchen and find that no water was coming out of the faucet or that there was nothing to drink in the refrigerator, then I would start to explicitly think about what I wanted and how I might get it. In that moment, an explicit belief and desire would begin to exist in my mind and would then take on the primary explanatory role in any ensuing action. In effect, Dreyfus accepts that the Humean theory of motivation is correct in the cases of "breakdown," in which our normally smooth, unreflective activity is interrupted but maintains that these cases of breakdown are the exception rather than the rule and any positing of mental states working behind the scenes to bring about our actions in the normal course of our everyday activities is unjustified given a careful description of the phenomena in question.

The Heideggerian theory of motivation that I have been developing here would be contrasted with the Humean theory in a different way than that proposed by Dreyfus. I agree with Dreyfus's claim that explicit mental states are primarily not present in our actions, but I would suggest a potentially more satisfying way and more radical way of explaining the role of explicit beliefs and desires in the explanation of actions. It seems odd and excessively complicated to claim, as Dreyfus does, that there are two different ontological structures of motivation—nonreflective skillful coping when things are going as planned and the Humean view of motivation with explicit beliefs and desires bringing about actions when there is a breakdown. Essentially, this sort of bifurcation runs afoul of a sort of philosophy of action version of Ockham's razor—do not multiply modes of agency without necessity.

I think that a cleaner and more plausible way of explaining the appearance of explicit beliefs and desires is as follows. As laid out in the previous sections, Heidegger's conception of agency contains from the ground up a conative aspect and an orienting aspect, much as the Humean theory does. I would suggest that there is nothing wrong with calling these aspects of motivation "desires" and "beliefs," respectively, and acknowledging that they are always at work in bringing about our actions, but only as long as it is remembered that, from the Heideggerian view, we cannot interpret desire and belief primarily as discrete, explicit mental states. "Desire" in the Humean theory becomes in the Heideggerian theory the sense of being pulled toward various things, people, and activities that matter, while "belief" becomes the way we take on various self-understandings that allows things to show up as desirable. There is always this dynamic at play in the course of our actions, even if, as Dreyfus maintains, it is relatively rare for us to reflect on our actions and explicitly articulate this feeling of being pulled toward something by saying, "I have a desire for X, and I believe that doing Y will get me X." So, we need not maintain that there is the sharp structural change in the nature of agency when we switch from unreflective skillful coping to reflective, deliberative action as Dreyfus claims. Instead, we can adopt Heidegger's general stance toward much of the language used in mainstream philosophy—it does indeed point to legitimate underlying phenomena, but it has been distorted by the presupposed overly mechanistic, ontic (in Heidegger's terms) understanding of human existence. The tendency to talk about desires and beliefs as discrete mental states that can serve as cogs in the process of bringing about an action is paradigmatic of this mistaken ontological presupposition that fundamentally dynamic and reciprocally interactive aspects of human existence as such are to be fit into the same mechanistic ontology that we have used to understand the natural world in the modern era. In one of the few passages where he specifically addresses the existence of particular mental states, Heidegger states, "Dasein's Being reveals itself as care. If we are to work out this basic existential phenomenon, we must distinguish it from phenomena which might be proximally identified with care, such as will, wish, addiction, and urge. Care cannot be derived from these, since they themselves are founded upon it" (SZ, 182). Here he indicates that his preferred term to capture underlying ontology of human existence, "care," which I showed can be traced back to his early lectures on Aristotle, cannot be reduced to any particular mental phenomena like willing, wishing, urges, etc. Instead, he contends that all of these descriptions of specific mental states that might be associated with the conative component of action are founded upon the underlying structure of care. Heidegger does not seem to want to say that we never experience things like a wish or an urge (he does refer to them as phenomena), but he does seem to claim that our experience of these mental states must be understood in terms of care rather than the other way around.

We can show how this would work with an example. Imagine again a scenario where I am sitting at my desk working and explicitly say to myself, "I have a real desire for a burrito right now." That is, I have the phenomenological experience of some discrete urge to get a burrito well up within me. I then say to myself, "I believe that the Mexican restaurant on the corner of my block is open and has burritos." It is quite plausible to assume that the combination of having this desire and this belief gives rise to my action of walking down the block to my local Mexican restaurant. I constructed the example this way to make it as clear a case as possible of a phenomenological experience of explicit mental states bringing about an action; that is, there is no encounter with something in the environment that might solicit a particular response. On the Dreyfusian view, it seems that he would hold that there has been some breakdown here (maybe an absence of burritos in my office) that gives rise to the explicit desire and belief that combine to bring about my action. First, it strikes me as odd and a bit forced to consider these cases as instances of a breakdown. Must we consider it a breakdown every time we do not have what we want immediately in front of us? Second, it seems odd if the Dreyfusian view would contend that if I had walked to the restaurant unreflectively, my action would have some different underlying structure that could not be captured by referencing desires and beliefs. Is the structure of motivation for my action somehow fundamentally different if I just jump out of my chair and head out the door to the Mexican restaurant without a distinct experience of any particular mental states that bring about the action? According to my account, the answer to both of these questions would be "no." I would say that we do not need to have a breakdown to legitimately experience explicit mental states related to action, but the experience of these explicit mental states also does not signify that they have an underlying role in bringing about action. As discussed in the previous section, in this sort of case, the "desire" for a burrito can be understood as my feeling pulled by my having been thrown into understanding myself as a being who needs food. My particular response to this pull is oriented by my understanding of myself as, perhaps, a resident of a culturally diverse, gentrifying urban neighborhood, an understanding which would make the corner Mexican restaurant stand out as the place to go to get burritos. Talking about specific desires and beliefs is merely one way of describing these underlying components of agency that fits better with a more mechanistic understanding of human existence. This is I why I contend that my view is both simpler and more radical than Dreyfus's. I am not willing to make even the partial concession to the psychologistic view that Dreyfus does.

The Distinction between Activity and Passivity

Finally, one of the standard motivating questions in philosophy of action is the question of what criteria we use to distinguish between actively doing something and having something done to us.[36] The thought is that a good theory of action would provide a clear way to distinguish activity from passivity. We can see that the Humean theory of motivation provides a clear-cut way to distinguish between "actions" in the true sense of the term and things that are done to us. The main criterion would be the existence of desire and belief combinations that bring about the movements in question. For example, I could reach out, grab the cup in front of me, and take a drink of water because I have a desire for something to drink and the belief that something potable is in that cup. This would clearly count as my action. However, we could imagine a (slightly) science-fiction scenario in which I am unconscious and a skilled neurosurgeon is able to implant electrodes in my brain that give them control of my muscle responses, and in so doing, they could manipulate my body into making the same exact physical movements. In this case, the same physical movements would not count as my action because they are not brought about by my desire and belief.

From the Heideggerian point of view, the strict opposition of activity and passivity is misguided. Everything we do is shot through with passivity insofar as the conative component of every action is a response to something—something in the world that shows up as desirable, or as we have seen, those fundamental aspects of our being to which we are obligated to respond. This is not to say, however, that Heidegger is endorsing some form of behaviorism here. As he puts it, "Being-there is taken with that which is there in the world with being-there itself—*from without*, but from without *in the sense of the world as the wherein of my being*" (GA 18, 197–198). Our actions are solicited "from without," but as I have shown here, that solicitation is only possible when we take on various self-understandings that make distinctions between which actions are important and which are not. This is why Heidegger says that we are pulled "from without," but only insofar as the world we exist in has been structured for us by the various for-the-sake-of-whichs toward which we are projecting ourselves.

Accordingly, there is no way to clearly distinguish between an agent doing something and having something done to the agent. Heidegger sometimes uses the unusual term *Bewegtheit* to refer to the movement of human existence instead of the normal term for movement, *Bewegung*. The most literal translation of *Bewegtheit* would be "movedness," and I think this is meant to capture the sense in which the human agent is neither being moved nor doing the moving. Instead, the movement of our actions arises out of this interaction between the agent and the environment. When discussing the *pāthe* in the *Basic Concepts of Aristotelian Philosophy*, Heidegger states, "In *pāthos*, Aristotle sees, with the facts regarding *motion*, not so much the passive, but that something *occurs for me*" (GA 18, 194–195/131). Notice the careful wording of this statement. Heidegger wants to avoid the overly passive, or behavioristic, reading of claiming that encountering something from without does something *to* us that prompts motion, instead describing this experience of being moved as something that happens *for* us, implying some participation on our part. Finally, I want to finish the discussion in this chapter with a passage from Heidegger's early *Phenomenological Interpretations of Aristotle*: "The movedness [*Bewegtheit*] of factical life can be provisionally interpreted and described as *unrest*" (GA 61, 92–94/70). Heidegger thinks of life as fundamentally in motion, in a state of unrest. To be alive is to be continually moving, being pulled toward performing those actions that stand out as meaningful, but this unrest is, again, a "movedness," which cannot adequately be understood as either passive or active. As we will see in the next chapter, to ask about what initiates motion, and whether the agent can truly be said to initiate their own motion, is a secondary question for Heidegger. It is better to understand life as a constant flow of activity and movement guided by the orienting aspect of human agency.

As with the discussion of the direction of fit of beliefs and desires, this point about activity and passivity might also appear to be somewhat tangential at first glance. Again, though, I will hope to show in subsequent chapters that this has quite important implications for the Heideggerian views I develop here. Making that basic distinction between actions as the things we do versus processes that we undergo lends itself to asking about the causes of some activity. It can make sense to think that we can draw a distinction between activities that have some internal cause, thinking of these as true actions, and activities that have an external cause, which would be thought of more as processes that we undergo. Furthermore, once we think of actions as being defined by the right sort of causes, it is just a small leap further to conceive of freedom in terms of causality as well. So, my intention is to head off this string of plausible intellectual leaps (I do not think they are implied by any sort of logical necessity) by undercutting the action/passivity distinction at the level of the fundamental structure of agency, thereby setting the Heideggerian account of agency and freedom developed here on a different path.

NOTES

1. David Hume, *A Treatise of Human Nature* (Oxford: Clarendon Press, 1978).
2. Donald Davidson, "Actions, Reasons, and Causes," in *Essays on Actions and Events* (Oxford: Oxford University Press, 2001).
3. Robert Audi, "Intending," *The Journal of Philosophy* 73, no. 13 (1973).
4. Michael Smith, "The Humean Theory of Motivation," *Mind* 96, no. 381 (Jan. 1987).
5. Neil Sinhababu, *Humean Nature: How Desire Explains Action, Thought, and Feeling* (Oxford: Oxford University Press, 2017). See also his articles "The Humean Theory of Motivation Reformulated and Defended," *The Philosophical Review* 118, no. 4 (2009); "The Desire-Belief Account of Intention Explains Everything," *Nous* 47, no. 4 (2013).
6. Davidson, "Actions, Reasons, and Causes," 4.
7. The published English translation version of this lecture course is composed of Heidegger's notes from which he gave the lectures and student transcripts of the lectures themselves (*Basic Concepts of Ancient Philosophy*, trans. Richard Rojcewicz, Bloomington, IN: Indiana University Press, 2008). The student transcripts do not appear in the original *Gesamtausgabe* volume for this lecture course (GA 22) but were instead added by the translator, Richard Rojcewicz, in order to clarify and expand upon Heidegger's fairly minimalist notes. I have assumed that the student transcriptions provide a reliable account of Heidegger's interpretation of the matters under discussion and will mostly cite them when referring to this lecture course instead of Heidegger's actual notes. Since there is no corresponding *Gesamtausgabe* page number for these transcripts, citations for them will appear in end notes with the same format as other non-*Gesamtausgabe* references. When I do cite Heidegger's actual notes, that citation will have the normal parenthetical reference to *Gesamtausgabe* volume and page number.
8. Heidegger, *Basic Concepts of Ancient Philosophy*, 228.
9. Heidegger, *Basic Concepts of Ancient Philosophy*, 228.
10. Heidegger, *Basic Concepts of Ancient Philosophy*, 228.
11. Lawrence Hatab, in his *Ethics and Finitude: Heideggerian Contributions to Moral Philosophy* (Oxford: Rowman and Littlefield, 2000), 124–128, also discusses this connection between Aristotle's notion of *ōrexis* and Heidegger's account of care (*Sorge*) in *Being and Time*. Similarly, Christiane Bailey, in her "The Genesis of Existentials in Animal Life: Heidegger's Appropriation of Aristotle's Ontology of Life," *Heidegger Circle Proceedings* 1, no. 1 (2011): 199–212, provides a good account of the development of Heidegger's analysis of the fundamental components of Aristotle's views on animal life into Heidegger's fundamental structures of Dasein in *Being and Time*.
12. Cf. Aristotle's *De Anima* (433a27 and 433b10) and *De Motu Animalium* (701b33).
13. Aristotle, *De Anima*, in *Readings in Ancient Greek Philosophy*, ed. Patricia Curd, S. Marc Cohen, and C. D. C. Reeve (Indianapolis, IN: Hackett, 2011).
14. Heidegger, *Basic Concepts of Ancient Philosophy*, 228.
15. Martha Nussbaum argues for this view of Aristotle's account of the movement of animals in her essay "The Role of Phantasia in Aristotle's Explanation of Action"

in her book *Aristotle's* De Motu Animalium (Princeton, NJ: Princeton University Press, 1978), 221–269.

16. Heidegger, *Basic Concepts of Ancient Philosophy*, 228.

17. Heidegger, *Basic Concepts of Ancient Philosophy*, 229.

18. Here I am using Terence Irwin's translation of the *Nicomachean Ethics* (Indianapolis, IN: Hackett, 1985).

19. Heidegger, *Basic Concepts of Ancient Philosophy*, 230.

20. Heidegger, *Basic Concepts of Ancient Philosophy*, 229.

21. It is probably worth noting that "understanding" is not a completely off-the-mark translation of *noūs*, which Heidegger claims plays the role of distinguishing in his articulation of the Aristotelian account of human action.

22. See the various essays collected in Steven Crowell's *Normativity and Phenomenology in Husserl and Heidegger* (Cambridge: Cambridge University Press, 2013), John Haugeland's, "Truth and Rule-Following" in *Having Thought: Essays in the Metaphysics of Mind* (Cambridge, MA: Harvard University Press, 1998), and Golob's aforementioned *Heidegger on Concepts, Freedom and Normativity* for recent examples of this emphasis on norms.

23. Hubert Dreyfus, *Being-in-the-World: A Commentary on Heidegger's* Being and Time, *Division I* (Cambridge, MA: MIT Press, 1991), 155.

24. Dreyfus, *Being-in-the-World*, 159.

25. I am grateful to several participants in the 2019 meeting of the Heidegger Circle for voicing their doubts and pressing me on this point, especially Kevin Aho, with whom I carried on a further discussion over email.

26. Dreyfus, *Being-in-the-World*, 94–95.

27. Bailey also defends this point about the seeming willingness of Heidegger to see human and animal life as sharing basic ontological structures. See, again, Bailey, "The Genesis of Existentials in Animal Life: Heidegger's Appropriation of Aristotle's Ontology of Life."

28. Heidegger, of course, means *lōgos* here not in the narrow sense of assertion or even language more broadly, but rather as that fundamental capacity to experience the world as a structural whole, in which we can encounter entities as meaningful. Kevin Aho provides a helpful explanation of logos used in this sense in his article, "Logos and the Poverty of Animals: Rethinking Heidegger's Humanism," *The New Yearbook for Phenomenology and Phenomenological Philosophy* VII (2007): 1–18. In chapter 3 I will return to Heidegger's conception of *lōgos* with a particular view to thinking about what it implies for the role of deliberation in human action.

29. Davidson, "Actions, Reasons, and Causes," 4.

30. Charles Guignon suggests such a distinction between mere deeds and proper actions in his "Heidegger's Concept of Freedom: 1927–1930," in *Interpreting Heidegger: Critical Essays*, ed. Daniel Dahlstrom (Cambridge: Cambridge University Press, 2011), 86. Mere deeds come about just from doing what one (*das Man*) does in certain situations, and Guignon implies no further analysis is needed. Of course, as the title of his article states, his main concern is what Heidegger means by freedom, which we will consider in chapter 4, so he is more interested in the implications of the distinction between deeds and action from that perspective.

31. There can also obviously be other examples of apparently nonteleological activities aimed at self-distraction that do not involve technology, but these technological examples were the ones that immediately came to my mind. Richard Polt provides an excellent analysis of the distractive possibilities of online activities using Heidegger's account of inauthenticity in his "A Heideggerian Critique of Cyberbeing," in *Horizons of Authenticity in Phenomenology, Existentialism, and Moral Psychology*, eds. Hans Pedersen and Megan Altman (Dordrecht: Springer, 2015), 181–199.

32. Smith comments on this tendency among supporters of the Humean theory and endorses it ("The Humean Theory of Motivation," 50–54).

33. This skepticism about the role of explicit mental states in action is not unique to the Heideggerian or even more broadly phenomenological perspectives. Some recent influential works in Analytic philosophy of action also take a similar antipsychologistic stance. For example, both Jonathan Dancy, in his *Practical Reality* (Oxford: Oxford University Press, 2000), and Michael Thompson, in his *Life and Action* (Cambridge, MA: Harvard University Press, 2008), argue that we should not insist that the motivation for action ultimately be explained by reference to some particular, explicit desire.

34. Dreyfus, *Being-in-the-World*, 76.

35. Dreyfus, *Being-in-the-World*, 78.

36. See Harry Frankfurt's remarks on this in his "The Problem of Action," *American Philosophical Quarterly* 15, no. 2 (Apr. 1978): 157–162.

Chapter 2

The Heideggerian Argument against Causal Theories of Action

In this chapter we will turn to the consideration of causal theories of action. In the middle of the twentieth century, there were a number of prominent philosophers who offered noncausal, Wittgenstein-inspired theories of action.[1] However, in contemporary work in philosophy of action, the most commonly held, though not unchallenged, view is that human actions are best explained by a causal analysis of how various mental states bring about our actions.[2] Davidson, whose Humean theory of motivation was briefly discussed in the first chapter, is most often credited with turning the tide in favor of causal theories of action with the 1963 publication of his "Actions, Reasons, and Causes." Indeed, if one thinks that actions come about through the combination of a belief and desire, it is a reasonable step to claim that the way a belief/desire combination brings about an action is causal in nature.[3] Remember that Davidson defines acting for a reason as follows: "(a) having some sort of pro attitude toward actions of a certain kind and (b) believing (or knowing, perceiving, noticing, remembering) that [an] action is of that kind."[4] Later in this essay, he makes it clear that a "primary reason for an action is its cause."[5] Following shortly after Davidson in the early 1970s, we find the publication of other influential works defending causal theories of action like Alvin Goldman's *A Theory of Human Action* and Arthur Danto's *Analytical Philosophy of Action*. More recently, there have been supporters of causal views who disagree with the strict Humean nature of Davidson's account. In *Intentionality*, John Searle makes the case that it is intentions, rather than belief/desire pairs, that serve as the direct cause of actions.[6] Similarly, Alfred Mele, in his *The Springs of Action*, argues that belief/desire pairs by themselves are insufficient to produce an action and must be accompanied by an intention to act.[7] However, the basic picture is still the same—actions are caused by some combination of discrete mental states.

This brief sketch of the history of the preeminence of causal theories of action in recent philosophical work in this area is meant to allow me to show how the Heideggerian theory of agency can offer an alternative to mainstream views. The debate over the role of causality in our understanding of action is an interesting one in its own right, but it is of special interest to me in this volume, because I think this is the point where the classic free will debate takes hold. If one accepts the basic idea that our actions are best understood causally, it is a reasonable enough step to then question whether this means that our actions are causally determined. Once the debate is framed in terms of causal determinism, we tend to understand free will as the potential absence of such determinism and are locked into the conceptual framework of the current state of the debate—libertarianism versus compatibilism versus hard determinism. So, if I want to address the question of freedom from the Heideggerian point of view later in this volume, it is of crucial importance that I address the question of causality prior so as to lay the groundwork for changing the basic structure of the way we think about freedom.

Reading Heidegger's work, especially that of the late 1920s and early 1930s, where he most directly addresses this issue, it is clear that Heidegger rejects a causal understanding of human agency, but the exact nature of Heidegger's criticism of this approach and the alternative that he offers are not entirely clear. As briefly discussed in chapter 1, Dreyfus's interpretation of Heidegger is still one of the most influential accounts of Heideggerian agency, and Dreyfus does, at least in part, address causal theories of action. He plausibly claims that "it is generally agreed among analytic philosophers that our commonsense concepts of perception and action are causal concepts" and goes on to note that "[prominent analytic philosophers] Searle and Davidson agree that our concept of action is likewise causal—that an action is a bodily movement that has been caused in the right way by a mental state."[8] The main thrust of Dreyfus's criticism essentially stems from his antipsychologistic account of Heideggerian agency, according to which, as we saw, theories of action like those of Searle and Davidson incorrectly make the role of explicit mental states in human action fundamental and that a close, phenomenological analysis of our actions reveals that it is fairly rare for us to have explicit mental states that result in the performance of an action. In his words, "Not all human activity is deliberate, and therefore not all activity is caused by a self-referential mental state."[9] Instead, as discussed in chapter 1, Dreyfus proposes that we think of the majority of human actions as nondeliberative "skillful coping" with our environment—the performance of the myriad tasks we do on a daily basis that requires no explicit mental states. So, Dreyfus seems willing to admit that causal theories of action might have the correct approach to analyzing our deliberate actions in these moments of breakdown, but since the majority of our actions are not deliberative, the scope of these causal theories will be quite limited. Furthermore, Dreyfus claims that "mental-state intentionality is a derivative mode" that presupposes and is indeed founded upon a pre-reflective coping with the world.[10] In other words, even in the instances of breakdowns in which explicit mental states do seem to play some clear role in bringing about our actions, this is only possible given an already operative background of skillful coping.

More recently, Sacha Golob has made the case that Heidegger has a broadly Kantian view of the connection between causality and human action. According to Golob, "merely by making sense of oneself qua Dasein, one understands oneself in a way that is incompatible with viewing your actions as the outcome of external causal forces."[11] Golob finds Heidegger's account, as he interprets it, to be unsatisfactory, as he says that Heidegger "fails to address the question of the causal dependencies, as opposed to our understanding of those dependencies, which exist between Dasein and the biological or physical."[12] Putting the same point slightly differently, Golob continues, "If Heidegger is genuinely proposing that causal analyses or explanations in those domains be avoided or at least treated as of secondary importance, he needs to show that his own apparatus can fill the huge gaps that would result."[13] We need to get clear on what type of action would have a biological or physiological cause in a way that would be different from the more psychologistic actions associated with Davidson's view. The thrust of Golob's criticism seems to be that even if one argues that mental states are not causal factors in bringing about our actions, it is harder to deny that brute biological and/or physiological factors do not causally influence our actions. Consider the following case. After a long day at work, I am walking home and feeling very hungry. On my way there, I pass a fast-food restaurant, am hit by the overwhelming smells of hamburgers on a grill, experience an overpowering "urge" to go in and get food, and then I do, in fact, undertake the action of going in and buying food. It seems hard to deny that my hunger, even if not thought of as a mental state, is a cause of me going into the restaurant and getting food.

I think Dreyfus's account falls prey to Golob's criticism, as it seems odd to assert, as Dreyfus does, that causal explanations of action involving mental states are sometimes applicable and sometimes not. Dreyfus also leaves some gaps in his explanation of the derivative nature of the causal efficacy of mental states. He makes claims like, "temporary breakdown calls forth deliberate action and thus introduces 'mental content,' but only on the background of nonmental coping."[14] The implication seems to be that mental states are "derivative" because they appear fairly infrequently when there are breakdowns in the pervasive skillful coping that makes up the bulk of our existence. This is not really an explanation of the dependence of mental states on skillful coping. Rather, it is just a claim about the relative frequency of these two different modes of action. When the skillful coping mode of acting encounters obstacles, the causal model of action takes over, but Dreyfus seems to imply that both models are equally legitimate within their respective domains. He also does not explain how actions are brought about in skillful coping in a noncausal manner. Just because he rules out actions being caused by mental states, that does not rule out some other causes being operative in this form of agency.

Fortunately, I think Heidegger does provide more resources than either Dreyfus or Golob acknowledge for explaining how causal theories of action are insufficient and derivative and how causality nonetheless can figure into his account of human action. In particular, there are two important moves that Heidegger makes. The first is that he argues that causality (understood as efficient causality) is based on a conception of temporality that cannot be used to capture the structure of the lived temporality of human existence at a fundamental level. We find this argument in his 1930 lecture course, *The Essence of Human Freedom*, where Heidegger provides a detailed analysis and interpretation of Kant's account of freedom in the *Critique of Pure Reason*. By looking at this work, we can see that, contra Golob, Heidegger gives us more than the Kantian idea that it is impossible to think of our actions as causally determined from the first-person point of view. However, this seeming rejection of the application of efficient causality to the explanation of human action leaves us with Golob's criticism of Heidegger's view. This leads us to the second move that Heidegger makes. It is clear from several different works that Heidegger is seeking to recover a broader sense of what is responsible for things happening as they do, reminiscent of the Aristotelian four causes, to make it clear that the modern tendency to reduce causality to efficient causality is too narrow. In his essay "On the Essence of Ground," Heidegger makes the case that efficient causality is in fact only one aspect of a deeper, broader conception of bringing something about, which Heidegger refers to as "ground" (*Grund*) or "grounding" (*Gründen*). I will argue that here, Heidegger is giving us his account of how efficient causality fits into a broader understanding of bringing something about in such a way that efficient causality is not to be disregarded totally but also is not to be given explanatory priority with regard to human agency.

DIRECTION OF FIT AND THE DISTINCTION BETWEEN ACTION AND PASSIVITY

We can begin to see why Heidegger would reject causal theories of action by returning to some of the considerations from the end of the previous chapter—namely, the direction of fit of beliefs and desires and the distinction between action and passivity. As a reminder, the usual view of the direction of fit of beliefs and desires is that beliefs are to be revised so that they "fit" with how the world actually is, while desires prompt us to reshape the world so that it "fits" with how we want it to be. I argued that for Heidegger, the direction of fit is more or less reversed. The equivalent of "belief" on the Heideggerian view, what I call the orienting aspect of agency, polarizes the world in such a way that things, people, and actions stand out to us as meaningful. There is no world "as it actually is," as a sphere of action that exists completely independently of our engagement with it. The equivalent of "desire" on the Heideggerian view, the conative aspect of agency, is the pull we feel toward certain courses of action based on our interaction with the environment around us. "Desire" on this view is the world pulling on the agent, rather than the agent attempting to reshape the world. In part based on this understanding of the direction of fit of the orienting and conative aspects of action and their interdependence, I also showed why Heidegger undermines the distinction between action and passivity. One might think that the Heideggerian reversal of the direction of the conative aspect of action means that he is essentially claiming that our actions are actually more passive—we are merely pulled by our environment to do certain things without much in the way of agential volition. However, Heidegger does not see things this way, since we cannot be pulled toward certain courses of action without projecting ourselves toward the self-understandings that allow actions to stand out as meaningful. So, we are "passively" pulled toward actions, but only because we are "actively" projecting ourselves. This makes the attempt to draw a sharp distinction between action and passivity fundamentally misguided.

As discussed in the introduction to this chapter, there is a tendency to couple a Humean theory of motivation with a causal theory of action. Belief and desire pairs are thought of as internal cogs, whose presence initiates, and thus causes, the subsequent action. If this view were to be represented in a simple diagram, it might look something like this, where the arrow represents a causal connection:

Belief + Desire → Action.

Philosophers like Searle and Mele would argue that a belief/desire pair by itself is insufficient to cause an action and would add "intention" to the causal equation, perhaps looking something like:

Belief + Desire → Intention → Action.

However, the addition of the extra mental phenomenon of an intention does not alter the general idea that actions are caused by a linear causal chain of mental states.

The Heideggerian view, by contrast, does not admit of such a simple picture according to which actions can be explained and analyzed by unidirectional, linear causal chains. One might be tempted to say that the Heideggerian view merely reverses the causal order by claiming that something desirable is encountered in the environment (recall his reference to Aristotle's claim that the object of desire is the basis of motion), and it is this encounter that then causes an action aimed at obtaining the object of desire, effectively making a causal chain starting from the external, encountered object that might look like this:

Encounter with object of desire → Desire (Conative aspect) → Action.

However, things are not this simple for the Heideggerian view, since it is only by virtue of having a certain self-understanding that an object can appear as desirable in the first place. There is a bidirectional influence that probably cannot be captured in a simple diagram. One might be tempted to diagram it as:

Orienting aspect → Encounter with object of desire → Conative aspect → Action.

This picture, though, still cannot be correct. It does not make sense to say that the orienting aspect causes the encounter with the object of desire to occur. It would perhaps be most correct to say that the efficacy of the encounter with the object of desire is itself made possible by a certain self-understanding. In other words, the orienting component of action makes possible the arrow that connects the encounter with the object of desire and the experience of feeling pulled toward a certain course of action (the conative component of action). Maybe it could be argued instead that we should simplify the representation of the Heideggerian view to match the simple initial diagram of the Humean view:

Orienting aspect + Conative aspect → Action.

This could be correct insofar as I have argued in chapter 1 that the orienting and conative aspects are equally necessary and sufficient conditions for action to happen. However, this diagram leaves out the essential claim of the Heideggerian view that we are pulled toward performing actions by virtue of our interaction with the environment around us. What we are left with on the Heideggerian view, then, is the conclusion that if we are to stick to the structure of agency laid out in the first chapter, we cannot give a simple, linear causal explanation of our actions.

HEIDEGGER'S TEMPORAL CRITIQUE OF CAUSAL THEORIES OF ACTION

We can add more substance to this Heideggerian argument against causal theories of action by considering his views on the temporal structures of causality and human action. More specifically, he argues that our normal concept of causality has a temporal structure that is incompatible with the temporal structure of human agency, and indeed, human existence more generally. These considerations of temporality can make further sense of my diagrammatic Heideggerian argument against causal theories in the preceding section of this chapter.

In his earlier lectures prior to *Being and Time*, Heidegger does not spend much time directly addressing the issue of causality and its application to human action. The situation changes, though, once we get to his thought immediately following *Being and Time* in the late 1920s and early 1930s. There, we find some in-depth consideration of what is meant by causality and whether it is ontologically appropriate to apply this concept to human action. Heidegger is, of course, well aware that "causality" is an ambiguous term, taking on different meanings in different eras and for different thinkers. So, he specifies that in *The Essence of Human Freedom* course, he will approach the problem of freedom and causality using Kant's conceptual framework. For Kant, and I would suggest for most post-Kantian philosophers, the problem of free will is set up by the apparent difficulty of seeing how we, as humans, can act freely within the all-encompassing causal determinacy of the natural world. Heidegger maintains that in Kant's thought, there is a divide between the "causality of nature" and the causality of human action (GA 31, 144/105). However, Heidegger thinks that "Kant is inclined to treat natural causality as causality itself, thus to define the causality of freedom from the ground of natural causality" (GA 31, 192/134). In other words, Heidegger is claiming that Kant thinks of the causality of human action in terms of natural causality, making it so that there really is only one form of causality. When Heidegger discusses causality in general in this work, he is referring to Kant's natural causality.

What, then, is the natural causality being discussed here? Heidegger states bluntly that "causality means temporal succession" (GA 31, 150/108). To explain this, Heidegger outlines the standard Humean analysis of causality as follows:

> A cause is always the cause of an effect. That which is brought about we also call the outcome. An outcome is something that follows from something else. So to bring about, to effect, means to let-follow. As the effecting of the effect, the

cause lets something follow-on, and thus is itself prior. The cause-effect relation thus involves priority and outcome: the following-on of one thing from another, succession, which Kant conceives as temporal succession. (GA 31, 149/108)

I want to suggest that natural causality thought of in this way is roughly equivalent to the Aristotelian concept of efficient causality. I do not want to spend too much time exploring or justifying this equivalence, but I do want to assert it, since Heidegger moves between Aristotelian and Kantian conceptual frameworks (and I will as well in this chapter), and it is helpful to have some uniformity in terminology. After defining natural causality as temporal succession, Heidegger quotes Kant's claim that "all change (succession) of appearances is merely alteration" (GA 31, 175/124). This echoes Heidegger's discussion of Aristotle earlier in the lecture course, where he reminds us that for Aristotle, the "fundamental nature of movement is *metabolē*, change" (GA 31, 59/41). And we find in the *Physics*, Aristotle's definition of what has come to be called efficient causality as the "primary principle of change" (194b30).[15] There is, of course, an important difference between Aristotelian efficient causality and Kantian natural causality. Kant, writing after Hume, is positing natural causality as a necessary condition of our experience of the world, not a force or principle that we can safely assume actually exists in the natural world. Aristotle seems to have no doubts that such a principle is actually operative in the workings of the natural world. Nonetheless, both natural causality and efficient causality have the same formal structure—a cause is thought of as that which brings about alteration in temporally successive appearances or states of an entity.

This familiar connection between causality and temporal succession in efficient causality is not a problem for Heidegger in and of itself. However, Heidegger takes the further step of arguing that this understanding of time as succession is not suitable for understanding human existence at the most basic level. The understanding of time as succession "expresses the relationship between present things in time as a sequence (of nows); seen under this sequential aspect, every present thing *follows on from* something else present" (GA 31, 159/113). According to this conception of time, the present will be the currently existing "now." The future would be the "now" that does not yet exist, but which will arise from the present "now," and the past would be that "now" which was present, but no longer exists. In essence, then, Heidegger's approach is to demonstrate that human existence at the most basic level does not have this sequential temporal structure.

To understand Heidegger's argument, we need to again look at his analysis of human existence in *Being and Time*. In chapter 1, I showed how Heidegger's early focus on Aristotle and the motion of living beings gives rise to conception of human agency constituted by orienting and conative components, which reach their fullest development as disposedness (*Befindlichkeit*) and understanding (*Verstehen*) in *Being and Time*. Here, I want to return to these two fundamental components of human agency and now consider their underlying temporal structure. By way of explaining what he means by disposedness, Heidegger provides an analysis of what it is to have a mood (*Stimmung*), or more generally, to be attuned to the world around us (*Gestimmtsein*) (SZ, 134). He is clear that in talking about moods, he is not talking about the psychological description of various different moods, but, rather, he is concerned with analyzing what it means ontologically to be the sort of being that has moods. Perhaps the key ontological characteristic of moods is that "in having a mood, Dasein is always disclosed moodwise as that entity to which it has been delivered over in its Being; and in this way it has been delivered over to the Being which, in existing, it has to be" (SZ, 134). In other words, moods reveal that we are already affected by the world around us before any conscious thought about how we should feel or what things should matter to us. In this way, we can be said to be delivered over to the world in which we find ourselves and delivered over to certain facts about our own being over which we have no control. We can already see that moods, and disposedness generally, can be roughly seen as the past-directed aspect of human existence. And, as we have seen, Heidegger explains his conception of understanding by analyzing its structure in terms of what he calls projection (*Entwurf*) upon a "for-the-sake-of-which" (*Worumwillen*) (SZ, 145). Understanding, then, is seen as the future-directed aspect of existence.

 The next step is to show why human existence conceived of in terms of disposedness and understanding has a nonsequential temporal structure. Let us begin by looking at what it would mean to say that the future-directed aspect of our existence, understanding, has a nonsequential temporal structure.[16] When we consider the examples I have been using up to this point to illustrate what Heidegger means by "understanding" (e.g., projecting oneself toward the possibility of being a professor), we can see that there is a problem in thinking of the temporal structure of human existence, at least as conceived of by Heidegger, as sequential. If I am a graduate student, it makes sense to see being a professor as a future way of being that I will work toward making actual. At some point, if I do all the right things and have some luck, I will actually become a professor. At the point when I am hired and actually working as a professor, however, how does it still make sense for Heidegger to claim that I would be projecting forward into the possibility of being a professor? Would it not seem that I just *am* a professor now and that there is no need to see my existence as projecting beyond this? Heidegger recognizes the difficulty and makes it clear that he has something else in mind when he says that projection is a fundamental and essential aspect of human existence and that it is future-directed. He states, "'Future' here does not mean a 'now' that has *not yet* become 'actual' and which sometime *will be* for the first time" (SZ, 325, translation modified). This does make some sense when considering the above example of being a professor. As mentioned above, one can see taking on this possible way of being as something that is achieved at some definite point in time, that is, as a "now" that was not yet, but which has become actual. However, it is also true that being a professor (or being any sort of person) is different in significant ways from completing a task like writing a paper. Once a paper is finished, or made actual, there is nothing else to be done. Possibility has been fully converted to actuality with no remainder. On the other hand, being a professor is not something that has a specific point of completion. Even after initially obtaining a position as a professor, one must continually perform all of the duties and actions that make one a professor. It is indeed a continual projection of one's existence toward this possibility that is required, and such projection can never be understood as something that can be fully actualized in any particular moment.

It is, perhaps, a bit trickier to understand why Heidegger identifies *Befindlichkeit* as the past-directed aspect of our existence and why he thinks that this aspect of our existence also has a nonsequential temporal structure. We can begin with the first issue: understanding why one's disposition would be past-directed in its temporal orientation. Heidegger makes the claim that "understanding is grounded primarily in the future; one's "*disposedness*," however, temporalizes itself *primarily* in *having been*" (SZ, 340, translation modified). By way of explanation, he states, "The thesis that 'one's disposedness is grounded primarily in having been' means that the existentially basic character of moods lies in *bringing* one *back to* something" (SZ, 340, translation modified) and attempts to show why we might think this by once again turning to an analysis of fear. Fear would seem to be a prime counter-example to the claim that our moods are fundamentally directed toward the past. In most (if not all) normal experiences of fear, we are afraid that something will happen in the future and that it is precisely that possibility that some undesired event will occur at a future point in time that makes us afraid. Instead, Heidegger states:

> In fear the awaiting lets what is threatening *come back* to one's factically concernful potentiality-for-Being. Only if that to which this comes back is already ecstatically open, can that which threatens be awaited *right back to* the entity which I myself am; only so can my Dasein be threatened. (SZ, 341)

The idea in this passage seems to be that we are only able to find specific things fearful in light of those potentialities for being through which we understand ourselves. For instance, if I read in the newspaper that the governor wants to cut the budget for public universities again, I might very well be afraid that this will come to pass, because such cuts could result in the loss of my job. What is revealed in this experience of fear is that a crucial part of who I am is being a philosophy professor. I then experience fear when confronted with a threat to the continuance of this possible way of being, a way of being that I must have already taken up to make possible my fear in the first place. This is why Heidegger can say that disposition is a "bringing one back to something," and as such, is in fact "grounded primarily in having been."

Now we can move on to understanding the second claim that the temporal structure of disposition is nonsequential. In pointing out that like the temporal structure of understanding, the temporal structure of disposition is nonsequential, Heidegger states, "With this 'before' we do not have in mind 'in advance of something' in the sense of 'not yet now—but later'; the 'already' is just as far from signifying 'no longer now—but earlier' " (SZ, 327). As we saw with understanding, to say that the projective aspect of understanding is future-directed does not mean making actual a state that currently does not exist. Here Heidegger makes the corresponding claim about the temporal structure of disposition. By saying that disposition is past-directed (i.e., characterized by the "already"), he does not mean that in the experience of moods, we are directed toward some prior state that once existed, but now no longer does. In his words, "In the *disposition in which it finds itself*, Dasein is assailed by itself as the entity which it still is and already was—that is to say, which it constantly *is* as having been" (SZ, 328, translation modified). That is, in the experience of a mood like fear (as we saw above), those self-understandings that we have already taken up and that have already defined us are revealed. Disposition is past-directed not because it points to something that once was actual but is no longer but, rather, because it points to something that already was and continues to be. In fact, the temporality of disposition is further differentiated from a sequential temporality when we recognize that what "already was" in the experience of a mood is not something that ever was or that can even become actual. Instead, what already was in the experience of a mood is the future-directed projection toward some possible way of being that is not in itself ever completely actualizable.

With these considerations in place, we can see why Heidegger would not accept any account of human action that primarily involves a conception of causality that is based on a sequential temporality. The two key components of human existence—disposition and understanding—cannot be adequately understood, if one tries to analyze their structure in terms of a conception of temporality that sees time as a sequence of "nows." If this is the case, then any theory of action that relies exclusively on natural/efficient causality cannot be used to provide an adequate analysis of the fundamental structure of human existence and agency. This hopefully clarifies the considerations of the preceding section—why one is not able to give a simple causal account of action using the orienting and conative aspects of actions in a parallel way to the use of beliefs and desires in a Humean causal account. For Heidegger, neither component of action can be understood as a linear, sequential understanding of temporality, so that sort of linear causal analysis that posits the appearance of a belief and desire combination that causes a subsequent action is just fundamentally unsuitable for human agency.

Furthermore, I take the argument to go beyond Dreyfus's argument against causal theories of action. It is not just because discrete, explicit mental states do not, for the most part, exist in the course of our actions that causal theories fail. They fail, again, because the temporality assumed by natural/efficient causality does not match the temporal structure of human existence. Now, to be fair to Dreyfus, he does claim that causal explanations involving mental states are derivative insofar as they rely on a background of skillful coping. As I suggested earlier in this chapter, the nature of the dependency suggested by Dreyfus is unclear. The next section of this chapter will aim, at least in part, to better explain the nature of this dependency.

GROUNDING (*GRÜNDEN*) AS HEIDEGGER'S ALTERNATIVE ACCOUNT OF BRINGING SOMETHING ABOUT

At this point, it should be clear that Heidegger does not think that human agency can be understood in causal terms, and I hope to have shown that his reasons for rejecting a causal understanding of agency are different and more substantive than on Dreyfus's interpretation, even if there is the remaining issue of fleshing out Dreyfus's claim about the dependence of causal theories on skillful coping. However, as things stand now, I have not addressed how Heidegger can avoid the sort of criticism that Golob makes of his view—Heidegger seems to have no way explaining the seemingly straightforward causal efficacy of various biological and/or physiological factors on our actions. As discussed at the beginning of this chapter, a total rejection of a causal understanding of our actions would leave any Heideggerian theory of action in a very difficult position for the reasons that Golob points out. That is, Heidegger would have to provide some other ontological account of how our actions come about, if he is going to deny that actions are brought about through causality. Luckily for the Heideggerian view of agency, I do think Heidegger attempts to provide such an alternative, which is found primarily in his account of the concept of ground (*Grund* in German).[17] Heidegger's discussion of ground, as with so many of his other ideas, is not as clear or fully fleshed out as one might like, but I think that we can build out his work here in such a way as to provide answers to both the question of how standard causal theories are dependent on the underlying noncausal structure of agency and the question of how to account for the seemingly undeniable causal effects of some biological and physiological causes on our actions.

The concept of ground has some immediate intuitive plausibility as an alternative to causality. It is common enough, though perhaps a bit stilted, to talk about someone's grounds for acting in a particular way. Furthermore, *Grund* can also mean "reason," in the sense of "one's reason for acting."[18] As we have seen in the sketch of Davidson's views, it can make sense to explain actions by appeal to reasons in this sense, even if Davidson argues that reasons are causally efficacious, a move we will not follow here. Heidegger, though, is not just appealing to the common usage of *Grund* to build it up as a plausible alternative to cause. As with many of the new concepts Heidegger introduces in his early work, his own conception of *Grund* is something of an appropriation of Aristotle, in this case, Aristotle's concept of the four causes, as we will see as we proceed.

To begin to understand what Heidegger means by ground, we can look at his interpretation of the Ancient Greek concept of cause. This interpretation, as is often the case for Heidegger, is shaped by his etymological comments on the relevant terminology. The Greek term often translated as cause is *aītia*. In several different works, Heidegger focuses on the broader meaning of *aītia* as being responsible for something in a rather general sense.[19] In his essay "On the Essence and Concept of *Phūsis*," Heidegger states that *aītion* means "that which is responsible for the fact that a being is *what* it is" (GA 9, 245/188). Furthermore, "this responsibility does not have the character of causation in the sense of a 'causally' efficient actualizing" (GA 9, 246/188). In a similar vein, Heidegger states in "The Question Concerning Technology": "What we call cause [*Ursache*] and the Romans call *causa* is called *aītion* by the Greeks, that to which something else is indebted. The four causes are the ways, all belonging at once to each other, of being responsible for something" (GA 7, 16/7). Heidegger, following Aristotle, claims that it is necessary to go beyond the efficient causal history of something to really understand what is responsible for that thing being what it is.[20] With those preliminary remarks in mind, we can move to the consideration of Heidegger's concept of "grounding" as his alternative, noncausal account of how our actions are brought about, that is, his account of what is responsible for our actions being what they are. In his 1929 essay, "On the Essence of Ground," Heidegger identifies three different aspects of grounding: (1) grounding as establishing (*Stiften*), (2) grounding as taking up a basis (*Bodennehmen*), and (3) grounding as the grounding of something (*Begründen*) (GA 9, 165/127).

The first aspect of grounding, establishing, is clearly a parallel to understanding from *Being and Time* and what I have been calling the orienting aspect of agency. Using the language of *Being and Time*, Heidegger states that "establishing" is "nothing other than *the projection of the 'for-the-sake-of-which'* [*Worumwillen*]" (GA 9, 165/127). As we know from *Being and Time*, this projection of a for-the-sake-of-which establishes a world, that is, a relational context of significance in which things can make sense to us and can stand out as important and salient to us. As we have already discussed for Heidegger, he maintains that we are always projecting ourselves toward the enactment of a particular way of being, even if this way of being is neither definitive of our essence nor possible to fully actualize.

Heidegger next characterizes the second aspect of grounding, taking up a basis (*Bodennehmen*), as an "*absorption* by beings," in which "Dasein has taken up a basis within beings, gained 'ground'" (GA 9, 166/128). Again, this second aspect of grounding has a parallel in Heidegger's earlier characterization of human existence in *Being and Time*, but this parallel is perhaps a bit more difficult to make clear. In this case, what Heidegger means by "taking up a basis" can be understood by returning to his characterization of disposedness (*Befindlichkeit*), or what I have been calling the conative aspect of agency. Recalling the earlier analysis of disposition in terms of what it means to have moods, we know that for Heidegger it is not the case that we emerge in the world neutrally disposed or completely indifferent to things encountered in the world. Rather, we are already disposed toward the world in some way. We always encounter things in the world as mattering to us in one way or another. This leads to a natural, pre-reflective absorption in the things and events encountered in the world. It is this ability to always encounter things as mattering to us in one way or another that makes it possible for us to have reasons to act. Playing on the ambivalence of the word *Grund*, which can, again, mean "ground" or "reason," we can see why Heidegger maintains that it is through an "absorption" in the world that we "gain ground." That is, we gain some motivation to act.

One might think that this is the end of the story at this point. The previous section of this chapter established that the interaction between the conative and orienting aspects of agency that brings about our actions cannot be understood in causal terms due to the unique temporal structure of that interaction, and now we have the added detail that Heidegger calls the way this interaction brings about our actions "grounding" instead of "causing." However, Heidegger includes a third aspect of ground. This third aspect is the "grounding of something" (*Begründen*). It is considerably more difficult to interpret what Heidegger is going for with this concept of "grounding something," as there is no immediate parallel to anything in *Being and Time*.[21] I take the importance of *Begründen* to be that this concept seems to explain how Heidegger thinks causality fits into the overall structure of grounding, though it is difficult to interpret him on this point.

Heidegger claims that grounding something "means *making possible the why-question in general*" (GA 9, 168/129). He goes on to say that "all ontic discovery and disclosing must in its way be a 'grounding of something'; i.e., it must *account for* itself" (GA 9, 169/130). Putting these two statements together, I take Heidegger to be saying that the grounding of something is connected to the act of making claims about specific things and events, giving an account of why they exist or happen as they do. This aspect of grounding, unlike the previous two, is not referring to the larger issue of how there is a world at all in which things can make sense to us. Rather, the grounding of something is supposed to refer to our ability to make sense of specific things that we encounter in the world (hence Heidegger's use of "ontic" to describe this aspect of grounding). Heidegger seems to indicate that sometimes this appropriate account could take the form of an efficient causal explanation, as he says that in the grounding of something, "what occurs is the *referral to a being* that then makes itself known, for example, as 'cause' or as the 'ground of movement' [*Beweggrund*] (motive) for an already manifest nexus of beings" (GA 9, 169–170/130, translation modified). Notice the connection here between cause and the ground of movement (*Beweggrund*). This clearly echoes Aristotle's characterization of the efficient cause as that which brings about change or motion. When we encounter some state of affairs in the world, we might be inclined to ask why things are this way, and the answer to the why question would be some preceding event or state of affairs that could be seen as the efficient cause of the current state of affairs, that is, that which is responsible for the change that has brought them into being.

Indeed, Heidegger is aware that his discussion of grounding will make readers think of Aristotle and seems to indicate that his view differs from Aristotle's for two main reasons. In his words:

> Are we then restricting to three the four grounds discovered by the tradition . . .? The comparison cannot be made in such a superficial manner; for what is peculiar to the first discovery of the "four grounds" is that it does not yet distinguish in principle between transcendental grounds and specifically ontic causes. . . . The originary character of the transcendental grounds and their specific character of ground remain covered over beneath the formal characterization of "first" and "highest" beginnings. And for this reason they lack unity. Such unity can consist only in the equioriginary character of the transcendental origin of the threefold grounding. (GA 9, 170–171/131)

It appears that Heidegger is acknowledging that, like Aristotle, he is proposing a multifaceted understanding of bringing something about, but unlike Aristotle, Heidegger's account contains a transcendental differentiation not found in Aristotle's. I take the term "transcendental" here in the Kantian sense of providing the grounds for the possibility of something. When first introducing *Begründen*, Heidegger states:

> The projection of world indeed makes possible—although we cannot show this here—a prior understanding of the being of beings, yet is not itself a relation of Dasein to beings. And our being absorbed, which lets Dasein find itself in the midst of beings and pervasively attuned by them (though never without unveiling the world), is likewise not a comportment towards beings. Yet presumably both—in their unity as characterized—make intentionality possible transcendentally, and in such a way that, as ways of grounding a third manner of grounding: grounding as the grounding of something. (GA 9, 168/129)

This passage suggests that he thinks the interaction of projection and disposedness makes possible the grounding of some specific thing.

I admit to finding Heidegger's general position here a bit ambiguous. There has been a long-standing debate in the mainstream philosophy of action literature over whether claims that attribute causal efficacy to various mental states are really best understood merely as rationalizations for action without actually signifying the existence of any underlying ontological causal mechanism that brings about action.[22] That is, if someone claims that they went to the restaurant at the corner of the block because they had a desire for a burrito and a belief that that restaurant served burritos, that claim could be taken as a rationalization that makes the action intelligible but does not actually entail that there were underlying mental states that were the true causes of the action. Heidegger's association of grounding something with the "why question" and giving an account of why an event happened certainly seems to lend itself to this interpretation of his position. He might not think that grounding something really is equivalent to there being an actual efficient cause of an event, but rather grounding something is merely providing a rationalization that uses the structure of efficient causal explanation to make the event intelligible. Alternatively, he might be claiming that there are actual, ontological efficient causes of action whose efficacy is made possible only by the interaction of establishing and gaining ground, or in the terminology of the first chapter, the orienting and conative aspects of actions. In other words, Heidegger could be making a genuine metaphysical claim about how efficient causality works, or he could be claiming that efficient causal explanations are merely ex-post-facto rationalizations to make intelligible actions that are brought about solely through the noncausal interaction of the orienting and conative aspects of action.

I would say that as a matter of pure exegesis, it could be interpreted in either way. In the following section, I will make use of this ambiguity and argue that in some cases, the grounding of something involves merely a rationalization that makes an action intelligible, while in other cases, the grounding of something does involve an actual efficient cause. I want to keep the latter interpretation alive, since there is a problem with the reduction of causal explanation to rationalization, at least with regard to the Heideggerian view of agency that I am developing. If Heidegger is only talking about rationalizations that make actions intelligible but have no actual underlying referent that is causally efficacious, his view still seems open to the criticism from Golob discussed at the beginning of the chapter—the Heideggerian view of agency cannot deal with those cases where there genuinely does seem to be some specific efficient cause. In order to try to develop a better response to Golob's objection, then, I am going to read Heidegger as suggesting that there actually are efficient causes for actions on his view in some cases but that this sort of causality is made possible by the interaction of the other two aspects of ground.

Is this consistent with the conclusion of the previous section? That is, is it consistent to maintain that efficient causality has a different temporal structure than human existence while also maintaining that efficient causality can have some role in explaining human action? I suggest that for Heidegger, there is not necessarily an inconsistency here. The fundamental temporal structure of human existence that is essentially nonsequential corresponds to the establishing and absorption aspects of grounding. Efficient causal explanations of action are, as we shall see in the next section, legitimate when understood as being made possible by the structure of grounding in a particular case. However, efficient causal explanations cannot be seen as complete and ontologically adequate explanations of action if they are proposed as such in themselves and divorced from this larger framework.

DEALING WITH APPARENT EFFICIENT CAUSES OF ACTION

Heidegger is making a much broader metaphysical claim about the nature of causality and the role that human beings play in the constitution of the world, but for our purposes here, we can focus on the implications of Heidegger's views for our understanding of human agency. There are two different types of efficient causal explanations of action to consider here. First, there are the explanations of action that focus on the causal role that mental states play in bringing about our actions. This is the sort of causal theory of action that Dreyfus is concerned with undermining. Second, there are the explanations of action that focus on physiological or biological causes. These are the sorts of explanations that Golob emphasizes in his critique of Heidegger when he maintains that Heidegger's account lacks the resources to explain the causal influence of physiological or biological factors on our actions.

To begin with, we can consider Davidson's Humean causal theory, which again posits that it is combination of a desire and a belief that causes actions. We can see that the sort of causal analysis employed by Davidson does imply a temporal ordering of cause and effect, namely, the cause being the reason that precedes the effect, that is, the movement to perform the action. Given Davidson's own sophisticated work on causality, it is not clear that he would agree with the perhaps overly simplistic reading of reasons as efficient causes to be understood merely as the event temporally proceeding an action, but I will skip over those potential complications for now and assume that one could see reasons as straightforward efficient causes in the sense being considered here.[23] If we take this reading of a Humean causal theory, then from what has been established earlier in this chapter, we must say that this sort of theory cannot align with the fundamentally temporally nonlinear, noncausal Heideggerian theory of agency being developed. The question, then, naturally arises: what are we to make of this sort of causal Humean account from the Heideggerian point of view?

There seem to me to be two main possible ways of dealing with this sort of causal theory on the Heideggerian view. One, which Dreyfus seems to favor, is to say that explicit mental states like beliefs and desires only exist in cases of a breakdown in our coping with the world, and thus, it is only in these cases of breakdown that these mental states can be efficient causes of action. In instances of skillful coping, for Dreyfus, there are no discrete mental states operative that could serve as causes for actions. With what I have added to the Heideggerian account in this chapter with regard to the concept of grounding, the further step would be to say that even if beliefs and desires can be efficient causes of action, their causal efficacy is made possible by the underlying, noncausal interaction of the orienting and conative aspects of action. This more fully fleshes out Dreyfus's claim, discussed in the introductory section in this chapter, that mental states can only be efficacious if there is a certain level of background in place. The required background is precisely the underlying interaction of the other two components of grounding.

We can return to Davidson's example of flipping a light switch to illustrate how this might look. On Davidson's view, upon entering a dark room, I have a desire for the room to be lighted. I also have a belief that flipping the light switch will lead to the room being lit. The combination of this belief and desire gives me a reason to perform the action of flipping the light switch, and it is this reason that is the efficient cause of the action. The first question for Dreyfus would presumably be whether this action takes place in the course of normal skillful coping or in a case of breakdown in that coping. If I am in the midst of a normal routine, say, coming into a dark house after work, I would probably, on Dreyfus's view, unreflectively reach for the light switch after having walked in the door without ever forming a discrete desire or belief that could serve as the cause of the action. In this case of normal skillful coping, Dreyfus would categorize the Davidsonian account of a belief/desire pair causing the action as a mere rationalization that retroactively makes sense of the action without having any actual underlying causal referents.

However, suppose that we modify the scenario a bit, and instead of the action being a flipping of the light switch, we consider the lighting of a candle after a sudden power outage. In this case, the Davidsonian account would be almost the same. I have a desire for the room to be lit, and knowing that the power is out, I have a belief that lighting a candle is the best way to fulfill this desire. That belief/desire pair then causes my action of lighting the candle. If I am interpreting Dreyfus correctly, he would agree with the Davidsonian account here, since this is a clear instance of a breakdown in my normal skillful coping, during which discrete, explicit mental states can emerge and serve as causes of actions.

As I argued in the first chapter, however, there are reasons not to endorse Dreyfus's strict bifurcation of agency into the realms of unreflective skillful coping, which does not involve explicit mental states, and reflective action in cases of breakdown, which does involve explicit mental states. I suggested there that, on the Heideggerian view, instead of allowing that there can be explicit mental states like beliefs and desires operative in actions in some cases (but not others), we can understand "beliefs" and "desires" to be reifications of the orienting and conative aspects of action. In other words, "beliefs" and "desires" are the terms we use to try to capture the underlying ontology of action when we are operating with an overly ontic understanding of human existence. This is essentially the same reductive move that Dreyfus makes when analyzing skillful coping, but I suggested that it be applied more broadly to any form of action, reflective or unreflective.[24]

What does this reductive move imply then for my Heideggerian response to the Davidsonian view? Explanations positing beliefs and desires as efficient causes of actions are *merely* rationalizations. The terms "belief" and "desire" refer to the orienting and conative aspects of actions, which, as we have seen, bring about action in a noncausal fashion. A Davidsonian rationalization is an answer to the "why question" insofar as it does make our actions intelligible, but the intelligibility of this rationalization is made possible by the underlying interaction of the orienting and conative aspects. Again, we saw how this works in the first chapter, but we can now add a bit more nuance. Because I understand myself as a being who needs light to see, I experience the world in such a way that opportunities to light my environment stand out to me as meaningful. This provides a particular orientation to my existence and activity, thus allowing for the possibility of particular methods of creating light to exert a pull on me when they are encountered. This can explain why I would take the specific action of flipping a light switch when I walk into a dark room. If someone were to ask why I had flipped the light switch, I could say that I had a desire for the room to be lit and a belief that the flipping the light switch would accomplish this, but this reason for action only makes sense in light of my understanding myself as a being who needs light and thus as a being who would be drawn to flipping switches. Establishing and gaining ground as the two underlying aspects of grounding make possible the third aspect of grounding something, in this case, grounding the particular action of flipping the light switch by supplying a reason for why it was performed.

We can also see how this would work in the case of a more sophisticated action. Suppose I arrive to my office on campus several hours before I am scheduled to teach class. Upon entering my office, I turn on my computer and begin putting together my notes for the upcoming class. This action of writing notes on the reading for class discussion is still relatively simple but is more complex than Davidson's flipping of the light switch. How could we give a causal explanation of this action using Davidson's conception of action outlined above? Perhaps on the Davidsonian view we would say that I have a desire to teach a good class later in the day and that I have a belief that spending a fair amount of time working on my notes and lecture strategy prior to class is necessary for teaching a good class. The combination of this belief and desire forms a reason to work on my lecture that would be seen as the efficient cause of this particular action and would provide an answer to the "why-question." If someone were to come into my office and ask why I am working on my lecture, a sensible response to this question would be to say something like, "I want to make sure I have a good class this afternoon, and I believe having a well-prepared lecture is a necessary condition for that."

On my Heideggerian view, we could say that in this case the for-the-sake-of-which toward which I am projecting myself is my understanding of myself as a professor. We could say that if I were not to understand myself as a professor, the action of writing a lecture would not strike me as an important or significant action. In this way, my projection of myself toward a specific way of being establishes a world in which certain actions, events, and duties can make sense to me. It is my absorption in this context of relations structured by my understanding of myself as a professor that lets the action of writing a lecture matter to me. This second characteristic of being absorbed in this world is important, because it could very well be the case that I made the decision to be a professor and understood the duties involved in enacting that way of being, but felt no pull to actually perform some of the actions required to be this sort of person. By understanding myself as a professor, I will have gained grounds for action. That is, I will encounter events and actions as inherently meaningful and as mattering to me.

Building on this line of thought, we can see how Heidegger would think that a traditional causal understanding of the action of writing the lecture like

Davidson's is made possible by this interconnection of the three aspects of grounding. A desire to teach a good class only makes sense within a context in which I understand myself as a professor, that is, in a context in which teaching a good class matters to me. Similarly, a belief that writing a lecture before class is necessary to teaching a good class is something that makes sense only within the context of the norms that lay out what it is to be a professor. It is my commitment to understand myself according to these norms that would allow such a belief to make sense. In general, then, we can say that it is this larger context of significance, in which certain actions matter to me, and which is opened up by my projection toward a certain self-understanding, that allows efficient causal rationalizations of the Davidsonian variety to make sense in the first place, but these causal rationalizations are, again, merely rationalizations.

Now we can turn to the consideration of the other type of apparent efficient causes of action—the biological or physiological causes that are the focus of Golob's criticism of Heidegger. Recall the example that I gave at the beginning of the chapter to illustrate his point. After a long day at work, I am walking home and feeling very hungry. On my way there, I pass a fast-food restaurant, am hit by the overwhelming smells of hamburgers on a grill, experience an overpowering "urge" to get in and get food, and then I do, in fact, undertake the action of going in and buying food. Suppose that all of this takes place more or less unreflectively, in the mode of Dreyfus's skillful coping. We could try to analyze this action in Davidsonian terms and say that this "urge" is a pro-attitude, i.e., desire, which is coupled with a belief that going in and buying food will be a way of satisfying that desire. But if we stay consistent with the preceding discussion of the reduction of desires and beliefs to the conative and orienting aspects of action, we can easily dispense with that interpretation. I think the thrust of Golob's criticism is that even if we do not bring the causal role of mental states into the picture, there seems to be some clear causal influence on my actions here. I was unreflectively walking home, and then I encounter this smell of food, and I change my course of action and enter the restaurant. Even if we do not go so far as claiming that smelling the food causally determines my action, it seems hard to deny that I would not have changed my course of action if I had not smelled the food. In other words, that physiological or biological reaction to the smell of food seems to cause me to take this new course of action. This seems to be the crux of Golob's criticism, as he says:

> [Heidegger] fails to address the question of causal dependencies, as opposed to our understanding of those dependencies. . . . Heidegger surely assumes that Dasein's actions are not simply determined by the weight of its greatest desire as in a crude Humean model. But rather than providing a metaphysical account

of how that might be possible, Heidegger's response is to reject the vocabulary, "will", "desire", etc., needed to formulate the question.[25]

Effectively, he is saying that it is not enough to claim that causal explanations for action are always merely rationalizations without any underlying ontological referents. I hope I have already dealt with the last part of Golob's criticism, Heidegger's alleged rejection of the vocabulary of desire, by showing how that terminology can be made consistent with a Heideggerian account of agency, but Golob's first point in the quoted passage still stands. Even if my Heideggerian account can reduce purported mental causes of action to the noncausal interaction of the conative and orienting aspects of action, as of yet, I have provided no explanation of how my account can deal with these nonmental causes of action.

This is the point where I want to invoke the other interpretation of *Begründen* and argue that in these cases of seeming biological causes of actions, they really are efficient causes, but their causal efficacy is made possible by the underlying noncausal interaction of the conative and orienting aspects of action. That is, I want to argue Heidegger's account of grounding does fill that gap mentioned by Golob and provides a metaphysical account of how these types of causes work. Recall the previously cited passage that provides part of Heidegger's characterization of the grounding of something: "What occurs is the *referral to a being* that then makes itself known, for example, as 'cause' or as the 'ground of movement' [*Beweggrund*] (motive) for an already manifest nexus of beings" (GA 9, 169–170/130, translation modified). Here, he seems willing to claim that the grounding of something can refer to some actually existent event that can serve as the ground of movement for a subsequent action. Returning to the restaurant example, we could say that my smelling the food is the event that serves as the ground of my subsequent movement, the action of entering the restaurant, and as such, smelling the food would be the efficient cause of my action. I want to claim that the causal efficacy of the event of smelling the food is made possible by the underlying interaction of the conative and orienting aspects of action but is nonetheless a genuine efficient cause. I understand myself as a being who needs food to survive. This self-understanding orients my actions by making opportunities to acquire food stand out as important or salient to me. The conative aspect of action is what allows me to feel the pull of these opportunities when I encounter one. These two aspects together describe, at least in part, my existence in the world as a being for whom eating opportunities matter. This means that having food matters to me in a fundamental way and gives me grounds to act. The interaction of these two underlying aspects of agency makes it possible for the specific event of the smell of food emanating from the restaurant to cause me to adopt a new course of action.

Now, someone like Golob might very well not be convinced and would want to argue that this does not actually show that the interaction of the conative and orienting aspects makes this efficient causation possible; it is merely asserting this dependency. However, we can make Heidegger's case here by considering what might happen if we vary the way the orienting aspect operates. As discussed in chapter 1, there are some for-the-sake-of-whichs that we are simply thrown into and have no choice but to project ourselves toward. This seems to clearly apply to the understanding of myself as a being who needs food. It is also the case, though, that I must enact this aspect of my existence in a particular way. There are many ways that people enact the self-understanding of being a creature that needs food. Some people see eating as a way to express their religious beliefs through eating kosher or halal food, for example. Others might be vegetarian or vegan for ethical reasons. Still others might favor red meat and fried potato products as a way of expressing a certain "all-American masculinity." In any case, our existence as beings who need to eat is not manifested in a homogenous way. It is a general possibility that must always be taken up and enacted in a specific way. I would suggest that the efficient causal power of the urge to eat a hamburger is made possible by the specific way that I enact my being as a creature who needs food. I might identify with the above-mentioned American male identity when it comes to food, which allows the smell of the hamburger to have the causal power to bring about my action of eating at the fast-food restaurant. If I were a vegetarian, the smell would have had no effect, or it might very well have been repulsive and made me hurry home faster to get food I would find more suitable. It is my absorption in the world as a being who needs food combined with my projection toward a certain way of enacting this possibility that allows the smell of the food to have its causal power.

I will not run through other specific examples of this sort, but I think something like this account would also hold for other biological urges that are often thought of as efficient causes of our actions—sexual urges, fight/flight urges, etc. It would be easy to see how this would work on a general level with sexual urges. Everyone (except those who are asexual) has been thrown into an understanding of themselves as sexual beings, but as the expansion of the movement for LGBTQ rights has demonstrated, there are many different particular ways that people enact this self-understanding. The event of encountering another person whom one finds to be sexually attractive can be the efficient cause of a subsequent action only because of the underlying interaction of the conative aspect of action and the agent's particular enactment of their understanding of themselves as a sexual being. On my reading, then, Heidegger would not have to deny the causal efficacy of these sorts of biological urges, and he could still maintain that efficient causal explanations of action relying on biological efficient causes are derivative insofar as they are dependent on the other two components of grounding.

Even though this does not seem to be Golob's worry, it is worth pointing out here too that this interpretation of the grounding of something would also allow for there to be efficient causes for actions not involving a biological for-the-sake-of-which. We can turn to my running set of examples involving my understanding of myself as a professor to see why this is so. Suppose that I am doing some normal weekly grading of online homework assignments. I switch momentarily to check to see if anything new and interesting has been posted to social media. I see that one of my friends has posted a call for papers for an interesting upcoming conference they are organizing. Upon seeing that post, I switch from grading homework assignments to writing an abstract to submit to that conference. Again, here, it seems like that event of seeing the call for papers causes me to take up a new and different course of action—writing the abstract instead of grading homework assignments. On my account of *Begründen*, this event does count as a legitimate efficient cause of my subsequent action, but its efficacy is made possible by the underlying way in which my self-understanding as a professor allows such things to stand out as important and worth pursuing. When I was finishing my dissertation in graduate school with no certain academic job prospects, I remember very well how this understanding of myself as an aspiring professor began to lessen so that these calls for papers no longer exerted the same pull on me they once did when I fully identified with this way of being. After I was fortunate enough to secure a position as a professor, these events reemerged with the same salience they had prior to my doubts about my future in the profession.

CONCLUDING REMARKS

We can now attempt to summarize the results of this chapter. The first chapter's establishment of the way that the conative and orienting aspects of action interact in order to bring about actions already hinted at the difficulty of understanding action in simple causal terms from the Heideggerian point of view. By analyzing the temporal structure of causality and seeing that it does not align with the fundamental temporal structure of human agency for Heidegger, we were able to show in more detail exactly why Heidegger would reject causal theories of action. From there, we moved on to consider Heidegger's concept of grounding as a different, broader way of understanding what is responsible for actions being what they are. On my Heideggerian view, efficient causal explanations of the Davidsonian variety as seen as mere rationalizations that can serve to make actions intelligible, but I leave room for there to be genuine efficient causes of action when an event occurs that does change the course of an agent's actions. With these moves, I hope to have shown that a Heideggerian account of action need not take Dreyfus's path to criticizing causal theories of action that focus on mental states as efficient causes. Instead of claiming that mental states are causes of action only in those cases of breakdown in which explicit mental states emerge, my account does not need this bifurcated conception of agency according to which actions performed in skillful coping have a different structure than those performed in instances of breakdowns in that coping. On my account, all actions have the same basic structure. It is just that sometimes we cite mental states as explanatory reasons for acting, even though these mental states are merely reifications of the underlying aspects of agency. Reasons or explanations, thus, do not pick out anything that can serve as an actual efficient cause of an action and are merely rationalizations. Furthermore, a Heideggerian account of action need not fall prey to Golob's criticism concerning its inability to explain the influences of physiological or biological causes on our actions. The causal power of certain events to change the course of our actions is made possible by the underlying, noncausal interaction of establishing and gaining ground, or as I have been calling them, the orienting and conative aspects of action, respectively. In these cases, even though there is some causal influence on our actions, the explanation of our actions cannot be reduced to one that only relies on efficient causality.

As I said at the beginning of this chapter, I would like to think that my reconstruction of Heidegger's account of action here is interesting in its own right insofar as it attempts to show how explanation of action cannot be reduced to efficient causality while still being able to give efficient causality some role in action. However, what I see as the more interesting and important implication, if one considers my Heideggerian account plausible, is that if we move away from understanding human agency solely in terms of efficient causality, we would also need to rethink of our understanding of freedom and responsibility, which traditionally have tended to be understood purely in terms of efficient causality. I will turn to this rethinking in the second half of this book, but these initial chapters provide the foundation for what follows by deconstructing some traditional assumptions about agency and pointing toward what Heideggerian accounts of freedom and responsibility could look like.

NOTES

1. Here I am thinking of works such as Anthony Kenny's *Action, Emotion and Will* (London: Routledge, 1963), A. I. Melden's *Free Action* (London: Routledge, 1961), R. S. Peters's *The Concept of Motivation* (London: Routledge, 1958), Peter Winch's *The Idea of a Social Science* (London: Routledge, 1958), and Charles Taylor's *The Explanation of Behaviour* (London: Routledge, 1964).

2. Giuseppina D'Oro and Constantine Sandis provide a helpful overview of this history of causal theories in philosophy of action in their article "From Anti-Causalism to Causalism and Back: A History of the Reasons/Causes Debate," in *Reasons and Causes: Causalism and Anti-Causalism in the Philosophy of Action*, eds. Giuseppina D'Oro and Constantine Sandis (New York: Palgrave Macmillan, 2013), 7–48.

3. Though I do think it is plausible and common to make the move from endorsing the Humean theory of motivation to also endorsing a causal theory of action, I do agree with Smith when he argues that the Humean theory does not logically entail the causal theory in the strict sense of the term. See Smith, "The Humean Theory of Motivation," 43–44.

4. Donald Davidson, "Actions, Reasons, and Causes," in *Essays on Actions and Events* (Oxford: Oxford University Press, 2001), 3–4.

5. Davidson, "Actions, Reasons, and Causes," 12.

6. John Searle, *Intentionality: An Essay in the Philosophy of Mind* (Cambridge: Cambridge University, 1983), especially chapters 3 and 4.

7. Alfred Mele, *Springs of Action: Understanding Intentional Behavior* (Oxford: Oxford University Press, 1992), especially chapters 7 and 8.

8. Hubert Dreyfus, *Being-in-the-World: A Commentary on Heidegger's* Being and Time, Division 1 (Cambridge, MA: MIT Press, 1991), 55.

9. Dreyfus, *Being-in-the-World*, 57.

10. Dreyfus, *Being-in-the-World*, 59, 85.

11. Sacha Golob, *Heidegger on Concepts, Freedom and Normativity* (Cambridge: Cambridge University Press, 2014), 209.

12. Golob, *Heidegger on Concepts, Freedom and Normativity*, 211.

13. Golob, *Heidegger on Concepts, Freedom and Normativity*, 211

14. Dreyfus, *Being-in-the-World*, 76.

15. Aristotle, *Physics*, trans. Terence Irwin and Gail Fine, in *Readings in Ancient Greek Philosophy: From Thales to Aristotle*, Fourth Edition, eds. S. Marc Cohen, Patricia Curd, and C. D. C. Reeve (Indianapolis, IN: Hackett Publishing, 2011).

16. In the attempt to deliver such an explanation, I will rely heavily on William Blattner's excellent work on Heidegger and time, *Heidegger's Temporal Idealism* (Cambridge: Cambridge University Press, 1999), especially chapter 2: Originary Temporality.

17. There has recently been a move in Analytic metaphysics to develop the notion of grounding as alternative to causal explanation. A substantive comparison of the Heideggerian notion of ground with that developed by Kit Fine in his "Guide to Ground," in *Metaphysical Grounding*, eds. Fabrice Correia and Benjamin Schneider (Cambridge: Cambridge University Press, 2012), 37–80, might very well be interesting and worthwhile, but such work is outside the scope of my project here.

18. Steven Crowell emphasizes this meaning of *Grund* in his work on Heidegger's views on agency and responsibility. See his chapter "Conscience and Reason," in *Normativity and Phenomenology in Husserl and Heidegger* (Cambridge: Cambridge University Press, 2013), especially pages 206–213.

19. In Henry George Liddell's and Robert Scott's authoritative, *A Greek Lexicon*, "responsibility" is given as the first definition of *aītia* (http://www.perseus.tufts.edu

/hopper/text, accessed May 29, 2018), which suggests Heidegger is on reasonably solid interpretive ground here.

20. To be fair to Dreyfus, he does seem to recognize that Heidegger has some neo-Aristotelian account of causality at work in his thought, as Dreyfus mentions the existence of three distinct types of causality: physical, governing, and existential causality (*Being-in-the-World*, 191). However, as far as I can tell, Dreyfus never really develops this line of thought more fully or ties it explicitly into Heidegger's work.

21. There might be some parallels to Heidegger's account of how the temporal present arises out of the interaction of disposedness and understanding.

22. See D'Oro and Sandis, "From Anti-Causalism to Causalism and Back," especially pages 23–27, for a synopsis of this debate.

23. I am thinking of Davidson's "Causal Relations," in *Essays on Actions and Events* (Oxford: Oxford University Press, 2001), 149–162, and "Mental Events," in the same volume, 207–224. It is in that latter essay that he lays out his influential account of anomalous monism.

24. I will say a bit more about how beliefs as discrete, explicit thoughts can fit into the Heideggerian picture in the next chapter, which develops an account of the role of deliberation in action.

25. Golob, *Heidegger on Concepts, Freedom and Normativity*, 211.

Chapter 3

The Role of Deliberation in Heideggerian Agency

The structure for this chapter will differ somewhat from the first two chapters. In chapter 1, I started with a brief explanation of the Humean theory of motivation, a view which has occupied a prominent place in mainstream work on the philosophy of action, in order for it to serve as a contrast to my Heideggerian theory of motivation. In chapter 2, I started with a brief explanation of causal theories of action, which, again, are quite prominent in mainstream work on philosophy of action, in order to show how a primarily noncausal Heideggerian account of agency would represent a significant break from and an alternative to these theories. With regard to the role of deliberation in agency, though, the situation is rather different. I am not sure that there are any sufficiently prominent views in mainstream philosophy of action to serve as useful contrasts here. It seems that sometimes the nature of deliberation is treated as a separate philosophical topic, frequently referred to as practical reasoning. So, there are influential works in the philosophy of action—such as Davidson's "Actions, Reasons, and Causes"; Smith's "The Humean Theory of Motivation"; and Mele's *Springs of Action*—that are almost exclusively focused on the mechanism by which actions are brought about and spend little time considering what role (if any) deliberation plays. There are, of course, also very important works in the philosophy of action that do give an account of what deliberation is and what role it plays in action, such as Jonathan Dancy's aforementioned *Practical Reality* and Christine Korsgaard's *Self-Constitution: Agency, Identity, and Integrity*.[1] In any case, I am left without a clear sense of there being a dominant-enough position in the mainstream literature to serve as a useful contrast to the Heideggerian view that I develop.

There is an additional issue here as well. I hope to have shown in the previous chapters that even though Heidegger never explicitly laid out a "theory of motivation" or a "critique of causal theories of action," there are enough resources in his work that substantive Heideggerian accounts in these areas can be reconstructed. I think the situation is different with a Heideggerian account of deliberation. While Heidegger has a great deal to say about language, broadly construed, and there has been an enormous amount of scholarship on Heidegger's understanding of language, Heidegger says little about deliberation or practical reason, and Heidegger scholars have correspondingly said little about this as well.[2] Indeed, it may very well make sense for scholars to take this lack of discussion of deliberation on Heidegger's part to imply that deliberation just does not play a major role in action for Heidegger. As we have already mentioned in prior chapters, in his commentary on *Being and Time* and in numerous articles before and after, Dreyfus developed an influential interpretation of Heidegger's conception of human action, and the main point that Dreyfus draws from Heidegger's thought is that most of our everyday actions take the form of skillful coping—a form of action in which explicit mental states play no role and no explicit deliberation takes place. On his view deliberation appears in our actions only when there has been some sort of disturbance to the flow of ordinary skillful coping. As an example, we can consider the action of opening a locked door. Normally, I would be able to take the right key out of my pocket, fit it into the lock, and turn the handle without any sort of explicit, conscious reflection about what I am doing. Suppose that I insert the key into the lock, but the door does not open. On Dreyfus's view, I would enter the stage of what he calls deliberate coping.[3] I am not yet explicitly deliberating about what I should do now, but I am now explicitly focused on the action of opening the door. Now suppose that several more attempts to open the door fail. At this point, I have encountered a more serious breakdown in my skillful coping and must now deliberate about what should be done.[4] For example, I could ask myself whether I do in fact have the right key, and then if I don't have the correct key, if I should call a locksmith, etc.

Indeed, for Dreyfus, as he lays out in the later article, "What Could Be More Intelligible Than Everyday Intelligibility? Reinterpreting Division I of *Being and Time* in the Light of Division II," authentic agency for Heidegger is best understood as that of the expert, who acts well without reflecting or deliberating, implying that reflective, deliberative action is a derivative mode of agency. In his words:

> The expert driver, generally without paying attention, not only feels in the seat of his or her pants when speed is the issue—the driver knows how to perform the appropriate action without calculating and comparing alternatives. On the off-ramp, his or her foot just lifts off the accelerator or steps on the brake. What must be done, simply is done.[5]

The expert, for Dreyfus, is someone who is so in tune with the situation of action that they do not need to deliberate but rather straightaway "see" what action is called for. He connects this with Aristotle's account of the *phronīmos*, the agent possessing the virtue of *phrōnesis*, suggesting that Division II of *Being and Time* is Heidegger's attempt to appropriate Aristotle's conception of *phrōnesis*. On Dreyfus's reading, Aristotle's *phronīmos* too is someone who acts with an intuitive grasp of the situation and does not rely on norms or rules for how one should act. He claims, "Because there are no rules that dictate that what the *phronīmos* does is the correct thing to do in that type of situation, the *phronīmos*, like any expert, cannot explain why he did what he did."[6] The implication here is the expert, the authentic agent, cannot provide reasons for their action and cannot explain it to anyone else.

And it is not only Dreyfus who maintains that there is a strict division between skillful coping and deliberative action. Other Heidegger scholars influenced by Dreyfus's account assume this position as well. For instance, Steven Crowell says:

> Heidegger analyzes the way that disturbances in the smooth flow of my activities can occasion a transition in my dealings with things: from their being "available" things become merely "occurrent"; accordingly, I no longer simply deal with them but rather—at the extreme—merely stare at them. Such disturbances provide the occasion for deliberation—that is, for technical, strategic, and prudential consideration of what is to be done.[7]

Crowell here is clearly following Dreyfus in maintaining that deliberation is only occasioned by "disturbances" in the normally smooth flow of our activities, implying that deliberative action is a different form of action. Similarly, Mark Wrathall, in his "Autonomy, Authenticity, and the Self," states that the "deliberative weighing of reasons, far from being the distinguishing feature of consummate action, is a mark of action impaired."[8] Wrathall is at least close to implying Dreyfus's view that the nondeliberative action of the expert is what should be taken as the optimal mode of agency, with any action involving deliberation being seen as lesser or "impaired."

And it should be acknowledged that there is not just the relative lack of discussion of deliberation in Heidegger's work to motivate Dreyfus's reading. There is a textual basis for Dreyfus's strongly nondeliberative interpretation of Heideggerian agency in Division II of *Being and Time*. There, Heidegger says things like this: "The Situation cannot be calculated in advance or presented like something present-at-hand which is waiting for someone to grasp it. It merely gets disclosed in a free resolving which has not been determined beforehand" (SZ, 307). This passage seems to imply that the authentic agent does not plan or calculate in advance with regard to how they will act in a given situation. Rather, authentic agency is about resolving to act in a certain way in the concrete situation itself. In a similar vein, when discussing the call of conscience, Heidegger says: "The call does not report events; it calls without uttering anything. The call discourses in the uncanny mode of *keeping silent*" (SZ, 277). It is certainly plausible to interpret this passage as claiming that hearing the call of conscience, a necessary component of being authentic for Heidegger, does not involve any specific action-guiding instructions, nor does it prompt the agent to provide justification for their actions. The call instead says nothing. This fits with the passage quoted immediately above, and Dreyfus's interpretation, in that it also portrays the authentic agent as heeding this impulse to act in a situation without any preceding deliberative process.

I want to structure this chapter, then, not as a contrast between the Heideggerian view of deliberation and some prominent view in mainstream philosophy of action. Instead, I will structure this chapter as an attempt to develop a way to fit deliberation into the Heideggerian account of agency in contrast to Dreyfus's nondeliberative account. In the first chapter, we looked at Dreyfus's account of the role of mental states in action (or lack thereof, as the case may be), and in the second chapter, we considered his critique of causal theories of action from this point of view of denying a major role for mental states in action. In both cases, I have tried to argue that there is something right about Dreyfus's approach but also that we can provide a Heideggerian account of agency that is more plausible and more grounded in Heidegger's texts than the one Dreyfus gives. In this current chapter, I will again argue that Dreyfus's view is somewhat correct, but, again, we can do more to develop an account of deliberation in Heideggerian agency that is more plausible and more defensible even if I acknowledge that it is probably stretching Heidegger's texts too far to try to develop an extremely robust account of deliberation.

I believe it is important to show that deliberation can play an important role in Heideggerian agency for reasons beyond trying to "score scholarly points" by favorably contrasting my own view with the Dreyfusian one. There are, I believe, some serious implications for the Heideggerian account of agency if Dreyfus is right to claim that deliberative action will always be a derivative, or impaired, in Wrathall's words, mode of action for Heidegger, which in turn leads to the claim that nondeliberative action is somehow superior. The first problem is that such an account might not capture the phenomenology of action very well. There are two facets of this problem. There has been recent research undermining Dreyfus's claim that expert action is purely nondeliberative.[9] Furthermore, there seem to be reasonably mundane actions for which deliberation seems integral, not a marker of a lack of ability to skillfully cope. For instance, in the course of my activity of writing this book, it would be odd if I automatically sat down each day and poured words onto the page without any reflection or deliberation. Perhaps a poet "inspired by the muses" might write in this fashion, but for us normal mortals, it seems odd to insist that an intellectual activity like writing a lengthy work of philosophy is better performed when there is no deliberation whatsoever. Or, to give a different sort of example, suppose that I am meeting up with a friend for dinner. It would be very strange if the action of going to dinner with a friend takes place with no deliberation concerning the time and location. This example is different, since there is obviously an element of interpersonal coordination, but if the paradigm of action is the nondeliberative expert, it is hard to see how such an agent could switch to deliberative action when planning with another person, unless every social activity of this sort is to be classified as a breakdown in the normal course of our skillful coping.

The second main problem comes out in the now-classic critique of Heidegger by Ernst Tugendhat. Tugendhat shares Dreyfus's view that the Heideggerian account of action, especially authentic action, really does not have a serious role for rational deliberation. For Tugendhat, though, this is a major problem for Heidegger's account. Tugendhat worries that Heidegger seems to leave us with only a nondeliberative resolute decision regarding which action to pursue, which precludes any serious discussion of evaluative, that is, moral or rational, standards of an action. If one, when acting most authentically, unreflectively throws oneself into one course of action over another, how are we to render any moral judgment of the agent? Tugendhat sees this as a feature, not a bug of Heidegger's thought, as he says, "But it is not accidental that in Heidegger's thought, words like 'right' and 'should' are missing."[10] This criticism that Heidegger advocates a form of decisionism has, of course, been a fraught issue for him and those offering sympathetic interpretations of his work since *Being and Time* was first published and continues to raise questions about the potential amorality of Heidegger's philosophical work and his own personal moral failings.

My hope, then, is that by showing how there is a more expansive and integral role for deliberation in the Heideggerian conception of agency than the Dreyfusian allows, I can enhance the plausibility and desirability of my Heideggerian account of agency by virtue of its ability to better capture the phenomenology of deliberation in action and to allow for a Heideggerian response to the sorts of criticisms raised by Tugendhat, though the full development of this response will have to wait until chapter 5 and my discussion of Heideggerian responsibility.

INCORPORATING DELIBERATION INTO THE HEIDEGGERIAN ACCOUNT OF AGENCY

In general, I will make the case that deliberation for Heidegger can be thought of as an aspect of the general orienting component of action. By doing so, this will show that deliberation is, contra Dreyfus, built into the structure of human agency at the fundamental level and that deliberative and nondeliberative actions share the same basic structure.

Perhaps the most obvious textual stumbling block for Dreyfus's argument for the nondeliberative nature of action is the fact that in *Being and Time*, Heidegger claims that discourse (*Rede*) is one of the fundamental existential structures of human being (SZ, 161). Of course, Heidegger is unclear about the status and nature of discourse compared to the two other fundamental structures—disposedness and understanding—and there has been plenty of scholarly debate about how to interpret the place of discourse in the overall analysis of Dasein in *Being and Time*. I will not pretend to settle the larger debates about the nature of discourse, but I do take Heidegger's assertion of its status as equally fundamental as disposedness or understanding to be a prima facie reason to be skeptical that he really thinks the paradigmatic instances of agency are nondeliberative, though it remains to be clarified what Heideggerian deliberation would look like.

As was my strategy in chapter 1, I do think that we can gain some clarity on his views in *Being and Time* by considering his earlier lectures on Aristotle. In his 1924 lecture course, *The Basic Concepts of Aristotelian Philosophy*, Heidegger spends a good deal of time analyzing the famous Aristotelian definition of human beings as *zōon lōgon ēchon*. At the most general level, he claims, "When the Greeks say that the human being is a living thing that speaks, they do not mean, in a physiological sense, that he utters definite sounds. Rather, the human being is a living thing that has its genuine being-there in conversation and in discourse" (GA 18, 107–108/74). Here he is already using being-there, *Dasein*, as his expression for human existence, and he is saying that this existence is fundamentally connected to conversation and discourse. Of special interest for our purposes, Heidegger also connects language to action at a basic level, as he states: "The being of human beings . . . has the character of speaking: *prāxis metā lōgou*" (GA 18, 102–103/71). Once again, he is saying that human existence has speaking as its essence, but more particularly, human existence is action (*prāxis*) in the midst of language (*metā lōgou*). Not only is human existence in general characterized by discourse and language but human action also is fundamentally characterized by language. It is easy to see why, when writing *Being and Time*, it is natural for Heidegger to include discourse as a fundamental existential feature of Dasein, even if he is not quite sure what to do with it.

Again, as discussed in chapter 1, Heidegger, in his lectures on Aristotle, analyzes Aristotle's conception of desire, *ōrexis*, and I have attempted to show how this analysis can lay the groundwork for understanding the general Heideggerian account of agency. Now we can consider how Heidegger connects *ōrexis* and language in his interpretation of Aristotle. Heidegger points out that hearing is also an essential possibility implied by speaking. After all, what good would it do to speak if none of us could hear each other? Again, he does not limit the ability to hear to just the cognitive processing of uttered sounds but rather connects hearing with *ōrexis* and action: "[A human being] does not hear in the sense of learning something, but rather in the sense of having a directive for concrete practical concern. This ability to hear is a determination of *ōrexis*" (GA 18, 110–111/76). This makes sense if we remember the analysis from chapter 1. There, we saw how Heidegger, in his early lectures, uses the more physical language of feeling pulled or inclined to take certain courses of action that stand out as significant or important to us. Now he is saying something similar insofar as certain courses of action "call to us," and this ability to "hear" is what allows us to be motivated to act in particular ways.

One might be tempted to think that Heidegger is merely changing his metaphors here, and passages like those quoted above do not really mean that he thinks discourse plays a central role in our actions. However, there are other places where he specifically discusses deliberation and its function in action. He says of deliberation that it "is a 'seeking,' a *zētesis*, a being-after a definite view that I want to achieve. Through deliberating, I want primarily to come to the *tēlos* of a *dōxa*" (GA 18, 141–142/96). The aim of deliberation here is coming to definite view of what action is to be performed. Interestingly and importantly, Heidegger refers to this view of the action to be performed as a *dōxa*, commonly translated as "belief" or "opinion." Heidegger often does discuss *dōxa* in the more traditional epistemic context, as when Plato gives an account of the difference between mere belief (*dōxa*) and true knowledge (*epistēme*). Heidegger also, though, at times uses this less psychologistic, more perceptual sense of *dōxa*. He states, "*Dōxa* designates, first of all, the 'view of something,' but at the same time it means, for the most part, 'to have a view'" (GA 18, 136–137/93). And then in the *Plato's Sophist* lecture course, he claims, "What is most proximally there is not yet known in the sense of a cognition; instead consciousness has a determined view about it, a *dōxa*, which perceives the world as it for the most part appears and shows itself, *dokeī*" (GA 19, 12–14/9). He makes the connection between *dōxa* and the verb *dokēo*, one of whose usages is "to seem."[11] Thus, *dōxa* in its fundamental form for Heidegger is having a view of things encountered in the world as they seem, as they appear. Deliberation aims at coming to some view of how things are in the world such that this view can guide action.

We can now start to see how this conception of deliberation maps onto the general structure of agency developed in chapter 1. As we established there, actions happen through the combination of a conative component that provides the impetus to act and an orienting component that articulates the world in such a way so as to allow us to find certain actions meaningful. Deliberation is part of the fuller characterization of the orienting component of action. It is what allows us to form a definite view of the situation of action such that certain actions stand out as meaningful, or in the language being used here, such that the conative component is able to "hear" certain actions calling to it. A "belief" here is not first and foremost a discrete mental state in which one holds a particular propositional claim to be true, but rather, if we are to talk about beliefs on the Heideggerian account of agency, they are to be understood as a way in which the situation of action comes into view after the process of deliberation. Beliefs thought of as mental states in which one holds a particular proposition to be true are, as stated in chapter 1, reifications of the more fluid and experiential way in that a situation is articulated such that certain actions exert a pull on the agent.

Now we can turn to the consideration of deliberation in *Being and Time*. Again, deliberation does not show up much in this work, but there are a few places where Heidegger explicitly mentions deliberation that can be used to piece together how it fits into a Heideggerian account of agency. To start with, he maintains that deliberation is a form of interpretation, stating:

> In one's current using and manipulating, the concernful circumspection which does this "surveying", *brings* the ready-to-hand *closer* to Dasein, and does so by interpreting what has been sighted. This specific way of bringing the object of concern close by interpreting it circumspectively, we call "*deliberating*". (SZ, 359)

This is consistent with his claims in the earlier lecture courses that the aim of deliberation is to produce a certain view, *dōxa*, of what is to be done. By talking through the situation of action and what is to be done, the agent is able to make certain objects or actions stand out as significant for the achievement of the ultimate aim, or to make the object appear "closer" in the terminology used in the above passage. As Heidegger says a few lines further down, "deliberation illumines Dasein's current factical situation in the environment with which it concerns itself" (SZ, 359). He in turn characterizes interpretation as the possibility of understanding (*Verstehen*) to develop itself (SZ, 148). By this he means that interpretation is the further "working-out of possibilities projected in understanding" (SZ, 148). If understanding is the initial projection of ourselves toward some possible way of being that first structures the relations of significance that make up the world, then interpretation is the process of further refining and articulating what is already laid out in this initial projection. Heidegger emphasizes the way explicit interpretation is grounded in his basic conception of understanding by saying that in an explicit interpretation of something as something, the "'as' does not turn up for the first time; it just gets expressed for the first time, and this is possible only in that it lies before us as something expressible" (SZ, 149). Furthermore, "this does not require that the understanding of equipment be expressed in a predication. The schema 'something as something' has already been sketched out beforehand in the structure of one's pre-predicative understanding" (SZ, 359). Here Heidegger is again maintaining that the initial projections toward a for-the-sake-of-which provides the structure for our experience of the world in terms of possibilities for action and things useful for those actions. When we try to verbally articulate an interpretation of the situation of action, this interpretation is really already grounded in the pre-predicative articulation of situation by our underlying projection. Extending this to the consideration of deliberation more specifically, Heidegger says, "The involvement-character of the ready-to-hand does not first get discovered by deliberation, but only gets brought closer by it in such a manner as to let that *in which* something *has* an involvement, be seen circumspectively *as* this very thing" (SZ, 360). In this passage he is confirming that deliberation is the sort of interpretation sketched out above; that is, deliberation makes clearer and more fine-grained the articulation of the situation of action already established by projecting ourselves toward a particular self-understanding.

I recognize that I am wading into a much larger debate here about how to understand Heidegger's views on language. There are those, such as Cristina Lafont, who read Heidegger as claiming that language is fundamental to any disclosure of beings in the world.[12] In other words, Lafont reads Heidegger's assertion in *Being and Time* that *Rede* is equally fundamental with disposedness and understanding means that the way we encounter anything in the world as meaningful is made possible by language, with the implication being that language is *the* fundamental aspect of shaping how we articulate the world. There are others who argue that, at least in *Being and Time*, Heidegger means for discourse to be a further articulation of the intelligibility of entities in the world already established by our practical engagement with the world. This certainly seems to be Dreyfus's view. He claims that discourse is indeed dependent on disposedness and understanding, stating that "telling [discourse] is not on a par with the other two aspects of Dasein's openness. Rather, telling [discourse] refers to the way the whole current situation is Articulated by coping so as to be linguistically expressible."[13] Other scholars such as Mark Okrent and Taylor Carman are more or less in alignment with Dreyfus's reading. Okrent says, "Language is a kind or species of worldly contexture, and there could be a non-symbolic, non-linguistic world. But there could be no language, no system of sign-relations, unless there were world, a system of equipmental relations."[14] Similarly, Carman maintains that, for Heidegger, "linguistic meaning is parasitic on a kind of pragmatic signification that has nothing directly to do with signs or words."[15] I will not argue for one interpretation over the other here as the overarching correct way of reading Heidegger on language and discourse. Instead, I will merely say that I agree with the Dreyfus/Okrent/Carman position here as far as deliberation is concerned. On the view I am developing here, deliberation is a further working out of that prelinguistic significance in any situation of action that is already present due to the self-understandings toward which we are projecting ourselves. And as I will argue in the proceeding section, I do think it is consistent to say that deliberation is dependent on the articulation of the situation of action by understanding without also having to hold, as Dreyfus does, that deliberation occurs only in cases of breakdown and that deliberative action is somehow a lesser form of action.

If the preceding considerations provide evidence for thinking that deliberation does have a substantial role in action for Heidegger and does not just occur in cases of breakdown, and it establishes that the aim of deliberation is the formation of a view that allows a specific course of action to stand out as most important, we still do not know what exact form deliberation takes on Heidegger's view. Again, we can go back to Heidegger's early lectures to begin to get a sense of what this would look like. In the *Plato's Sophist* lecture course, Heidegger discusses two different forms of deliberation found in Aristotle's *Nicomachean Ethics*. The first type of deliberation is associated with the virtue of *téchne*, the knowledge that guides our productive activity, while the second type of deliberation is associated with the Aristotelian virtue of *phrónesis*. Heidegger characterizes the first form of deliberation as follows: "The deliberation of *téchne* relates simply to what contributes to the production of something else, namely, the *érgon*, e.g., a house" (GA 19, 47–49/34). He fleshes this out a bit further by claiming that this sort of deliberation has a conditional form: "If such and such is to come to be, then this or that must happen" (GA 19, 49–50/35). In other words, the focus of the deliberation of *téchne* is how to produce a certain object or complete a certain task, and it takes the form of talking through what is required to achieve that aim. This sort of deliberation allows us to come to a view, belief (*dóxa*), of what action is best suited to lead to the end product and allows that action to stand out as most salient or meaningful.

He says something very similar in *Being and Time* when defining deliberation: "The scheme peculiar to this [deliberation] is the 'if-then'; if this or that, for instance is to be produced, put to use, or averted, then some ways and means, circumstances, or opportunities will be needed" (SZ, 359). Heidegger connects deliberation of this sort back to understanding, the orienting component of action, as he says, "But if deliberation is to be able to operate in the scheme of the 'if-then', concern must already have 'surveyed' a context of involvements and have an understanding of it" (SZ, 359). This passage, as discussed above, supports the view that deliberation is a further working out of the articulation of the world around initially established by the projection toward some particular self-understanding. It might seem odd that Heidegger repeatedly frames deliberation more in the language of formal logic with his focus on the centrality of conditional statements for deliberation. I suspect, though, that this is just his way of making deliberation match up with the "in-order-to" structure of our experience of the world. As we have discussed in prior chapters, we experience the world in terms of possibilities for actions and things encountered in the world as potential means for performing these actions. Saying that deliberation has an "if-then" structure just means that we deliberate in terms of, "If I want to achieve this end, then I should use that means."[16] I do not think that deliberation always has to take this literal conditional form for Heidegger, but rather he is indicating that deliberation is essentially instrumentalist, that is, characterized by means-end reasoning. Talking through the possible options for action in this way allows one course of action to emerge as the best one to achieve the agent's end and thus exert the most pull on the agent.

We can see how this works using his example of building a house. This is, I would suggest, an example of a very complex action or series of actions that would be hard to explain on a purely nondeliberative, Dreyfusian model. Even if one supposes that I am a very skilled general contractor with plenty of experience building houses, it would be odd if I set straight away to building a house with no deliberation whatsoever, and it would be odd if we labeled any deliberation about how specifically to build the house to be some sort of breakdown in my ability to skillfully cope with the world around me. We might start with an explanation of this action in terms of the general conative and orienting aspects of action as developed in chapter 1. I understand myself as a being who needs shelter from the elements, so the action of building a house stands out to me as important and exerts a pull on me. Now, just talking about the action of building a house seems much too broad to capture the way that specific actions would exert a pull on me in the actual process of building. By this I mean that just saying that I am pulled toward the action of building a house provides very little direction in terms of what specific action I should undertake at any given moment. This is where deliberation plays the role of providing a more fine-grained articulation of the situation of action so as to let more specific actions appear as salient and exert a pull on me. I might start with something like, "If I want to build a house, then I need to buy land upon which to build it." This leads to the task of buying land for a house acquiring a salience and significance that draws me toward it. That might lead to me then thinking, "If I want to build a house on that land, I need to clear it of trees." Now the action of cutting down trees has appeared as salient and important for me to undertake. We can obviously see how this sort of deliberation can be extended through the whole process of building the house. At each stage the end product of the house orients my action, but deliberation allows for the particularized interpretation of the situation that makes specific intermediary actions exert a pull on me. Without deliberation letting all of the appropriate intermediary actions appear as significant, I am not sure that an agent could just perform the action "building a house," even if, again, the agent is a supremely skilled homebuilder.

Now we can consider the second main type of deliberation found in our everyday actions—that of *phrōnesis*. What is different about the deliberation of *phrōnesis* is that it is concerned not with the proper action required to produce some object or complete a task (e.g., building a house) but rather is concerned with the being of the agent themselves. Heidegger states that "[i]n the deliberation of the *phronīmos*, what he has in view is himself and his own acting" (GA 19, 49–50/35). In contrast to the deliberation of *tēchne*, the "deliberation of *phronesis*, however, relates to this *ērgon* insofar as it contributes to the deliberator himself" (GA 19, 47–49/34). This deliberation has the same conditional form as that of *tēchne*, but now the deliberation is concerned with what sort of actions one must undertake to be a certain type of person. In Heidegger's words, the "deliberation of *phrōnesis* is, furthermore, a certain drawing of conclusions: . . . if I am to behave and be in such and such a way, then . . ." (GA 19, 49–50/35). The implication is that in order to be a particular type of person, one must behave in certain ways. If I understand myself as a professor, for instance, then I could deliberate about whether to use my free time over summer break to, for example, radically overhaul my syllabi for the coming semester or write another chapter for this book. This sort of deliberation leads to the formation of belief, a view on the situation of action, that allows, say, the action of preparing my syllabus to stand out as mattering to me and pulls me toward performing it. Here, however, the deliberation is not about how best to create the desired end product, in this case the syllabus. Rather, the deliberation is about which action lets me best enact this particular self-understanding. The deliberation is guided by my understanding of my identity and which actions best contribute to the enactment of that identity.

I do think that Heidegger sees the deliberation of *phrōnesis* going a bit beyond this too. I will return to a fuller consideration of this idea in chapter 5, but I did want to introduce it now, since it does have to do with how he understands deliberation. As established above, Heidegger maintains that the deliberation of *phrōnesis* pertains to the being of the agent deliberating, and I suggested we understand this in terms of the agent's deliberating about which actions best allow them to enact particular self-understandings, but Heidegger also says that, the "*bouleūesthai* [deliberation] of the *phronīmos* concerns the Being of Dasein itself, the *eū zēn*, i.e., the right and proper way to be Dasein" (GA 19, 47–49/34). The ultimate aim of the deliberation of *phrōnesis*, then, is not merely the determination of the best way of enacting a specific self-understanding but rather the best way of being human as such. This sort of deliberation can still be understood in the "if-then" structure suggested above, taking the form of something like, "If I want to enact being human in the best way, then I must act in such and such a way." I think that is this the form of deliberation that is characteristic of authentic agency as Heidegger understands it in *Being and Time*, but again, this will be explored more fully in chapter 5. For now, I just want to establish that there seem to be three different types of deliberation for Heidegger: (1) the deliberation of *technē* concerned with how to create a certain end product, (2) the deliberation of *phrōnesis* concerned with how to enact a particular self-understanding, and (3) the deliberation of *phrōnesis* concerned with how to enact the proper or best way of being human.

We are now in a position to better address one of the potential concerns raised in chapter 1—how to understand cases of conflicting actions on the Heideggerian view of agency. It might seem that the Heideggerian account I have been developing would provide no resources to explain how an agent would end up taking one course of action over another when it is not possible to do both. These cases of conflicting actions can involve either form of action discussed here—*poīesis* or *prāxis*. Using Heidegger's example of building a house once more, we can see how this would work in the case of *poīesis*. What I want to produce is a house that is secure from the elements insofar as I understand myself as a being that needs shelter. If I want a house that does provide shelter from the elements, then I must put some sort of siding on it. I might deliberate about whether wood siding or aluminum siding would be best for achieving this desired result, and I cannot do both. This deliberative process that weighs the relative merits of the two competing options can again take the form of conditionals. For example, I might say, "If I use wood siding, then I can do it myself, but if I use aluminum siding, then it will be more durable." This deliberative process results in the formation of a "belief," a view of the situation of action, that allows the action of putting up one siding to appear as more desirable than the alternative. What this deliberative process does is to allow, through a more refined process of articulation, the action of putting up one siding to have more pull on me than the possible alternatives, but it is not essentially different from the pre-reflective articulation of our situation that takes place in Dreyfus's skillful coping.

Returning to the example of understanding myself as a professor, we can see how the same process could play out with conflicting actions aimed at enacting a particular self-understanding. Suppose that at the end of the day, I only have one hour to devote to work-related activities. I could spend that hour working on my own research, or I could spend it working on my class lecture for the next day. I might say, "If I understand myself as a professor, then I really need to have some sort of lecture for class tomorrow, since not having anything for class would constitute a total failure to uphold my duty to my students. If I put off working on my own research for a day, then I can still make up for that later." Again, this sort of conditional deliberation allows me to arrive at a view of the situation of action in which a particular action exerts a greater pull on me, in this case, the action of working on my class lecture.

Before moving on, there is one further point I want to add concerning the basic structure of deliberation for Heidegger. It might very well strike a reader who is familiar with Heidegger's later work that the form of deliberation described here is more or less synonymous with what Heidegger will later call "calculative reasoning." And indeed, in his later work, Heidegger frequently rails against the pernicious and ubiquitous nature of calculative reasoning, exhorting us to move beyond it to a different mode of thinking. Is it, then, misguided to make calculative reasoning central to his general account of agency? I would argue not. It should be remembered that deliberation, even in his early work, is not constitutive of language or thinking as a whole. As I have tried to make clear, it is the form of language that is involved in action. Also, in Heidegger's early work, he is attempting to give a phenomenological description of our everyday agency as it is "proximally and for the most part," to use his oft-repeated phrase. He might very well be right in his later work to argue that our everyday existence should not be as beholden to calculative thinking, but that does not detract from the plausibility of the claim that it is in fact the operative mode of reasoning in much of our daily lives.

RESPONSE TO THE DREYFUSIAN VIEW

At this point, we can clarify the response to the Dreyfusian account of Heideggerian deliberation and highlight the differences with the account developed here. When we deliberate, we are engaged in articulating the situation of action in such a way that a certain course of action will appear as more salient than alternatives by the end of the deliberative process. Deliberation will have allowed this action to matter most to us. Seen in this way, explicitly deliberative action is not a completely different type of action brought on only by a breakdown in our skillful coping with the world around us. Instead, explicitly deliberative action and pre-reflective skillful coping can both be understood as having the same basic structure: both rely on an articulation of the situation of action by our projection toward some possible self-understanding, but in the case of deliberative action, a bit of further articulation is required for a certain course of action to appear salient and actually call us into action. If the view of deliberation presented here is right, then there is reason to reject the further claim made by Dreyfus that deliberative action is a derivative, less authentic form of action. Rejecting this claim then also allows us to reject Dreyfus's account of authentic action as being that of the nondeliberative expert.

A defender of the Dreyfusian view might want to step in here and make the case that my view still does make a sharp distinction between deliberative and nondeliberative action. Maybe my view makes a distinction between situations where there is a course of action that is immediately salient requiring no explicit deliberation (Dreyfus's skillful coping) and situations where no single course of action immediately stands out as salient, but rather one only emerges through the process of deliberation. Is not the latter case just a different way of saying that this is a breakdown of our normal "mindless" agency that now requires explicit deliberation? While there is a difference between having explicit deliberation operative in action and not having explicit deliberation operative, I want to hold the line and maintain that there really are not two wholly distinct forms of action here. In the following passage, Heidegger is explaining when a truly theoretical attitude emerges in our dealings with entities encountered in the world:

> When we are using a tool circumspectively, we can say, for instance, that the hammer is too heavy or too light. Even the proposition that the hammer is heavy can give expression to a concernful deliberation, and signify that the hammer is not an easy one—in other words, that it takes force to handle it, or that it will be hard to manipulate. But this proposition *can* also mean that the entity before us, which we already know circumspectively as a hammer, has a weight—that is to say, it has the property of heaviness. . . . We now have sighted something that is suitable for the hammer, not as a tool, but as a corporeal Thing subject to the law of gravity. To talk circumspectively of "too heavy" or "too light" no longer has any "meaning"; that is to say, the entity in itself, as we now encounter it, gives us nothing with relation to which it could be "found" too heavy or too light. (SZ, 361)

There is obviously a lot to unpack here, but what I take to be the most important point for the considerations in this chapter is that deliberation does not signify the complete breakdown of the situation of action and the appearance of the theoretical attitude. Deliberation still takes place within that context of action. When I say something like, "If I want to pound in this small nail, then that hammer is too heavy," I am still operating within a certain context of action, and that sort of "if-then" deliberation allows one hammer to appear as too heavy and perhaps allows another hammer to appear as the right weight to achieve the desired outcome. In either case it is the deliberation that allows the hammer(s) to appear as a suitable instrument with which to perform the action at all. As with the Dreyfusian view concerning the role of mental states in action, I would say that with regard to deliberation, we again do not need to posit two different structures of agency: one for nondeliberative action and one for deliberative action. My view has the virtue of being able to explain deliberative and nondeliberative action from out of the same basic structure of agency.

Furthermore, as I alluded to in the example of building a house, in my view, one need not be committed to Dreyfus's claim that true experts act without deliberation, and this, indeed, is the mode of agency we should strive for in all of our actions. In my view, there is no problem with admitting that experts can and do deliberate about complex actions, like building a house or writing a long philosophical treatise, and the existence of deliberation in such cases does not indicate a breakdown in their expert, skillful coping but is instead integral to their performance of the action. This is not to say on my view that deliberation is essential for a higher mode of action or that deliberative action is somehow better than nondeliberative action. In my view, the presence of deliberation does not determine whether a mode of action is lesser or greater. Heidegger does distinguish between authentic and inauthentic action, but on my account, as we will see in chapter 5, this distinction does not hang on the presence or absence of deliberation.

CROWELL'S INTERPRETATION OF THE ROLE OF DELIBERATION IN ACTION

As mentioned at the beginning of this chapter, Steven Crowell, in contrast to Dreyfus, does think that there is a substantive role played by deliberation in the Heideggerian account of agency, and there are some similarities between Crowell's view and my own. Crowell, as I have done in this chapter, points out Heidegger's claim that discourse (*Rede*) is one of the fundamental aspects of human existence. Unlike Dreyfus, who, as we have seen, equates authentic action with the nondeliberative action of the expert, Crowell argues that authentic existence is characterized by engaging in the practice of giving reasons for one's actions. On this view, formulating justifying reasons for actions and sharing them with others so as to be answerable for one's actions are the core of authentic agency. I will postpone a thorough discussion of Crowell's account of authentic agency until chapter 5. Here I want to focus on how Crowell generally thinks of Heideggerian deliberation and point out some differences between his view and mine.

Crowell agrees with the view I have been developing here in general terms, as he says that "deliberation involves making explicit what belongs to understanding—the in-order-tos grounded in the practical identity at stake in my smoothly functioning practice."[17] However, the specifics of Crowell's account differ in several respects from mine. As is indicated in the passage quoted here and the one in the introductory section of this chapter, while he shares my view that deliberation is concerned with the further articulation of the situation of action already established by the projection toward a particular self-understanding, Crowell assumes the correctness of Dreyfus's claim that deliberation only occurs when there is a breakdown in our normal "smoothly functioning practice." I hope to have shown in the preceding section that one need not read Heidegger as being committed to this view, and indeed, removing this aspect of the Dreyfusian account of Heideggerian agency better matches the phenomenology of action generally.

Crowell also maintains that there are two different types of deliberation for Heidegger, which, as I have also claimed, correspond to the different modes of action of *poīesis* and *prāxis*. However, Crowell thinks that only the form of deliberation associated with *poīesis* has the "if-then" structure. In Crowell's words,

> His [Heidegger's] account of deliberation need not be limited to the sort of instrumental reasoning characteristic of making.... This sort of reason is not well expressed as an in-order-to; I do not attend the violin recital in order to be a good father but for the sake of being one.[18]

I do not think that much hangs on this, but I thought it was worth noting my disagreement on this issue. As stated above, I think the deliberation of *prāxis* can take the same "if-then" form of that of *poīesis*. On my reading, both *prāxis* and *poīesis* have a teleological structure—they are forms of actions aimed at some end. So, deliberation in both cases is concerned with coming to see a specific course of action as the best way of achieving that end. The difference is in the nature of the end involved in each type of each. The end of *poīesis* is some product that is external to the agent and can be finished, whereas the end of *prāxis* is a way of being of the agent themselves. In *prāxis* the agent is enacting a particular self-understanding, "making" themselves a certain type of person, even if, as discussed in chapter 2, there is no end product here that can definitively be said to be finished. It is a constant and never fully actualized process of making ourselves into certain types of people. Again, I do not think much hangs on this disagreement, but as I have argued with regard to various aspects of Dreyfus's view, I would prefer to have a more streamlined account of agency when possible and to cut out any unnecessary addition of different modes of action, deliberation, etc.

The other discrepancies between my view of deliberation and Crowell's emerge in the following passage:

> Things (including my own beliefs and desires) will present themselves as salient, as "weighty" or not.... If I am finally moved to act "in spite of" the way I feel about things "because" it is what reasons demands, this is possible only if I am so disposed that I can feel the weight of the reasons brought forward.[19]

Crowell is still describing deliberation as the process by which actions come to be seen as "salient," as I do, but is now doing so in the more explicitly cognitive and logical language of weighing reasons. Further fleshing out what he means by deliberative reasoning, he says:

> First, reasoning is a discursive practice in which something is offered or given—support for one's judgment, justification for one's behavior. Second, that which is given, the reason, is itself something . . . *speaks for* something else—not in the sense of speaking in place of something but in the sense of telling in favor of it.[20]

Again, Crowell's terminology shifts toward that of logical reasoning through his use of terms like "justification." While I think Heidegger might accept that his account of deliberation provides the foundation for the more formal sense of logical deliberation being alluded to by Crowell, I think Heidegger would object to the claim that this is fundamentally what deliberation is about. And Crowell himself acknowledges this, as he says:

> Far from seeing an intimate connection between discourse and reason, such as one might find in contemporary attempts to link linguistic meaning to truth-conditions or to spell out the semantics of language with the help of logic, Heidegger argues that the logical forms of language—*apophansis*, predicative assertion—are parasitical on a more primordial sense of *logos* as "letting be seen."[21]

As seen above, I would say that while Heidegger initially focuses on conditional "if-then" statements as the paradigm for practical deliberation, this need only be understood in a loose sense. The "if-then" statements are meant to convey the way we see actions as means of achieving an end, whether that be the creation of some product in the case of *poīesis* or the enactment of a certain self-understanding in the case of *prāxis*. As I will argue below, there is some sense of a rational structure at work in this deliberation, but it need not rise to the level of explicit claims that can be represented in symbolic logic or even a substantive weighing of competing reasons. In my view, Heideggerian deliberation can be more loosely discursive—a talking about possible actions that ultimately results in seeing the situation in a way such that one action stands out as the most salient. I would suggest this way of thinking about it fits better with our actual experience of deliberation in practice as well. There can be situations where we make lists of pros and cons and use that to allow some course of action to emerge as the most salient, or there can be instances where we employ a logically valid modus ponens/tollens type of deliberation that allows an action to emerge as most important. However, there are also plenty of situations where it might only take a quick single thought to accomplish this. For instance, on the occasions when I head out for work and realize that I have left my phone at home, I only have to say to myself, "If I go without my phone for the whole day, my wife will not be able to get ahold of me." Based on my understanding of what it is to be a good husband, that single statement by itself is enough to allow the action of turning around and going to retrieve my phone to have a pull on me and stand out as the most important course of action in that moment.

I believe Crowell is interested in pushing his interpretation of Heideggerian deliberation in the direction of logical justification through giving and weighing reasons so that he can then develop an account of authentic agency centered on this process that serves as a response to the sorts of criticisms raised by Tugendhat. On Crowell's account, an authentic agent can give reasons for their actions, thereby achieving a level of answerability and rational justification for their actions. This shows that the authentic agent does in fact employ a deliberative process that is bound by the normative standards of rationality (contra Tugendhat's criticism). But again, I will put off the substantive consideration of this picture of authentic agency until chapter 5.

The final difference that I want to note here between Crowell's account and mine has to do with the connection between deliberation and beliefs and desires in the overall structure of action. In the passage cited above, Crowell states, "Things (including my own beliefs and desires) will present themselves as salient, as 'weighty' or not." He seems to be suggesting that deliberation allows beliefs and desires themselves to appear as more or less salient. I recognize that he is nowhere claiming to give a comprehensive theory of motivation, as I have tried to do in chapter 1, and this might seem like a trivial bit of nitpicking, but if one does think about his claim from the perspective of a comprehensive theory of motivation, it seems wanting. Is his claim that deliberation is a component of action that takes place apart from specific beliefs and desires, implying that beliefs and desires can be the subject of deliberation rather than treating actions themselves as the proper subject of deliberation? If so, this seems at last inelegant, if not somewhat misguided. Suppose that I am working late into the night and experience a sudden desire for pizza, even though I had a full dinner several hours ago. I might very well think that it is unhealthy for me to eat pizza in these circumstances and, thus, might engage in some internal deliberation about the prudence of going down the block to the pizza place that is open late. However, it seems to me that the deliberation here is not about the *desire* for pizza. Similarly, the deliberation is not about the *belief* that eating pizza would be unhealthy in this circumstance. The deliberation, rather, is about the *action* of going to get pizza or the *action* of eating pizza. This is why I think my account of the Heideggerian theory of motivation and deliberation's role in that is at least cleaner and more elegant than what Crowell is implying. Again, in my view, the deliberation is a further refinement of the orienting component of action and is aimed at producing a view of the situation of action, a "belief," that allows a certain course of action to stand out as meaningful, to exert a pull on the agent. In the case of making a late-night pizza run, it might be as simple as saying to myself, "If I get pizza now, then I will make it harder for myself to continue to lose weight." Given my understanding of myself as a health-conscious person or as a fit person, this might be enough to establish a view of the situation of action such that I stay in my office working, or instead of getting pizza, go find some fruit to snack on in the kitchen. This shows again how the orienting component of action can channel and guide that fundamental tendency we have to be pulled toward various actions.

RESPONSE TO TUGENDHAT'S CRITICISM

Now we are at the point where I can start building a response to Tugendhat's criticism, though again, a fuller response will come in chapter 5, since it is there that I will deal with the issue of deliberation in authentic agency, which seems to be the real crux of the issue for Tugendhat. Here, however, I will lay the foundation for that later response by showing how I see a rational standard for deliberation operative in the sort of deliberation discussed in this chapter. If we think of the deliberation of *téchne* as a means-end reasoning about what action or object is best suited to achieve a goal, there are clear standards of good and bad deliberation here. If I am trying to cut new boards to replace the flooring on my deck, and I am drawn to the action of grabbing a jigsaw, which has a small blade and is not suited for making long, straight cuts, I can be said to have deliberated poorly, even if my deliberation did not take the explicit form of, "If I want to cut these boards, I should use a jigsaw." If I am trying to get my first-year students in an introductory course interested in philosophy, and when deliberating about how to structure my syllabus, I conclude that I should assign them Kant's *Critique of Pure Reason* as the first week's reading, then again, I can probably be said to have deliberated poorly. The "goodness" or "badness" of the deliberation depends on whether or not it makes the object or action needed to complete the task stand out as significant, as the one that in fact we ended up being drawn toward.

We can say something similar for the deliberation associated with *phrōnesis*. There might be different ways of successfully enacting various self-understandings, but there are also ways that people can clearly fail to enact their operative self-understanding. In the *Plato's Sophist* course, Heidegger, when describing good deliberation as characteristic of *phrōnesis*, states, "it is part of *euboulía* [deliberating well] not only to posit the *télos* as *agathōn* [the good] but to be *agathōn* [good] in each of its steps. In every step the *euboulía* must be directed in such a way that it has the *agathōn* in view and discusses all the circumstances and occasions with regard to it" (GA 19, 154–155/106). In other words, deliberation is good when it is directed toward the end to be achieved and correctly articulates the situation of action in terms of this end, in this case, the enactment of a particular self-understanding. When deliberation fails to do this either by not being directed toward the proper end or by incorrectly articulating the situation of action such that an action not consistent with the proper end stands out as most salient, the deliberation can be said to be bad. My deliberation can be seen as rational (good) or irrational (bad) depending on whether it leads me to see actions in alignment with the enactment of my operative self-understandings as salient or if it fails to do this. For instance, to use Aristotle's example, if I understand myself as a doctor, and when deliberating about how to handle patients coming in complaining of vague chronic pain, I conclude that I should prescribe unnecessarily large amounts of dangerous painkilling drugs to my patients, then something is wrong with my deliberation. Perhaps my deliberation is not aiming at enacting the self-understanding of being a doctor at all here, even though that is clearly what the situation calls for. Or, it could be the case that my deliberation is aimed at enacting being a doctor, but it is misguided in terms of what actions lead to successfully enacting this way of being. If I truly understand what it is to be a doctor, that sort of action should not be appearing as the sort of action I ought to pursue, since we understand a doctor as someone who seeks to improve the health of patients, not push them unnecessarily toward potentially dangerous and addictive drugs.

Now, Tugendhat's criticism does go deeper than this. He acknowledges that Heidegger could allow for the rational judgment of technical deliberation involved in creating a product or the deliberation involved with enacting a certain self-understanding. The real problem comes from Heidegger's account of authentic agency. He is especially worried that Heidegger sees authentic action as completely devoid of any rational deliberation or evaluative standards by which it could be judged and, indeed, thinks this is what makes authentic action better. As mentioned in chapter 1, for Heidegger, in the experience of anxiety, all of the significance that normally allows actions to stand out as meaningful drops away, and Heidegger says that we are left with making a resolute choice in this moment. He is often taken to mean that in this state of anxiety, we recognize the distance between ourselves and any particular self-understanding. This distance allows us to now choose which self-understanding we are going to identify with going forward, and this results in us having the possibility of "owning" our actions in a way we did not before this experience of authenticity. The issue is that if our self-understandings are what provide the context in which we can deliberate (over, for example, how best to be a professor) and the rational standard for judging such deliberation, it seems that in authentic agency, deliberation is not possible, and there would be no rational standard to judge it even if it were. Again, I will only offer a promissory note that will be redeemed in chapter 5, but my general strategy will be to argue that being an authentic agent is a self-understanding that we can take on that can involve deliberation and does provides some rational standard by which we can judge that deliberation to succeed or fail, even though being an authentic agent is not defined by public norms or biological characteristics of human existence in the same way that the self-understandings we have been discussing are.

NOTES

1. Christine Korsgaard, *Self-Constitution: Agency, Identity, and Integrity* (Oxford: Oxford University Press, 2009).

2. Steven Crowell is a notable exception to this, and I will consider his views on the nature of deliberation for Heidegger and its general role in a Heideggerian account of agency later in this chapter.

3. Hubert Dreyfus, *Being-in-the-World: A Commentary on Heidegger's* Being and Time, Division 1 (Cambridge, MA: MIT Press, 1991), 71.

4. Dreyfus, *Being-in-the-World: A Commentary on Heidegger's* Being and Time, *Division I*, 72.

5. Dreyfus, "Could Anything Be More Intelligible Than Everyday Intelligibility?: Reinterpreting Division I of *Being and Time* in the Light of Division II," *Bulletin of Science and Technology* 24, no. 3 (June 2004): 268.

6. Dreyfus, "Could Anything Be More Intelligible Than Everyday Intelligibility?: Reinterpreting Division I of *Being and Time* in the Light of Division II," 269.

7. Steven Crowell, *Normativity and Phenomenology in Husserl and Heidegger* (Cambridge: Cambridge University Press, 2013), 202.

8. Mark Wrathall, "Autonomy, Authenticity, and the Self," in *Heidegger, Authenticity, and the Self: Themes from Division Two of* Being and Time, ed. Denis McManus (New York: Routledge, 2015), 196.

9. See Gunnar Breivik's "Skillful Coping in Everyday Life and Sport: A Critical Examination of the Views of Heidegger and Dreyfus," *Journal of the Philosophy of Sport* 34, no. 2 (2007): 116–134. There, Breivik, among other things, contests Dreyfus's claim that high-level athletes do not deliberate while competing in their sports. Barbara Gail Montero makes a more in-depth argument against the Dreyfusian claim that explicit thought is absent in expert action in her *Thought in Action: Expertise and the Conscious Mind* (Oxford: Oxford University Press, 2016).

10. Ernst Tugendhat, "Wir sind nicht fest verdrahtat: Heidegger's 'Man' und die Tiefendimensionen der Gründe," in *Aufsätze: 1992–2000* (Frankfurt am Main: Suhrkamp, 2001), 144.

11. Liddell and Scott, *A Greek-English Lexicon*, accessed January 4, 2020, http://www.perseus.tufts.edu/hopper/text.

12. Cristina Lafont, *Heidegger, Language, and World Disclosure* (Cambridge: Cambridge University Press, 2000).

13. Dreyfus, *Being-in-the-World: A Commentary on Heidegger's* Being and Time, *Division I*, 217.

14. Mark Okrent, "Equipment, World, and Language," *Inquiry* 45, no. 2 (2002): 202.

15. Taylor Carman, "Was Heidegger a Linguistic Idealist?," *Inquiry* 45, no. 2 (2002): 212.

16. It is not uncontroversial to view deliberation or practical reasoning as essentially instrumentalist, but Candace Vogler provides a good argument in favor of the instrumentalist account of practical reason in her *Reasonably Vicious* (Cambridge, MA: Harvard University Press, 2002).

17. Crowell, *Normativity and Phenomenology in Husserl and Heidegger*, 202.

18. Crowell, *Normativity and Phenomenology in Husserl and Heidegger*, 291.

19. Crowell, *Normativity and Phenomenology in Husserl and Heidegger*, 202.

20. Crowell, *Normativity and Phenomenology in Husserl and Heidegger*, 200.

21. Crowell, *Normativity and Phenomenology in Husserl and Heidegger*, 200.

Chapter 4

Heideggerian Freedom and the Free Will Debate

The traditional philosophical debate surrounding the nature of freedom has typically focused on the question of what it means to have free will and whether it is reasonable to conclude that human existence is such that we could have free will. This debate has grown and shifted and moved to the consideration of hyperspecific questions, so I will not pretend that I can address all important facets of the debate here. There are two particularly central aspects of the free will debate that I will make the focus of this chapter. As Robert Kane puts it in his Introduction to *The Oxford Handbook of Free Will*: "These two features of the personal or practical standpoint are pivotal to what has traditionally been called free will: we believe we have free will when (a) it is 'up to us' what we choose from an array of alternative possibilities and (b) the origin or source of our actions is in us and not in anyone or anything else over which we have no control."[1]

Taking the latter issue first, it makes sense to think that in order to be free, we, as agents, have to be the source or origin of our actions. This is where the question of causal determinism takes root and gives rise to doubts about our freedom. The mainstream philosophic and scientific traditions have, over the past several centuries, mostly converged on the idea that to be the source of something is to be its cause. So, if we can say that we, as agents, are the cause of our own actions, then it seems that we can say that we have freedom. Unfortunately, as Kant pointed out, we cannot think of a cause that brings about a future state of affairs without also positing an earlier state of affairs that caused it. And this is the problem of free will in its modern form—we conceive of freedom as being the cause of our own actions but also have to understand that this implies a causal chain that extends beyond any of us as individual agents, making it seem like it is not possible to truly be the origin of our actions.

While I clearly cannot do justice to enormous range and complexity of views that have emerged in the modern free will debate, I do want to provide a sketch of the basic conceptual framework as I see it along with some particularly influential responses to the problem from individual philosophers. The aim is, as in earlier chapters, to provide a sense of the mainstream philosophical debate surrounding freedom to show how the Heideggerian account I develop connects to it at some points, while going in different directions at others. The general libertarian position is that there are at least some instances when our actions are not causally determined by outside factors beyond our control, implying that we can, again, at least sometimes be the origin of our actions. Roderick Chisholm, in his "Human Freedom and the Self," proposed a different sort of causality, agent (or immanent in his first formulation) causality, that would allow us to conceive of our actions as being self-caused without having to extend that causal chain out into some external realm that is beyond our control. In Chisholm's words, "If a man is responsible for a particular deed, then, if what I have said is true, there is some event, or set of events, that is caused, not by other events or states of affairs, but by the agent, whatever he may be," and, "when an agent, as distinguished from an event, causes an event or state of affairs, then we have an instance of immanent causation."[2] This is essentially the tendency mentioned by Heidegger to understand freedom in terms of a different sort of causality than natural causality, which we discussed briefly in chapter 2. Kane defends a different sort of libertarian position that eschews positing a different sort of agent causation.[3] Instead, Kane argues that there are certain moments where we are genuinely and completely evenly torn when making a decision. All of the causal factors in the agent's background (their character, developed preferences, previous experiences, etc.) that make them choose one path of action might be exactly evenly balanced by a different set of causal factors that push them toward an alternative path of action. In these moments, Kane thinks, the only thing that can tip the balance in favor of one action or another is the will of the agent themselves. These actions are truly free, and moreover, these shape the character and experiences of the agent going forward, so we can say that the agent has some responsibility for the formation of their character that will have a causal influence on their future decisions.

Then there are compatibilists, or soft determinists, who argue that even if our actions are causally determined by causal chains that extend beyond our control, there can be some meaningful sense of freedom or responsibility attributed to us as agents. For instance, Harry Frankfurt, in his "Freedom of the Will and the Concept of a Person," lays out what has come to be called a hierarchical account of action.[4] We have normal desires for things that bring about our actions, called first-order desires by Frankfurt, but we also can have desires about which desires will bring about our actions, which

Frankfurt calls second-order desires or volitions. In other words, he claims that we can be said to have a free will when we have a second-order desire for the first-order desire that actually causes our actions, even if it is causally determined that we have these desires. When the desire that we want to move us is in fact the one that brings about our action, then we have free will in the sense that we are doing what we want. Frankfurt uses the example of a willing addict to make his point. Someone with a powerful drug addiction would presumably have a first-order desire for the drug, and this first-order desire would cause them to use the drug. However, it is possible that they could have a second-order desire to have that first-order desire move them to act. An addict with this alignment of first- and second-order desires would have free will on Frankfurt's view. Having the right sort of causal structure internal to the agent bringing about the action makes it so that the action is performed with a free will, even if, again, there is a causal chain that extends beyond the agent that leads to the specific desires the agent has. John Martin Fischer has also put forward an influential compatibilist view.[5] Unlike Frankfurt's view that is interested in whether higher-order desires align with lower-order desires, in Fischer's view, the key consideration is whether or not an action is brought about, or caused, by a "reasons-responsive mechanism." By this, Fischer means that the process through which the action is brought about must be responsive to reasons; that is, the agent's decision about which action to perform could change in light of new, relevant information. For instance, if I decide to leave work to drive home early, because I saw that it would start snowing heavily at my normal departure time, this action would be reasons-responsive insofar as my decision-making process was receptive to the new information about the incoming inclement weather. Fischer maintains that actions of this sort, which are brought about by a process that is reasons-responsive in this way, are to be considered free, even if it is causally determined that I will be provided with that new information at exactly that moment and that I will change my course of action in exactly that way upon receiving that information. His view is similar to Frankfurt's in that they both can be agnostic about the truth of determinism while holding that free will can be defined by some specific causal structure internal to agent in the process of performing the action.

Now, the other main focus of the free will debate mentioned by Kane is the idea that in order to be free, we must be able to do otherwise. It is a common intuition that in order to say that an agent is free, it must be possible for them to pursue alternative courses of action, and Kane himself argues for this intuition, making the case that free will is exercised in those moments of indeterminism when it is completely up to the agent to pick which action to pursue. Frankfurt, though, famously challenged this intuition in his "Alternate Possibilities and Moral Responsibility."[6] There, Frankfurt constructs examples that he takes to show that there are at least certain hypothetical situations where we would intuitively be inclined to say that an agent acted freely, even if they truly did not have the possibility of taking a different course of action. Fischer agrees with the general thrust of what are now called Frankfurt-type examples and provides one of his own.[7] Fischer asks us to imagine an undecided voter about to cast their ballot. Unbeknownst to the voter, a progressive neuroscientist has implanted a chip in their brain so that if it is detected that they will vote for the Republican candidate instead of the Democrat, the chip will override the voter's decision and make them vote for the Democrat. In this case, the voter decides to vote for the Democrat anyhow, and the chip never influences their action. Frankfurt would argue that this action of voting for the Democrat was still free, even though the voter had no possibility of doing otherwise, presumably because the voter had a second-order desire that the first-order desire to vote for the Democrat be the one that moves them to act. Fischer agrees with Frankfurt that this action could very well be free in spite of the lack of ability to pursue an alternate action but has different reasons for this judgment. For Fischer, the action of voting for the Democrat is free if the voter arrives at that decision through a reasons-responsive process, even if the implanted chip eliminates any possibility for the agent to do otherwise.[8]

At the other end of the spectrum, hard determinists like Derk Pereboom have been willing to bite the bullet and argue that there is no way of salvaging the idea of free will.[9] Instead, we should accept the fact that all of our actions are causally determined in a way that makes it impossible for us to be the source of our actions. Pereboom structures his argument as an attack on both compatibilists and libertarians. If he can show that both of these positions are unsatisfactory, that leaves hard determinism as the only plausible view. With regard to compatibilism, Pereboom shows what he finds to be an inconsistency with both Frankfurt's and Fischer's views by returning to examples where a neuroscientist could remotely exert control over an agent's actions. Frankfurt and Fischer both agree that an agent acts freely if their action is brought about with the right structure internal to the agent in the process of acting, but both also agree that if a neuroscientist were to interfere with the action and, say, change a second-order desire to match a first-order desire in Frankfurt's case or change the way in which the agent responds to reasons in Fischer's case, then the action would no longer be free. Pereboom argues that if determinism is true, our genetic makeup and other factors well outside of our control will have already determined which second-order desires we have and how/if we act in reasons-responsive ways in a manner that is quite similar to the hypothetical neuroscientist meddling contemporaneously in the process of action. If that is right, then we should have no reason to think Frankfurt- or Fischer-style compatibilism really preserves any meaningful sense of free will or responsibility. With regard to libertarianism, Pereboom argues that a libertarian view like Kane's that relies on the existence of some moments of indeterminacy is not successful, since maintaining that free actions are those that are not determined by any prior causal factors makes those actions appear quite random. Normally, we think for actions to be free, we must have some control over them, which would be negated if our actions were random. Pereboom does not think that agent-causation views suffer from the same logical issue, but rather he argues that we have no evidence to show that agent-causation actually exists, and absent such evidence, we should assume that it does not.

This, then, completes my sketch of the conceptual framework of the current free will debate. What I want to emphasize here before turning to the Heideggerian account of freedom is that all of these influential responses to the problem of free will share the assumption of a causal theory of action, that is, that our actions are fundamentally to be understood in causal terms.

My aim in this chapter is to build up the Heideggerian conception of freedom that follows from the conception of agency that I have developed up to this point and to contrast Heidegger's concept of freedom with the prominent positions in the mainstream free will debate sketched above. My goal is not necessarily to make Heidegger's thought fit neatly within the conceptual framework of the mainstream debate but rather to show more clearly what the Heideggerian stance would be on these central concerns in the free will debate and to show how Heidegger provides us with a very different understanding of freedom and, as we will see in chapter 5, responsibility. I will start by laying out what I take to be Heidegger's general understanding of freedom in the late 1920s and early 1930s. Once that task is accomplished, I will proceed to consider the Heideggerian response to Kane's two main questions of the free will debate. Although there will be significant differences between the Heideggerian view I develop and the mainstream compatibilist views like those of Frankfurt and Fischer, I will ultimately argue that like these compatibilists, for Heidegger, it is possible for us to be the origin of our actions and that it is not required that we can pursue alternative courses of action to be free.

THE HEIDEGGERIAN ACCOUNT OF FREEDOM

The first thing to point out is that Heidegger pointedly does not use the phrase "free will" but instead prefers to talk about "freedom." Given our considerations in previous chapters, it should already be somewhat clear why he does this. Earlier in the philosophical tradition, the will was seen as a specific faculty of the soul or mind that pushes us into action. Such a faculty would be considered free if there were no external force determining which actions it pursued, and the free will debate took shape around the attempt to determine whether the will was in fact free in this sense. Contemporary philosophers have largely dropped the idea that there is some specific faculty called the will and have instead, as we have seen, proposed various mental states and associated phenomena as the impetus for action. The free will problem then gets to be construed in terms of whether or not these mental phenomena are determined by external forces. Heidegger, of course, would not accept the existence of a special faculty of the will either, but moreover, as I hope to have shown, he would have misgivings about pinning the conative force behind our actions on any discrete mental states that function like springs in a mechanical process. Indeed, on my reconstruction of his views, the conative force driving our actions is not purely in the mind of the agent at all but rather is the pull toward the performance of certain actions that arises through the interaction of agent and environment that cannot fundamentally be understood in terms of efficient causality.

With that initial bit of terminological clarification out of the way, we can turn to the task of figuring out what freedom is for Heidegger. Several scholars have made the case that there are two different senses of freedom developed by Heidegger in the late 1920s and early 1930s. I think the distinction between these two different types of freedom is essentially right, and it provides a good general framework for working out a plausible conception of freedom from this era of Heidegger's thought. My approach going forward in this chapter will incorporate aspects of what all three scholars have said on this topic, but, of course, I will also be charting my own course a bit and deviating from or adding to their interpretations.

Charles Guignon refers to the concept of freedom found in *Being and Time* as "human freedom," by which Guignon means the sort of freedom we think about in the context of normal human actions.[10] Beatrice Han-Pile refers to this first sense of freedom as ontic or existentiell freedom, as, again, this deals more with the question of what it means to be free in the course of our concrete, everyday activities.[11] Sacha Golob calls this sense "freedom^2."[12] All three interpret this sense of freedom as being aligned with authentic existence as described in *Being and Time*. For the sake of terminological clarity, I will refer to this first sense of freedom as existential freedom. Here, the central issue is Heidegger's oft-repeated idea that when existing authentically, we "choose to choose." It is this second-order choice that occurs in authentic action that makes actions free. Of course, more needs to be said to flesh out what exactly Heidegger is referring to with this focus on second-order choice and why this second-order choice is constitutive for a certain kind of freedom. I will return to the consideration of this existential freedom later in this chapter and in the next; for now, though, I will just provide a sketch of what is mostly familiar to Heidegger scholars at this point. We can get the basic gist of existential freedom by considering the following passages. When discussing anxiety (*Angst*), the mood Heidegger associates with authentic existence, he says, "Anxiety makes manifest in Dasein its *Being towards* its ownmost potentiality-for-Being—that is, its *Being-free* for the freedom of choosing itself and taking hold of itself" (SZ, 188). Similarly, when talking about the projective aspect of authenticity, anticipation of death, he claims:

> When, by anticipation, one becomes free *for* one's own death, one is liberated from one's lostness in those possibilities which may accidentally thrust themselves upon one; and one is liberated in such a way that for the first time one can authentically understand and choose among the factical possibilities lying ahead of that possibility which is not to be outstripped. (SZ, 264)

Furthermore, he goes on to state:

> Free for its ownmost possibilities, which are determined by the *end* and so are understood as *finite*, Dasein dispels the danger that it may, by its own finite understanding of existence, fail to recognize that it is getting outstripped by the existence possibilities of Others, or rather that it may explain these possibilities wrongly and force them back upon its own, so that it may divest itself of its ownmost factical existence. (SZ, 264)

For Heidegger, anxiety is the mood in which all of the usual significance of our activities and entities that we encounter in the world drops out. In the passage quoted above, he is saying that it is this collapse of significance that affords us the distance that makes it possible for us to choose (perhaps for the first time) who we want to be, and thus to take hold of our existence. Something similar happens in the anticipation of death. We become radically individualized through the awareness that dying is something that no one else can do for us. Ultimately, our existence cannot be reduced to the self-understandings that we have taken to be definitive for ourselves, and again, we are provided with that distance from our ordinary, everyday self-understandings so that we are capable of affirmatively choosing to be defined by certain possible ways of being rather than simply having drifted into them. That is why I am referring to this as existential freedom. This sense of freedom in *Being and Time* has obvious parallels to conceptions of freedom that we find in the canonical existentialists like Kierkegaard, Nietzsche, and Sartre, even if Heidegger suggests freedom is more of a choice of the set of normative constraints that one will abide by for one's actions rather than suggesting freedom is about more radically reconfiguring the norms by which one acts, as might be the case with Nietzsche or Sartre. Heidegger's existential freedom also shares with these thinkers the idea that freedom is about breaking out of the unreflective conformity to prevailing social standards and making one's existence one's own.

The second sense of freedom is broader, and its connection to human action is not as immediately obvious. Guignon calls this second sense of freedom "freedom as letting be," while Han-Pile calls it ontological freedom. Golob refers to this sort of freedom as "freedom[1]."[13] Guignon in particular points out that Heidegger, after *Being and Time*, starts using freedom to refer more and more frequently to the freeing up of entities. In other words, freedom is the space that lets entities manifest themselves as what they are. I will adopt Han-Pile's practice of referring to this sort of freedom as "ontological freedom" going forward, since it has to do with the being of entities in the world. In this chapter I will primarily focus on the ontological conception of freedom for three primary reasons, which will become clearer as the chapter progresses. The first is the simple fact that after *Being and Time*, discussion of the existential conception of freedom becomes much less frequent, and Heidegger seems more and more focused on fleshing out the ontological conception of freedom. While I have maintained throughout this volume that I will not constrain myself to following Heidegger slavishly, it does seem clear that ontological freedom is increasingly what he sees as the more important type of freedom for his thought going forward, and that should carry some weight in my interpretation, perhaps especially as something of a corrective to the outsized weight that existing Heidegger scholarship has placed on existential freedom. The second reason for focusing on ontological freedom is that I think it allows for a more satisfactory Heideggerian response to the central issues of the mainstream free will debate than a primary focus on existential freedom does. Finally, we will see that ontological freedom is actually the condition for the possibility of existential freedom, so ontological freedom should have philosophical pride of place.

Now we can begin trying to sort out what Heidegger means when he starts using freedom in the ontological sense, that is, more in this sense of freeing up entities, rather than the existential sense of choosing oneself in one's actions. The conception of ontological freedom is already used in *Being and Time*, even if it perhaps takes a backseat to all of the evocative claims that Heidegger makes about existential freedom is his discussion of the various key aspects of authenticity. In Division I, when introducing the idea of the for-the-sake-of-which and its importance in providing the context of significance that is the world, Heidegger says, "Letting an entity be involved, if we understand this ontologically, consists in previously freeing it for its readiness-to-hand within the environment" (SZ, 85). Later, in the 1930 essay, "On the Essence of Truth," Heidegger in a more explicit manner than in *Being and Time* equates freedom with letting beings be what they are, as he claims that "freedom for what is opened up in an open region lets beings be the beings they are. Freedom now reveals itself as letting beings be" (GA 9, 188/144). Heidegger cautions against an overly passive reading of the phrase "letting beings be," as he says that this "does not refer to neglect and indifference but rather the opposite. To let be is to engage oneself with beings" (GA 9, 188/144). So, now we have the idea that freedom consists in engaging with beings so as to let them be what they are. To understand how this is supposed to work, we can look at the 1929 essay, "On the Essence of Ground," and the 1928 lecture course, *The Metaphysical Foundations of Logic*. In both of these works, Heidegger equates freedom with transcendence. In *The Metaphysical Foundations of Logic*, he says, quite explicitly, "Dasein's transcendence and freedom are identical" (GA 26, 237–239/185). Furthermore, transcendence "casts something like the 'for-the-sake-of' projectively before it" (GA 9, 163/126). And with the use of this sort of language (e.g., "projection" and "for-the-sake-of"), we see the connection back to his analysis of Dasein in *Being and Time*.

We have already thoroughly discussed Heidegger's conception of the for-the-sake-of-which as a self-understanding toward which one can project oneself and the importance of this idea for a Heideggerian account of action. Now it is important to note that after *Being and Time*, he explicitly and repeatedly equates the projection toward a for-the-sake-of-which with freedom, particularly ontological freedom. We have also already discussed how various scholars have emphasized the importance of norms for defining each for-the-sake-of-which, but that earlier discussion primarily focused on how the norms that define the various self-understandings we take up can make actions appear as important for us, which thus allows us to be pulled to take up certain courses of action. When considering ontological freedom, Heidegger really does focus on the ontological import here—the way in which this sort of freedom opens up a space for beings to manifest themselves as what they are. In chapter 1, I used the example of a chalkboard being badly placed from *The Fundamental Concepts of Metaphysics* to make the point about how our commitment to various self-understandings opens up a space for things in the world to manifest themselves (GA 29/30, 497–502/343–345). In that earlier chapter, we also discussed how the norms that define our self-understandings allow for this space. Remember that Heidegger maintains that it is objectively correct that the chalkboard is poorly placed, but that the possibility of making such a judgment relies on there being teachers and students, with certain expectations. For the sake of simplicity in chapter 1 and a desire not to introduce too many interconnected concepts too quickly, I left out the connection to freedom for Heidegger. However, now I can point out that he sees freedom as the opening of that space for the board to manifest itself as badly placed.

Despite the shift in focus to the ontological importance of projection toward a for-the-sake-of-which, I want to argue that this does not wipe away the practical import of such projection as laid out in earlier chapters. In other words, the ontological sense of freedom is still connected to normal, everyday agency by virtue of ontological freedom's opening up a space in which certain actions are significant for us. Even though he is primarily concerned with how beings manifest themselves in his discussion of freedom and projection in *The Fundamental Concepts of Metaphysics*, Heidegger still at times hearkens back to earlier lecture courses where he is more explicit about considering human action. For instance, in *The Fundamental Concepts of Metaphysics*, he remarks that the "essence of understanding consists precisely in distinguishing (it has been regarded in terms of *krīnein* from time immemorial)" (GA 29/30, 517–518/356). As we have seen, in earlier Aristotelian lecture courses, Heidegger would frequently characterize all life, including that of humans, as being primarily characterized by *kineīn* (moving) and *krīnein* (distinguishing). Our projection toward certain possible ways of being creates distinctions between different possible actions. It makes some appear beneficial and worthwhile, others detrimental, and others do not even register and remain in the background of insignificance. In this lecture Heidegger also pointedly keeps making the claim that the human mode of being open to things encountered in the world is comportment (*Verhaltung*) as opposed to the mere behavior (*Benehmen*) associated with animals. Furthermore, in the essay "On the Essence of Ground," he states that "all forms of comportment are rooted in transcendence" (GA 9, 163/126), while also maintaining in the *Metaphysical Foundations of Logic*: "If we now pose the problem of transcendence in connection with the problem of freedom, we must not take freedom in a narrow sense, so that it pertains to *prāxis* in contradistinction to *theorīa*. . . . [T]he problem is the common root of both intuition, *theoreīn*, as well as action, *prāxis*" (GA 26, 236–237/184). These passages make it clear that while he is shifting the emphasis to the ontological dimension of freedom in the late 1920s, Heidegger does not mean to sever the concept from the practical realm entirely.

Seen in this way, the ontological sense of freedom as freeing up runs very deep into the structure of our everyday agency. It is not just when we exist authentically and achieve freedom in the existential sense that we can be said to be free from Heidegger's point of view. It is really the case that ontological freedom is a necessary condition for any sort of action. This holds even for inauthentic existence in which, for Heidegger, I have merely drifted into a certain self-interpretation that then lets certain actions matter to me. I might have never explicitly chosen to understand myself as professor and just kind of drifted into that role as the obvious next step after graduate school, but I would still need an implicit commitment to that way of being for the actions that I perform on a daily basis to manifest themselves as significant in any way. Insofar as we act at all, we are "free" in the ontological sense of the term. Golob makes this same point, as he claims that "there is a crucial sense in which even the most inauthentic agent is still defined by the first-person normative perspective of 'mineness'."[14]

FREEDOM, CAUSALITY, AND BEING THE ORIGIN OF ONE'S ACTIONS

Now we are in position to see how we can formulate a Heideggerian response to the question about whether we are the source of our actions or not. As laid out at the beginning of this chapter, from the perspective of the mainstream free will debate, the main ways of addressing this question all rely on a causal understanding of human agency and the resulting concern about causal determinism. After all, if our actions are a product of a series of causal chains that extend well beyond ourselves and our control, it does not seem like we can be the true source of our actions. What, then, are the options for addressing this question from the perspective of the Heideggerian view of freedom?

One option is to focus on Heidegger's concept of existential freedom, as defined above. This is essentially the approach taken by Guignon as he argues that the Heideggerian account of freedom, understood as existential freedom, undermines the basic question of the normal free will debate. To show how this would work, he uses the example of putting on a certain pair of shoes. In Guignon's words:

> If someone asks me whether I am wearing the shoes I have on of my own free will, the proper response is not "Yes," but rather "What makes you ask? Is there something strange about wearing these shoes that I didn't see? Are they inappropriate in this situation? The issue of free will does not arise in such a case, because, quite simply, these are my shoes, the shoes I wear, and it makes no more sense to ask whether I put them on this morning of my own free will than it makes to ask whether I was determined to put them on by forces beyond my control (perhaps some sort of shoe police).[15]

He goes on to explain as follows:

> Heidegger would say, I think, that these deeds are not really actions in the full sense of that word, and so not really part of what I freely do as an agent. This is so because merely enacting roles in the public world is, for the most part, simply a matter of doing what everyone else does, a matter of doing things unreflectively in accordance with the norms and conventions regulating such doings.[16]

Guignon makes a distinction between true actions and mere deeds and suggests that we are only really interested in the question of freedom when it comes to true actions. On his view, we are only truly agents, and thus truly free, when we make a second-order choice to identify ourselves with our actions and self-understandings, as he claims: "Instead of drifting into the familiar activities approved by the conventions of the public world, the resolute individual fulfills her ability-to-be free by identifying herself with a specific range of choices while recognizing that, in doing so, she is renouncing others."[17] The implication is that the traditional debate over free will that worries about the causal determination or lack thereof for mundane actions like putting on shoes is just beside the point. The important thing to consider are these moments where the agent chooses to choose and makes themselves the ground for their actions.

This is not a wholly unsatisfactory or implausible way of addressing the issue of being the source of actions. As discussed at the beginning of the chapter, libertarians like Chisholm and Kane do not say that every action is free but instead argue that in certain cases, there can be a different way of bringing about an action that is not causally determined. Perhaps even closer to Guignon's view is that of Frankfurt. Frankfurt essentially says that we should not worry about whether our actions are causally determined and should instead focus on the relation between our first- and second-order desires. If these desires are appropriately aligned, then we can say an agent's will is free regardless of any background causal factors. Guignon, indeed, says something very similar, claiming that existential freedom for Heidegger is a "specific sort of relation an agent has toward being an agent" and that the "same actions may be seen as free or unfree in different situations, depending on the person's relation to his or her action."[18] That said, I do think there is something unsatisfactory about Guignon's approach. It seems to run back into Golob's critique of Heidegger's account of agency that we discussed in chapter 2. Golob, remember, claimed:

> [Heidegger] fails to address the question of causal dependencies, as opposed to our understanding of those dependencies. . . . Heidegger surely assumes that Dasein's actions are not simply determined by the weight of its greatest desire as in a crude Humean model. But rather than providing a metaphysical account of how that might be possible, Heidegger's response is to reject the vocabulary, "will", "desire", etc., needed to formulate the question.[19]

And it seems like Guignon is doing the same thing Golob accuses Heidegger of—merely stating that any possible causal dependencies do not really matter to how we understand freedom without providing any alternative explanation of what is going on in apparent cases of causal influence on our actions.

There is another way that Heidegger scholars have attempted to deal with the question of causal determinism. The basic idea here is that we can take a reflective distance from immediate causes of our actions, thereby transforming those from brute causes that necessarily determine certain actions to normative constraints that we feel we should obey. Crowell suggests something like this when he says, "To have care as one's being—to be an issue for oneself—means to see things in normative terms, to understand one's factic inclinations in relation to the very idea of 'what is best,' of better and worse. This is to treat them as only *potentially* my reasons—that is to treat them as normative reasons rather than causes."[20] Golob similarly claims that for Heidegger, "to be free is to operate under normative rather than merely causal restraints."[21] Both Crowell and Golob seem to be dealing with the issue of potential causal determinism from Heidegger's point of view by maintaining that our being is such that we can turn causes into normative reasons for action. In the following section, I will consider how this is supposed to work in a bit more detail, but here, I just want to focus on this idea more generally. The thought seems to be that by recognizing a potential cause for action as something I can allow to move me or not, this makes that potential cause something that I can consider in light of my chosen self-understanding and see it as something that should or should not move me to act. Using the example of seeing a stack of papers to grade again, I could, upon seeing those papers, immediately and unreflectively sit down at my desk and start grading them. In this case, seeing the papers would be a brute causal determinant of my action, thereby making my action unfree. Alternatively, on the Crowell/Golob view, I could establish a reflective distance from the event of seeing the papers and decide that sitting down at my desk and grading them is something that I should do in light of my understanding of myself as a professor. This transforms the brute causal determinant into a normative reason for action. The problem, though, as with Guignon's approach, is that it seems like maintaining that causal determinants can be transformed into normative reasons for action again runs into Golob's criticism that the Heideggerian account of agency is unable to account for actual causal influence on our actions. Indeed, Golob formulates this criticism precisely because he reads Heidegger as advocating the idea that freedom is about transforming causes into normative reasons.

I think there is a more satisfactory, fuller response to the concerns of the mainstream free will debate that can be given from the Heideggerian point of view, focusing on ontological as opposed to existential freedom. In chapter 2 I laid out Heidegger's argument against causal theories of action. As a reminder the key issues discussed there were as follows. The way that the conative and orienting aspects of action interact does not lend itself to easy, linear causal analysis. The reason for this on the Heideggerian view is that there is a mismatch between the temporality assumed by efficient causality and the temporality operative in the fundamental aspects of human agency. Efficient causality is based on the idea that the cause is that which temporally precedes the effect, that is, based on a conception of time as a linear progression of "nows." By contrast, both the conative and orienting aspects of agency exhibit a nonlinear temporality and, thus, cannot be understood in terms of efficient causality. Despite this, I argued, contra Golob, that Heidegger's concept of grounding does provide a way to understand how the noncausal interaction of the conative and orienting aspects of agency makes possible both rationalizations of action in terms of the causal efficacy of mental states and the actual causal influence of events on our actions in certain cases.

While I did not bring up the connection in chapter 2 so as not to unnecessarily muddy the waters at that point, Heidegger very explicitly equates freedom with grounding. He states that "freedom as transcendence, however, is not only a unique 'kind' of ground, but the *origin of ground in general. Freedom is freedom for ground*" (GA 9, 165/127). Here he is claiming that freedom is the basis for grounding as such in its threefold structure. If this is the case, and it is grounding that makes it possible for there to be efficient causes of actions, then the implication is that it is ultimately freedom itself that makes it possible for actions to have causes. And this indeed is what Heidegger claims. In "On the Essence of Ground," he maintains that "only because transcendence consists in freedom can freedom make itself known as a distinctive kind of causality in existing Dasein" (GA 9, 164/126). Because freedom is understood as that fundamental openness that allows the world to manifest itself at all, it is also the basis for the possibility of any causal understanding of the world or any causal understanding of our actions as humans.

What, then, to make of the question of determinism? Heidegger states:

> In this interpretation of freedom arrived at in terms of transcendence there ultimately lies a more originary characterization of freedom than that which determines it as spontaneity, i.e., as a kind of causality. The beginning of something by itself provides only the negative characterization of freedom according to which there is no determinative cause lying further back. (GA 9, 164/126)

From the perspective of the traditional free will debate, freedom is seen as an absence of a prior cause external to the agent. In the quoted passage above, Heidegger does not seem to be completely denying the legitimacy of such an understanding of freedom, but rather, he is maintaining that it is derivative and depends on the account of ontological freedom that he is providing. At the very end of *The Essence of Human Freedom*, Heidegger puts this idea even more succinctly and emphatically, stating: "*Causality is grounded in freedom. The problem of causality is a problem of freedom and not vice versa*" (GA 31, 303/207). Here, he is clearly maintaining that a causal understanding of our actions is made possible by freedom, which we now understand to be equivalent to grounding. So, we need to understand any causal account of our actions and free will out of the fundamentally noncausal structure of grounding/freedom. To try to understand free will first in causal terms is to get it backward on Heidegger's view.

Now we are in a position to build up the Heideggerian response to the central issue of being the origin of actions. To begin with, we can consider whether we can say that we are the origin of actions when it comes to unreflective, mundane actions performed in the mode of Dreyfus's skillful coping. Returning to Guignon's example of putting on shoes, if we emphasize the role of ontological freedom in our everyday actions, then when answering the question, "Are we free when putting on our shoes?," the answer from the point of view of my Heideggerian account of freedom would be "yes." Freedom is equivalent to grounding, which in turn is the interaction of the conative and orienting components of action. We are free insofar as we, even in inauthentic existence, have committed to certain self-understandings and have freed up individual actions so that they matter to us. We are the ground or origin of our actions from this point of view, even with regard to insignificant actions like putting on shoes. It might be my understanding of myself as an athlete that lets the action of putting on running shoes matter, or it might be my understanding of myself as a beach lover that lets the action of putting on flip-flops matter to me. In either case, I am the ground of my actions in Heidegger's sense of the term insofar as I have committed, even if only implicitly, to understanding myself in one of these ways.

My account is able to go further than Guignon's here insofar as I am able to say definitively that we are the ground for even our everyday actions that have not been endorsed through a second-order choice. I would suggest that this is a more satisfactory response to the concerns of the mainstream free will debate than Guignon's. As we have seen, Guignon denies the significance of the question of freedom for a certain category of mundane actions (deeds in his terminology). On my account, there is no problem saying that we perform these actions freely in the sense of ontological freedom opening a space in which these actions can be meaningful to us and can exert a pull on us. In contrast to the Crowell/Golob view that causes are transformed into normative reasons when we act freely, on my account, I can allow that there are actual causal influences on our actions, even external events that are efficient causes that might set an action in motion, thereby avoiding Golob's criticism of the Heideggerian views' inability to account for actual causal influence. This makes my account, then, a more satisfactory response to the mainstream concerns about causal determinism than the Crowell/Golob view as well.

Still, though, this does not entirely address the worry about determinism. Suppose one accepts my argument that we can be the ground for our actions in the way just described and that being the ground for actions is fundamentally noncausal. If I also maintain that there are at least some cases where there are legitimate efficient causes of action, as I do to fend off Golob's criticism, it seems that determinism could still be an issue for the Heideggerian account of agency. We can return to the example I initially used in chapter 2 to illustrate the issue here. I used the example of walking home from work, smelling hamburgers cooking at a restaurant, and then going into the restaurant to get a hamburger. I made the case that the event of smelling the hamburgers is indeed an efficient cause of my resulting action of entering the restaurant. I would not have gone into the restaurant without the experience of that smell. This is a point where the determinist could press their case. Encountering the smell of the hamburgers is an event that is outside my control. This event itself has prior efficient causes that are outside of my control. Maybe the restaurant opened its back door because their air conditioning was not working; maybe I am walking home instead of driving because my car is in the shop being repaired, etc. Once these potential causal chains are elaborated and laid out, it might seem that my action in that moment really is determined by the interaction of all of these efficient causes that exist completely beyond my control.

I think it is fairly clear at this point what the Heideggerian response would be according to my account. It is perfectly legitimate to say that the event of smelling the hamburgers caused my action of entering the restaurant. It is also perfectly legitimate to list prior events that serve as efficient causes of my smelling the hamburgers and develop chains of efficient causes for that event stretching as far back as one likes with the stipulation that each prior event causally determines the one that follows it. However, the efficacy of that final event of smelling the hamburgers is only made possible by the noncausal interaction of the conative and orienting components of action, and this interaction is what constitutes grounding and freedom for Heidegger. It is my understanding of myself as a being who needs food, the particular way I enact this understanding, and the way in which this understanding orients my activity so as to allow certain actions to exert a pull on me that makes it possible for the event of smelling the hamburgers to influence my action. As I mentioned in chapter 2, Heidegger wants to make a broader claim about the metaphysical status of causality, but again, for me here, I am only going so far as to lay out how causality works in the context of human agency. So, in the context of human agency for Heidegger, there could be a legitimate efficient causal account of why I pursued a particular action at a particular time, but the existence of such an account would not undermine the claim that I am the origin of my actions, since it is my commitment to enact my various for-the-sake-of-whichs in particular ways that allows the efficient cause to influence my action.

One might then ask whether all actions would have efficient causes on my Heideggerian view, with the understanding, of course, that the efficacy of these causes is made possible by grounding. It might strike us as odd to say that sometimes actions have efficient causes and sometimes they do not. Indeed, this was one of my repeated criticisms of Dreyfus's reading of Heidegger in the earlier chapters—that he advocated for a sharp division between two different ontological structures of action and two different types of agency. As far as I know, there is no strong textual evidence to indicate Heidegger's views on this question, but it seems to me that, in principle, he would have no issue with saying that there is an efficient cause for every action, as long as the ontological dependency of causality on freedom is remembered and the causal explanation is not to be taken as fundamental. This is similar to the consideration of the role of mental states in our actions from chapters 1 and 2. There I argued that there is not any difference in underlying ontology between actions where mental states are explicitly present and ones where they are not; talk of mental states is just a reification of those basic components of human agency that is sometimes given as a way to explain an action without referring to any actual change in the underlying ontology. So, if one wanted to pick some event that preceded every action and identify that event as the cause, that would be fine and would not change the underlying ontology of agency. Heidegger might, though, maintain that oftentimes the identification of some specific efficient cause is unnecessary or at least explanatorily unhelpful. Remember that he says of the third component of grounding, *Begründen*, that it makes the "why question" *possible*, which leads to a specification of a preceding state of affairs that serves as the "ground of motion," or efficient cause of the action. He does not say that there is some preceding state of affairs that can serve as the answer to the "why question" for every action. Consider my action of walking out to my car in the morning in order to drive to school. As we have seen, we can explain this action by saying that I understand myself as a professor (the orienting component) and, thus, the action of driving to school in the morning stands out to me as something salient and exerts a pull on me (the conative component). This might very well stand as a sufficient explanation for what brings about my action without specifying some event that could serve as an efficient cause. What would such an event even be in this case? My seeing that the clock now reads 8:00 AM? My finishing my breakfast? Maybe it does help answer the question of why I am going to the car if, for example, my wife asks why I am leaving, and I respond, "I just saw that it is 8:00 AM already." It could be the case that my seeing the clock triggers my motion to go out to the car. I suppose one could say that these events that immediately precede my action of going out to the car are efficient causes of my action, but the explanatory value added by such a specification seems minimal. In response, then, to the initial question I posed, I would say there would be nothing wrong from Heidegger's point of view in claiming that every action has an efficient cause. It is just that in all cases, its causal power is dependent on freedom, and in some cases, specifying an efficient cause does not add much to our understanding of the action.

THE NECESSITY OF ALTERNATE POSSIBILITIES FOR FREEDOM

Now we can turn to the Heideggerian response to the other key issue for the mainstream free will debate—the question of the necessity of alternative possibilities for having freedom. When focusing on existential freedom, one might very well conclude that Heidegger would agree with the idea that being free does require alternate possibilities, since he repeatedly emphasizes the importance of choosing, which seems to imply a choice between alternative courses of action or alternative possible self-understandings that would orient our actions. In the concluding section of this chapter, I will explain how I think existential freedom fits into this question. Here, though, I would like to again focus exclusively on ontological freedom. It is not immediately clear, given what was said in the preceding section, whether ontological freedom would require the ability to pursue alternative courses of action. I hope to have established that we are the origin of our actions insofar as we are the ground for our actions and that there can still be efficient causes of actions, even if the efficacy of those causes is made possible by ontological freedom/grounding. I want to make the case in this section that ontological freedom does not require alternate possibilities for Heidegger, not because our actions are causally determined in such a way that we cannot pursue alternative actions but rather because the self-understandings we take on bind us to taking certain actions.

To make this case, I will focus on the second half of *The Fundamental Concepts of Metaphysics*, where Heidegger engages in a lengthy analysis of animal behavior (*Benehmen*) and then spends the final sections contrasting that behavior with human comportment (*Verhaltung*). Human comportment, on his view, is different because we are free. I do not want to get into the assessment of the potential anthropocentrism of Heidegger's much-discussed assertion that animals are world poor, while we are world-forming, but rather, I would like to use Heidegger's analysis here to figure out how exactly Heidegger thinks humans are different from animals in order to have a better sense of what Heidegger means by ontological freedom and whether or not this freedom requires the existence of alternate possibilities.

Heidegger characterizes animal behavior as in terms of captivation (*Benommenheit*). While he is engaging in a bit of word play here with the shared root of *Benehmen* and *Benommenheit*, he is also saying that animals are taken over by their instinctual responses to what they encounter in their environment. Using the example of a bee's flight, Heidegger maintains that instead of having the sort of ontological freedom that is characteristic of human existence, the "bee is simply taken by its food. This being taken is only possible where there is an instinctual 'toward. . . .' Yet such a driven being taken also excludes the possibility of any recognition of presence. It is precisely being taken by its food that prevents the animal from taking up a position over and against this food" (GA 29/30, 352–353/242). This is why he goes on to claim that "beings are *not manifest* to the behavior of the animal in its captivity, they are not disclosed to it and for that very reason are *not closed off* from it either" (GA 29/30, 360–362/248). Not only does an animal engage in behavior without recognizing the presence of the objects which bring about its behavior, it also engages in that activity "*without* any so-called *self-consciousness* or any *reflection* at all, without any relating back to itself" (GA 29/30, 339–340/233).

Human comportment, by contrast, is characterized by an awareness of entities encountered in the world and a distance from those entities that allows them to manifest themselves. "As transcending," Heidegger says, "i.e., as free, Dasein is something alien to nature" (GA 26, 211–213/166). Furthermore, the "human being is a creature of distance!" (GA 26, 285/222). Humans have a "being open for . . . *of such a kind* that this being open for . . . has the character of *apprehending something as something*" (GA 29/30, 442–444/306). A nonhuman animal, by contrast, is open to its environment but "lacks the ability to apprehend as a being whatever it is open for" (GA 29/30, 442–444/306). He goes on to say, "Man's being open is a being held toward . . ., whereas the animal's being open is a being taken by . . . and thereby being absorbed in its encircling ring" (GA 29/30, 497–499/343). The idea here seems to be that animals are open to their environment, but they respond immediately and instinctually to stimuli presented to them and are not aware of the stimuli as stimuli. In human comportment we too are open to being moved by that which we encounter in the environment, but we are also able to hold (playing on *halten* as the root of *Verhaltung*) ourselves at a distance from those things that move us, and it is this distance that allows the things encountered to manifest themselves as what they are, allowing humans a *Spielraum* that animals do not have (GA 29/30, 491–493/339).

However, Heidegger does not merely seem to be claiming that humans are somehow exempt from causal determinism, while animals are not or that humans have the ability to make choices about how they will act, while animals do not. Instead, he repeatedly characterizes human freedom as having a "binding character" (*Verbindlichkeit*). Consider the following passage:

> Being open for . . . is from the very outset a *free holding oneself toward* whatever beings are given there *in letting oneself be bound*. The possibility, which

can become binding, of tuning in to beings, this relating to them in comporting oneself in such and such a way, is characteristic in general of every ability and comportment as distinct from capacity and behavior. In the latter we never find any letting oneself be bound by something binding, but merely a sphere of instinctual drives becoming disinhibited while remaining captivated. (GA 29/30, 496–497/342)

Here he seems to be characterizing the freedom found in human comportment not with the ability to act in a different way than one is pulled to act but rather with the phenomenon of "letting oneself be bound." Returning the example of being a professor, my projection toward being a professor binds me to a certain course of action. Insofar as I am a professor, I must teach courses, write papers, attend faculty meetings, etc. These actions are constitutive for what it is to be a professor, so in making a commitment to that particular way of being, I am letting myself be bound to finding these actions important and being moved to act in such a way that I perform these actions. I have the awareness of these actions as discrete phenomena that stand out by virtue of their significance from other actions, and I grasp (if only implicitly) the larger context made possible by my understanding of myself as a professor that makes these particular actions appear as significant. And there is still this sense that I can have a sort of distance from my actions, holding them apart as somehow other than myself, while still feeling obliged to perform them. For instance, to return to a slightly modified example from chapter 1, I could see the stack of student exams to be graded very much as an unwanted, external imposition on me, calling for my attention from the corner of my desk, and yet I would still feel bound to take up my pen and start grading.

In *The Fundamental Concepts of Metaphysics*, Heidegger explains this distance, lacking in animals, that we as humans have between ourselves and entities in the world by claiming that we have *lógos*, while animals do not (GA 29/30, 417–418/288). Here, however, I want to go in a different direction to explain the distance we feel between ourselves and the actions that exert a pull on us. I already introduced the basic idea here in the discussion of weakness of the will and how to account for that phenomenon on the Heideggerian account of agency. As humans we have the ability to understand ourselves as apart from any particular for-the-sake-of-which that we take on. We cannot be fully and completely identified with any particular self-understanding. Crowell suggests the same idea, as he claims, "freedom consists in the gap that opens up between any such goal-directed action in the world and the breakdown of all practical identities in *Angst*/death."[22] We can and do experience instances of complete breakdown when none of our normal self-understandings are operative and no actions show up as salient for us. This is the ultimate gap between ourselves and the actions that matter to us—the actions that usually matter just do not at all in these moments of breakdown. There is an infinite gap. For Heidegger, this awareness of the irreducibility of ourselves to any particular self-understandings is always there implicitly in our actions, even if we do our best to distract ourselves from explicit awareness of it most of the time. I want to suggest that this implicit awareness of the possibility of breakdown is what is responsible for this distance on an everyday basis too. Returning to the example of seeing the stacks of papers to grade, I feel a distance from the action, because implicitly I am aware that I do not fully identify with the self-understanding of being a professor. There is some distance between myself and this self-understanding, which means a distance can manifest itself between the actions that should exert a pull on me in light of this self-understanding and myself as an agent. This cannot happen for animals, since they do not (as far as we know) have the same possibility for an existential breakdown that human beings do.

There are still questions, though, regarding how exactly to understand freedom as letting oneself be bound and whether this sort of freedom still requires the ability to pursue alternate possibilities. There are several different ways that scholars have tried to flesh out what Heidegger means by "bindingness" and why it is important for his notion of freedom. Golob claims that it is the ability to be bound by norms that is the decisive difference between humans and animals. Golob says:

> It is because Heidegger, in this characteristically Kantian fashion, understands Dasein in terms of the ability to take on, respond to and assess normative commitments that he analyzes freedom as "self-binding": to be free is to operate under normative rather than merely causal restraints.... An animal, in contrast, lacks the "as" and the normative sphere which it characterizes; in Kantian terms, the animal is determined by its impulses without the ability to ask whether such impulses genuinely constitute reasons.[23]

For Golob, it seems that the distance we establish from the pull certain courses of action exert on us allows us to assess whether we should perform these actions, instead of experiencing the pull as a brute causal determinant as animals do. Even if we do ultimately feel bound to perform an action, as discussed in the preceding section, we experience this binding as a normative one rather than a causal one.

Sean Kelly and Hubert Dreyfus also articulate views of freedom in terms of bindingness that are a bit broader than Golob's view. For Kelly and Dreyfus, norms are, of course, important in terms of how our operative self-understandings are defined, and norms are often responsible for the way we feel bound to perform a certain action, but they both allow, as I argued for in chapter 1, the possibility of actions exerting a pull on us on the basis of more biological self-understandings. Beginning with Kelly's view, he states:

> The main difference between us and animals is that we can resist our motivation to respond to the environment in a way that animals cannot. Our freedom, then, consists always in letting ourselves be bound, simply because whenever we are bound by the environment it is a result of our not having resisted it. By contrast with Kant, then, Heidegger's is a kind of negative freedom—a freedom to resist what we are drawn to do. Our spontaneity acts for Heidegger as a check on our immediately motivated response to the environment.[24]

Kelly loosely references Heidegger here but is not engaged in serious exegesis of his work in this particular essay. Kelly is trying to sketch a view of what freedom would look like if one presupposes the sort of agency as skillful coping view developed by Dreyfus. For Kelly, it does seem that freedom involves the ability to pursue alternate courses of action.[25] He does talk, as I have throughout, of being drawn toward performing certain actions and suggests that freedom consists in the ability to "resist what we are drawn to do." He gives the following example to make this clear: "I can, in the midst of being immediately motivated to walk to the kitchen and make a cup of tea, nevertheless resist this motivation and decide instead to keep working at the computer."[26] The distance between ourselves as agents and the actions that exert a pull on us is important too for Kelly, as he states, "in order to resist the motivation to act in a certain way one must notice that one is so motivated."[27] The idea is that by being able to distance ourselves from the immediate pull an action exerts on us by becoming conscious of it, we can, unlike animals, neutralize the pull this action exerts.

Dreyfus, in one of the articles comprising his debate with John McDowell, "The Return of the Myth of the Mental," introduces the idea of "pervasive freedom," which appears to be something along the lines of what I am referring to as ontological freedom.[28] Dreyfus claims, contra McDowell, who locates freedom in the ability to step back from unreflective action, "unlike mere animals, we have a freedom not to exercise our freedom to step back but rather to let ourselves be involved."[29] He goes on to clarify this by stating, "Heidegger sees as essential the fact that human beings are free to open themselves to being bound—a freedom that animals lack because they are constantly captivated by their current activity and can never step back."[30] Dreyfus does not go much further than this, and since his aim here is to engage in this broader dialogue over the nature of action with McDowell, he does not tie his claim tightly to any specific passage(s) from Heidegger.

What are we to make then of these three different views? The reader might very well anticipate my response to Golob at this point. I do not think that Golob takes a stand one way or another on whether this sense of bindingness is compatible with being able to pursue alternative courses of action or not, but I want to point out again that according to my account, a response to normativity is not the only fundamental difference that Heidegger is going for between free human comportment and animal behavior. I say "only fundamental difference" here, because it is hard to deny that we are bound by and feel ourselves bound by normative commitments in a way that does not seem possible for animals. However, again, as I argued in chapter 1, it seems possible to construe the for-the-sake-of-whichs we take up in our projections not only in terms of social roles defined purely by adherence to sets of norms (e.g., being a professor); we also project toward various biological for-the-sake-of-whichs. Returning to the example of understanding of myself as a being who needs shelter, on the view I have been developing here, we would say that the actions that exert a pull on me in light of this self-understanding still do manifest freedom, even if there are not obvious normative constraints at work. My self-understanding binds me to the action of seeking a cave, cabin, overhanging rock, etc. when caught outside in a bad storm. It is not the experience of normative constraint that makes this a free action on Heidegger's view, but rather it is the way in which my self-understanding allows seeking shelter to stand out as important and, indeed, as something binding in this instance, even as I can recognize a distance between myself and the self-understanding of being a creature who needs shelter. I can still be said to let myself be bound to act in this way by at least implicitly recognizing this distance and letting it collapse.

We can now consider Kelly's view and his assertion that freedom as letting oneself be bound still involves the possibility of taking up alternate courses of action. I want to argue that for Heidegger, the ability to take alternate courses of action is not necessary, though, I do not want to go so far as to say that we are always bound to perform one specific action in any given situation. I leave open the possibility that we are capable of performing alternate actions in some (maybe even most) circumstances but that this is not the essence of freedom for Heidegger, as Kelly suggests. Heidegger does frequently discuss possibility in junction with freedom, but I do not think that he is using "possibility" here to refer to being able to do otherwise. Consider this (knotty and convoluted) passage: "What is projected in the projection *compels* us before what is possibly actual, i.e., the projection *binds* us—not to what is possible, nor to what is actual, but to *making-possible*, i.e., to that which the possibly actual in the projected possibility demands of the possibility for itself in order to actualize itself" (GA 29/30, 527–528/363). He continues a few lines down and states: "For whatever is possible does not become more possible through indeterminacy, so that everything possible would, as it were, find room and be accommodated in it. Rather whatever is possible grows in its possibility and in the force that makes it possible through *restriction*. Every possibility brings its intrinsic *restriction* with it" (GA 29/30, 527–528/363). These passages seem to imply that by projecting toward a for-the-sake-of-which, we make it possible for actions to bind us, and this is the essence of possibility, not the "indeterminacy" of being able to take a different course of action. Possibility, for Heidegger, even goes hand in hand with compulsion and restriction. My projection toward being a professor, for example, makes it possible for certain actions to not just exert a pull on me but also to feel genuinely binding for me. It could even be that in a particular situation, I am bound to take one specific action, if I am to make actual my enactment of being a professor. Now, as we discussed in chapter 2, being a particular sort of person is never a completed task; it requires a constant projection toward being that sort of person. Thus, as Heidegger says in the first passage quoted above, projection binds us to a constant making-possible. Crowell nicely explains what is meant by possibility here when he describes it as a "possibilizing," making it clear that through our projection toward various self-understandings, we are engaged in making the various options available in a situation stand out as possible grounds for action.[31] We continuously have to project toward some particular way of being, which makes it continuously possible for a set of actions to show up as significant for us, and indeed, as binding.

This leaves me, then, in agreement with Dreyfus's view, as far as it goes. Freedom as binding for Heidegger is not necessarily about being bound by norms, and it does not require an ability to reject the pull that certain actions exert upon us in order to perform alternate actions. The essence of freedom, rather, is the bridging or collapsing of the distance between ourselves and the actions that exert a pull on us in such a way that we let ourselves be bound to perform certain actions. I would argue that the agent need not explicitly recognize this distance between themselves and their actions or explicitly decide to let this distance collapse and bind themselves to performing certain actions. After all, I have maintained that on the Heideggerian view, we are free in the course of our everyday actions, since ontological freedom is the condition for the possibility of action; freedom is not something achieved only in those relatively rare moments of resolute decision, as in the view that prioritizes existential freedom. The important thing is that for humans, whether we recognize it or not in the moment, there is always a distance between ourselves and any particular self-understanding that is operative in orienting our actions. Each action is, thus, an instance of letting ourselves be bound.

There might still be a lingering worry about my claim that freedom does not require alternate possibilities for Heidegger. One might accept that there will be occasions where my self-understanding as a professor will bind me to perform one specific action and no other. However, there are plenty of other career paths that people take, and presumably changing careers (or retiring) would give me another set of norms that are constitutive for my identity and make a whole other set of actions present themselves as binding. So, even if there are specific actions that are binding in light of one self-understanding, one might argue that alternate actions are possible if one adopts a different self-understanding. However, this is again a place where the existence of biological for-the-sake-of-whichs is important to consider. I would suggest that there are certain biological ways of being that we are unable to change but that even with regard to these ways of being, we still have freedom in the sense being discussed here. To construct an extreme example to illustrate this point, suppose that we imagine someone on a small, deserted island that only has, say, bananas as a food source. Since the castaway understands themselves as a being who needs food to survive, and eating bananas is the only way to enact that understanding in this situation, it might truly be the case that there is no alternate course of action that they could take, since the castaway, as we all are, is thrown into understanding themselves as a being who needs food without being able to change this, and there is only one way to enact this self-understanding in this scenario. Even in this case, I would argue that the castaway is free in the Heideggerian sense discussed here. There is still a letting oneself be bound on the part of the castaway here, since they are not reducible to this particular self-understanding and maintain a distance from it, even as they are bound to enact it in some specific way. Letting this distance collapse by letting the action in question exert its pull is freedom, even if, again, there is no alternate course of action available. Again, I am not contending that there is only one course of action available to us in any given situation. Instead, I am claiming that even in a case where there genuinely is only one available course of action, freedom in Heidegger's sense is still manifested.

HOW DOES HEIDEGGERIAN ONTOLOGICAL FREEDOM FIT INTO THE FRAMEWORK OF THE TRADITIONAL FREE WILL DEBATE?

Given the Heideggerian understanding of freedom that I have worked out here, does the Heideggerian view fit in the roughly tripartite framework of the mainstream free will debate that divides views into libertarian, compatibilist, or hard determinist categories? As I have tried to show in this chapter, both the Heideggerian and mainstream discussions of freedom share the concern with the issue of whether and how we are the origin of our actions and whether alternative possibilities are required for freedom (though, I would not say that this is a central concern for Heidegger), but the responses to these concerns seem to diverge quite a bit. I ultimately do not think the Heideggerian view I develop here comfortably fits into any of these three categories, but I do still think it is potentially instructive to think through exactly why this is the case. To start with the easiest one, it seems clear that Heidegger is not a hard determinist. According to the Heideggerian view, it is not the case that the truth of causal determinism would imply that we are not the source of our actions. Freedom is, again, what makes possible causal determinism, so freedom is not eliminated by determinism.

If this rejection of hard determinism is right, then one might be tempted to swing to the opposite end of the spectrum and suggest that Heidegger is a sort libertarian, since I have argued that ontological freedom is operative in all of our actions, which allows us to say that we are always the origin of our actions. There is a similarity between Heidegger's view and agent causation libertarian views, as supporters of agent causation argue that there is another way of bringing about actions outside of the scope of natural causality that makes it possible for us to be the source of our actions, which is not totally dissimilar to Heidegger's account of freedom as grounding. However, I think Heidegger would be critical of any account of agent causation that does not do the work of actually developing a different structure for this type of causation that makes it something other than natural causality. Remember in chapter 2, we saw that Heidegger thinks a major problem with the mainstream free will debate is that when philosophers think of freedom of the will, they are merely transposing the idea of natural/efficient causality to an internal faculty. This would seem to be the criticism he would level against something like Chisholm's account of agent causation. With regard to Kane's libertarian view, the considerations of the preceding section should make it clear that Heidegger does not associate freedom with any sort of indeterminacy the way that Kane's view does, and Heidegger does not require an actual ability to do otherwise for an action to be free.

Finally, maybe one could say that Heidegger is a sort of compatibilist who could accept that all of our actions are determined by preceding efficient causes that are beyond our control while still maintaining that we have some kind of meaningful freedom, and like Frankfurt and Fischer, my Heideggerian account of freedom does not require the ability to pursue alternative possible actions. There is, again, something to this comparison. I do think, though, that mainstream compatibilist views assume that efficient causality is the best way to understand our actions at a *fundamental* level. What I mean by this is that they assume that at the deepest ontological level, our actions are produced by prior events that serve as causes of our actions, even if they remain agnostic about the truth of thoroughgoing determinism. A meaningful sense of freedom or responsibility is then achieved for thinkers like Frankfurt and Fischer when our actions are produced by the right sort of causal structure. As we have seen, for Heidegger, it would be misguided to say that the basic structure of agency can be understood in terms of efficient causality. It might be true that we can give an efficient causal account of why each action happened when it did, but this causal account is still dependent on the underlying freedom of the agent. So, the mainstream compatibilists can accept the possible truth of determinism and the fundamentality of causal theories of action and look to find a place for freedom and responsibility within that framework. Heidegger, conversely, might accept the truth of determinism but would still maintain this truth is ontologically dependent on a sense of freedom that is wholly separate from any chain of efficient causes. Freedom, for Heidegger, does not mean some particular configuration of the agent's mental states within a deterministic framework.

To conclude this section, I want to consider whether the Heideggerian view of freedom I develop here would also be subject to the same sort of criticism sometimes made of compatibilist views. One might think that this sort of freedom is not a very meaningful sort as it is consistent with the idea that we have no ability to do otherwise in our actions. Furthermore, this sort of freedom is always operative in the background of our everyday actions and is not the sort of thing that requires a profound decision about one's identity, as found in existential freedom. I think, though, upon a bit of reflection, it is clear that ontological freedom is extremely important for action and is quite meaningful. The phenomenological analysis that Matthew Ratcliffe puts forward in his *Expressions of Depression: A Study in Phenomenology* portrays depression as existing in a world in which there are no salient possible courses action; that is, depression is a state of unfreedom. Even though Ratcliffe has his reasons for not making Heidegger central to his account, instead focusing on Husserl and Sartre, what he describes there is quite similar to the Heideggerian view I develop here. In Ratcliffe's words, the "experience of freedom involves being presented with a world that offers various kinds of possibilities."[32] Nothing that a depressed person encounters shows up as a live possibility for action; nothing draws them into acting. Nondepressed individuals wake up every morning with an array of things that they are concerned with doing and set out to do them. The world is full of possible actions pulling the nondepressed toward pursuing them, and it is freedom in the sense that I have tried to articulate here that enables this experience.

In the end, then, by putting forth a conception of agency that has a reduced role for efficient causality, the Heideggerian view does not fit comfortably into the mainstream conceptual framework of the free will debate. However, instead of just making the blanket claim that the Heideggerian account of agency undermines this whole debate, I think my account of Heideggerian agency and freedom is better able to show the exact points of disagreement between the two views while still showing how they both are focused on the issues of being the origin of our actions and the necessity (or lack thereof) of possible alternative actions.

WHAT DO WE DO WITH EXISTENTIAL FREEDOM?

Throughout this chapter, I have mostly focused on ontological freedom for the three reasons provided earlier. Hopefully, support for the first two reasons has already materialized through the course of the development of this chapter. I have cited many passages from works from the late 1920s and early 1930s that show that Heidegger understands freedom more in the sense of ontological freedom at this point, supporting my claim that this sense of freedom is really the important one for him as he moves away from *Being and Time*. I also hope to have shown how a focus on ontological freedom can be used to develop a robust Heideggerian approach to the two central concerns of the mainstream free will debate. Indeed, I have argued that focusing more on the existential conception of freedom when tackling the question of the source of our actions leads to a less satisfactory approach than focusing on the ontological conception. The question still remains, though, what are we to make of existential freedom? Surely, scholars are on solid textual footing when they claim that such a conception of freedom is to be found in *Being and Time*, so it would seem irresponsible for me just to completely neglect consideration of it.

I think there are two possible ways of dealing with the place of existential freedom in the account I have been developing, the first more conservative, the second, which I will ultimately favor, more radical. The first path begins by considering the connection between ontological freedom and existential freedom. As I mentioned earlier in the chapter, my third reason for privileging consideration of ontological freedom here is that existential freedom is dependent upon ontological freedom for Heidegger. All three scholars I mention who have suggested such a differentiation between two conceptions of freedom in this period of Heidegger's thought (Guignon, Han-Pile, and Golob) try to connect these two different senses of freedom by appealing to Heidegger's references to transparency or self-disclosure in Division II of *Being and Time*. For instance, Heidegger claims that when existing authentically, "Dasein is revealed to itself in its current factical potentiality-for-Being, and in such a way that Dasein itself *is* this revealing and Being-revealed" (SZ, 307). When we gain this ontological insight, we then come to see that the nature of human existence is such that we must "choose to choose," or in my preferred Heideggerian expression of this, we must take over being a ground (this idea will be the focus of the latter half of chapter 5). Seen in this way, existential freedom is made possible by a special sort of ontological freedom. Through our ontological freedom generally, we open a space in which certain actions matter and exert a pull on us. In the case of existential freedom, our own ontological structure is revealed in such a way that we are pulled not to perform a specific concrete action, but rather, we are pulled to exist authentically in the general mode of action that is characterized by existential freedom.

However, I think it might be helpful to employ a recharacterization of what Heidegger is doing here. I would suggest that instead of talking about choosing to choose or taking over being a ground as a form of freedom, we deal with this idea under the heading of responsibility. Changing the designation to responsibility also allows us to see a connection between freedom (thought of as ontological freedom) and responsibility that somewhat parallels that found in the mainstream free will debate. In the mainstream debate, the primary question is typically whether or not we have free will. The secondary question then has to do with what sort of responsibility we have for our actions (if any) given the answer to that primary question about free will. The next chapter will focus on working out a fuller account of Heideggerian responsibility, but the general idea will be that once we understand freedom as that which opens a space that allows things to matter to us and exert a pull on us, responsibility is then best conceived as a responsiveness to that which exerts a pull on us. In the case of our everyday actions, this takes the form of responsiveness to the actions that should matter to us based on the self-understandings that make up the orienting component of our agency. In the case of authentic agency, the responsiveness in question involves responding to the call of conscience that pulls us toward authentic existence, which is in part characterized by "choosing to choose." Again, this will be developed more thoroughly in chapter 5, but this is the basis for my rationale of putting existential freedom under the overarching heading of responsibility.

NOTES

1. Robert Kane, "Introduction: The Contours of the Contemporary Free Will Debates," in *The Oxford Handbook of Free Will*, ed. Robert Kane (Oxford: Oxford University Press, 2002), 5.

2. Roderick Chisholm, "Human Freedom and the Self," Lindley Lecture Series (University of Kansas Department of Philosophy, 1964), https://kuscholarworks.ku.edu/bitstream/handle/1808/12380/Human%20Freedom%20and%20the%20Self-1964.pdf.

3. For a condensed version of Kane's view, see his "Libertarianism," in *Four Views on Free Will* by John Martin Fischer, Robert Kane, Derk Pereboom, and Manuel Vargas (Oxford: Blackwell, 2007), 5–43.

4. Harry Frankfurt, "Freedom of the Will and the Concept of a Person," in *The Importance of What We Care About* (Cambridge: Cambridge University Press, 1988), 11–25.

5. For the abbreviated version of Fischer's view, see his "Compatibilism," in *Four Views on Free Will* by John Martin Fischer, Robert Kane, Derk Pereboom, and Manuel Vargas (Oxford: Blackwell, 2007), 44–84.

6. Harry Frankfurt, "Alternate Possibilities and Moral Responsibility," in *The Importance of What We Care About* (Cambridge: Cambridge University Press, 1988), 1–10.

7. Fischer, "Compatibilism," 58.

8. Fischer, "Compatibilism," 78–79.

9. Derk Pereboom, "Determinism al Dente," *Nous* 29, no. 1 (March 1995): 21–45.

10. Charles Guignon, "Heidegger's Concept of Freedom, 1927–1930," in *Interpreting Heidegger: Critical Essays*, ed. Daniel Dahlstrom (Cambridge: Cambridge University Press, 2011).

11. Beatrice Han-Pile, "Freedom and the Choice to Choose Oneself in *Being and Time*," in *The Cambridge Companion to Being and Time*, ed. Mark Wrathall (Cambridge: Cambridge University Press, 2013).

12. Sacha Golob, *Heidegger on Concepts, Freedom and Normativity* (Cambridge: Cambridge University Press, 2014), 250.

13. Golob, *Heidegger on Concepts, Freedom and Normativity*, 249.

14. Golob, *Heidegger on Concepts, Freedom and Normativity*, 205.

15. Guignon, "Heidegger's Concept of Freedom, 1927–1930," 85.

16. Guignon, "Heidegger's Concept of Freedom, 1927–1930," 86.

17. Guignon, "Heidegger's Concept of Freedom, 1927–1930," 90.

18. Guignon, "Heidegger's Concept of Freedom, 1927–1930," 84, 85.

19. Golob, *Heidegger on Concepts, Freedom and Normativity*, 211.

20. Steven Crowell, *Normativity and Phenomenology in Husserl and Heidegger* (Cambridge: Cambridge University Press, 2013), 302.

21. Golob, *Heidegger on Concepts, Freedom and Normativity*, 202–03

22. Crowell, *Normativity and Phenomenology in Husserl and Heidegger*, 189.

23. Golob, *Heidegger on Concepts, Freedom and Normativity*, 202–03.

24. Sean Kelly, "Perceptual Normativity and Human Freedom," Philpapers Archive, accessed January 8, 2020, https://philpapers.org/archive/KELPNA.pdf, 7.

25. Han-Pile also claims that alternative possibilities are necessary for ontological freedom as she says that while she cannot provide a full account of ontological freedom, "for Heidegger, being ontologically free . . . entails that it has alternative possibilities," "Freedom and the Choice to Choose Oneself in *Being and Time*," 292. However, she states she will not pursue this claim further, since her focus is on existential freedom.

26. Kelly, "Perceptual Normativity and Human Freedom," 8.

27. Kelly, "Perceptual Normativity and Human Freedom," 8.

28. Hubert Dreyfus, "The Return of the Myth of the Mental," *Inquiry* 50, no. 4 (2007): 355.

29. Dreyfus, "The Return of the Myth of the Mental," 355.

30. Dreyfus, "The Return of the Myth of the Mental," 355.

31. Crowell, *Normativity and Phenomenology in Husserl and Heidegger*, 208.

32. Matthew Ratcliffe, *Experiences of Depression: A Study in Phenomenology* (Oxford: Oxford University Press, 2015), 161.

Chapter 5

Heideggerian Responsibility— Responsibility as Responsiveness

As was discussed in the preceding chapter, much of the mainstream free will debate assumes a causal theory of action and frames the problem of free will in terms of the issue of causal determinism. Correspondingly, responsibility is often understood in causal terms too. That is, the degree of responsibility that an agent has for their actions is related to the degree to which the agent can be said to have caused those actions or to have caused those actions in the right way. This connection of causality and responsibility seems to spread across the spectrum of different views on the question of free will and responsibility. For libertarians like Kane and Chisholm, the agents are completely responsible for actions that are not the product of prior deterministic causal chains, whether these actions arise in moments of genuine indeterminacy (Kane) or are brought about through agent (as opposed to natural) causation (Chisholm). Compatibilists like Frankfurt and Fischer think that even if actions are causally determined, agents can be responsible for their actions if these actions are produced by the right combination of causal factors in the process that brings about the action—an alignment of first- and second-order desires for Frankfurt or a reasons-responsive mechanism for Fischer. A hard determinist like Pereboom denies the existence of responsibility precisely because he does not think that agents can be the cause of their actions the way that libertarians do, and he finds the half-measures of the compatibilists logically inconsistent.

As should already be clear at this point, Heidegger does not think human agency can be understood in terms of efficient causality at the fundamental level, which implies that he would not understand responsibility in causal terms either. In this chapter, I will develop a Heideggerian understanding of responsibility that is explicitly noncausal. Instead of understanding responsibility in terms of causality, we can use Heidegger's thought to develop a conception of responsibility as responsiveness. This conception of responsibility focuses on the root word, "respond" (the German equivalent would be *Verantwortlichkeit* and *antworten*, "answer"), and interprets Heidegger as endorsing responsiveness, not being the cause of one's own actions, as the key aspect of responsibility.[1] There is some intuitive support for the plausibility of this general way of thinking about it too. We often think of a responsible person as someone who can be counted on to fulfill the duties and obligations expected of them. In this sense, we refer to someone as responsible when they show up for work consistently, take care of their children, keep their promises to friends, etc. In this case, responsibility is not about being the cause for one's actions in a way that is not determined by any external influence (as libertarians like Chisholm and Kane would have it) or having the right internal causal structure to one's actions (as compatibilists like Frankfurt and Fischer would have it) but rather by responding appropriately to solicitations for action in the midst of one's engagement with the world.

I want to start fleshing out this general idea by first considering to what exactly a responsible agent is responsive. As I mentioned at the end of chapter 4, on my account, I will posit two different modes of responsibility, each of which is characterized by a different form of responsiveness. I will call the sort of responsibility that is potentially exhibited in our everyday actions first-order responsibility. If an agent exhibits this sort of responsibility, that means that they are responsive to the pull to perform the actions necessary to enact their operative self-understandings. The first section of this chapter will be dedicated to more fully working out this conception of first-order responsibility and responding to potential problems for it. First-order responsibility, given everything I have developed thus far in previous chapters, should be fairly straightforward and easy to understand at this point. Second-order responsibility, though, will be a significantly more difficult concept to work out. I will make the case that second-order responsibility is to be understood in terms of the main aspects of authentic existence as laid out in *Being and Time*. The responsiveness in second-order responsibility is not the responsiveness to the pull to perform a certain action or even to take on a particular self-understanding. Instead, second-order responsibility is constituted by being responsive to enacting a different mode of existence or agency—authentic agency. This is why I decided to use the "first-order" and "second-order" designations. First-order responsibility has to do with everyday actions and the ways we can fail or succeed at enacting specific self-understandings, while second-order responsibility, as we will see, has to do with the meta-level issue of enacting a different stance toward one's being as an agent altogether. After working through the idea of first-order responsibility in fairly short order, the bulk of the chapter will be devoted to developing the idea of second-order responsibility.

FIRST-ORDER RESPONSIBILITY

This is another place in this work where I will stray a bit beyond Heidegger's texts. As readers familiar with Heidegger are certain to realize at this point, this sketch of first-order responsibility that I put forward seems very much like inauthentic agency for Heidegger. As we will see shortly, Heidegger maintains that agents acting inauthentically do not really manifest "responsibility" in the true sense of the term. So, Heidegger is not very much interested in trying to work out a sense of responsibility that could be achieved in our everyday, inauthentic action. However, I do think it is worthwhile to flesh this idea out a bit, even while lacking resources from Heidegger's texts to do so. The mainstream scholarship on responsibility is predominantly concerned with the question of responsibility with regard to everyday actions, and there has been an incredibly nuanced debate over what exact conditions are required for us to hold an agent responsible for their normal, mundane actions. While I acknowledge that I cannot put forward a fully defensible account of everyday responsibility that will cover the whole wide range of possible situations, I do want to try to at least show that the Heideggerian account of agency I develop here can have something to say on this front. It seems to me hyperbolic to claim that in everyday agency, the way we act most of the time in Heidegger's view, there really is no applicable conception of responsibility, and it makes the overall Heideggerian account of agency, freedom, and responsibility that I have been developing less appealing if I accept this aspect of Heidegger's views. This is why I want to introduce the distinction between first-order responsibility, which I have been discussing in this section, and second-order responsibility, which I will turn to in the following section. Second-order responsiveness or responsibility is meant to capture the sort of true, deep responsibility that Heidegger thinks is lacking in inauthentic agency, and which only emerges in authentic agency. However, I think that first-order responsibility is a perfectly fine concept to use when analyzing everyday actions as long as it is recognized that this does not count as responsibility in the fundamental sense for Heidegger on a strict reading of his text.

With that caveat in mind, we can see already how this conception of responsibility as responsiveness fits well with the Heideggerian account of agency developed here. We project ourselves toward various for-the-sake-of-whichs that in turn allow certain actions to be significant and to exert a pull on us. In order to successfully enact any given self-understanding, we must be responsive to the pull to perform certain actions. If I understand myself as a professor, but I fail to be moved to grade papers in a timely fashion, I am failing to be properly responsive, and thus am failing to be a responsible professor. In other words, the conative component in our action, that by which

I feel pulled to perform a certain action, must be in alignment with the orienting component, that self-understanding I have taken that lets certain actions stand out as meaningful.

As we have seen, many of the self-understandings that we take on are largely constituted by various social norms that we must act in accordance with to a large degree in order to successfully enact that self-understanding. There might be a tendency, then, to think of this sort of responsiveness as being responsive to the norms that we take to constitutive for the various self-understandings that we have taken on. If I feel drawn to grade papers, it is because I understand (implicitly or explicitly) that part of what it is to be a professor is to give students assignments and then evaluate those assignments. If I understand myself as bound by the norms that define being a professor, this action of grading papers should stand out to me as something meaningful and should exert a pull on me. I do, though, want to keep the primary focus on the idea that this sort of responsiveness is about responding to solicitations to perform certain actions. One reason for this is that, as I have tried to argue throughout, there can be some self-understandings that are not completely defined by social norms. For instance, I understand myself as a being who needs certain nutrients and caloric intake to survive. If I fail to eat, or if I eat very unhealthy food, it seems fair to say that I am not being a responsible eater, insofar as I am not drawn toward the actions that would allow me to successfully enact a self-understanding of this sort. While specific eating practices are certainly defined by norms, some aspects of what counts as an acceptable eating action are determined by biology. The second reason for maintaining the focus on responsiveness to the pull to perform certain actions is that this will make for a clearer contrast once we get to discussing second-order responsiveness later in this chapter. I will argue that second-order responsiveness, epitomized by authentic existence for Heidegger, involves not a responsiveness to a particular course of action but rather a responsiveness to the pull of certain mode of existence, namely authentic existence.

It should also be fairly clear how the conception of deliberation developed in chapter 3 fits into this idea of first-order responsibility. I still do not want to argue that deliberation is any way necessary for agency or necessary for first-order responsibility. Instead, as I explained in chapter 3, deliberation can be understood as a further refinement of the orienting component of action that can be employed during any course of action but does not have to be. Deliberation allows the agent to come to a view of the situation of action, a *dōxa*, that lets a particular action stand out as the one most worth pursuing. There is, according to my account, no difference in the ontological structure of agency when comparing deliberative and nondeliberative action. Deliberation, then, can be employed in the service of first-order responsibility.

For example, if I keep putting off grading my students' papers, I might say to myself, "If I do really want to be a good professor, I should get those papers graded and returned." That little bit of deliberation then might make the action of grading the papers acquire the salience necessary to make that action exert enough of a pull on me such that I actually do it. By performing this action, I am enacting the self-understanding of being a professor and being "responsible" in the first-order sense of the term. Recall as well in chapter 3 that, following Heidegger's interpretation of Aristotle, I proposed that there is a rational, evaluative standard supposed by deliberation. An agent can deliberate well or poorly. Good deliberation takes place in light of the correct grasp of the self-understanding that articulates the given situation of action and correctly picks out which action properly enacts that self-understanding. Poor deliberation fails in one or both of these regards. If, for example, I do not understand that being a professor requires me to provide assessment of my students' work and base my deliberation on that misunderstanding, my deliberation will not lead to the action of grading papers having a pull on me, and thus, this sort of bad deliberation will not aid in my achievement of first-order responsibility.

Again, it should also be relatively clear how ontological freedom connects to first-order responsibility. As laid out in chapter 4, ontological freedom is equivalent to grounding—that interaction of the conative and orienting components of action that opens up a space in which possible actions can appear as salient to us as agents. It is because of this articulation of the situation of action by ontological freedom that we can be responsible or irresponsible; that is, we can be responsive to the appropriate solicitations for action or not. It is my projection toward understanding myself as a professor that allows actions like grading papers, submitting my own work to conferences, or delivering lectures to stand out as important and worth pursuing. First-order responsibility is a way of talking about whether this is all functioning as it should, a way of talking about the success or failure to be drawn toward the actions that should exert a pull on me given my operative self-understandings. If an agent loses their ontological freedom, perhaps as occurs in cases of severe depression, as I suggest toward the end of chapter 4, then they lose the possibility of being responsible or irresponsible. The world just fundamentally does not manifest itself as offering any opportunities for action, as there are no operative self-understandings that allow actions to appear as meaningful. So, the agent without freedom cannot be judged in terms of their responsiveness to the actions appropriate for the enactment of their self-understandings. This shows the dependence of responsibility on freedom in a way that parallels the mainstream debate on free will and responsibility. Freedom, on my Heideggerian view, still is the necessary condition for responsibility. It is just that neither freedom nor responsibility is understood in causal terms.

Potential Problems for This Conception of Responsibility

I want to briefly consider some of the potential problems for this conception of first-order responsibility with regard to its usefulness in judging agents to be responsible or not in their everyday actions. Again, Heidegger does not provide much to work with here and probably would not even approve of my efforts in this regard, but I thought I should do a bit to try to address obvious concerns and make my formulation of this type of responsibility slightly more plausible.

Delimiting Irresponsibility as Compared to Not Being That Sort of Person

There might be a worry here about how to draw the line demarcating someone who is, for example, an irresponsible professor versus someone who just is not a professor. As I suggested above, if I understand myself as a professor and do not respond to the pull of the action of grading, then I am being irresponsible. Suppose, though, we extend this dereliction of duty and stipulate that I also no longer show up to class or attend any departmental meetings or events, though I still do some scholarly writing and still do claim to understand myself as a professor. Am I still merely an irresponsible professor at this point, or have I failed to perform so many of the necessary actions for being a professor that I just simply am not one?

I am not sure that there is an easy way to draw a line in these cases, but I also do not think that is necessarily a fatal flaw. It seems true to how things often happen in our lived experience that the degree to which we identify with certain self-understandings gradually fades out until those self-understandings no longer structure how we see the world at all. There is not necessarily one precise moment where one moves from irresponsibly enacting a self-understanding to simply no longer holding that self-understanding. For instance, when I was younger, I understood myself as a lover of live music. In light of that self-understanding, announcements of various concerts would stand out to me as meaningful and would pull me toward a certain course of action (buying tickets, seeing if friends also wanted to go, etc.). Now, that self-understanding is largely not operative for me anymore. The concert announcements come and go without eliciting any action, and indeed, oftentimes without standing out as meaningful at all. Perhaps at some point, it could have been said that I was being an irresponsible lover of live music when I first started to fail to be moved to go see certain performances, but now it seems more correct to say that this self-understanding is just not operative for me any longer, and I do not project myself toward this for-the-sake-of-which anymore.

I will consider this issue further in the section on second-order responsibility, but I do want to point out here that there are also self-understandings that cannot be dropped in this way. For instance, by virtue of being born, everyone must understand themselves as the child of some parents. Of course, there are many different ways of enacting the self-understanding of being someone's child that might largely be defined by cultural norms, but everyone must enact this possibility in some manner. Usually, we would say that someone who has cut off all contact with their parents despite the parents' desire for interaction, absent some extremely compelling reason, is not acting responsibly as a child. If someone is not responsive to the pull of the actions of calling one's parents, going to dinner with them, visiting over the holidays, etc., then these are grounds for judging one to be an irresponsible child. I would suggest that this judgment holds even if the agent in question firmly rejects the identification with being a child to argue that they should not be bound by this self-understanding.

Unchosen Self-Understandings

That consideration of self-understandings that one cannot opt out of leads to the next potential problem. One might object that it seems unduly harsh to say that someone is not a responsible agent if they fail to be responsive to the solicitations for actions that should exert a pull on them given the norms of self-understandings that they have not chosen or over which they have no control. In our normal usage of the concept of responsibility, we often think it unfair to hold someone responsible for something over which they have no control. On Heidegger's account, we often either unreflectively drift into certain self-understandings or are thrown into them without having had a chance to ever reflectively choose them. For instance, one of the examples we have periodically used throughout is being a creature who needs shelter. This is a self-understanding we have all been thrown into without the possibility of reflectively choosing it beforehand. Is it fair, then, to maintain that someone who lacks the responsiveness to the sort of actions required by the standards of this self-understanding is not responsible?

Toward the end of chapter 4, I suggested that, despite other differences, there are some parallels between the Heideggerian view of freedom and mainstream compatibilist accounts in that both argue that we can be free even when it is not possible to pursue an alternative action. If that parallel is extended to considerations about responsibility, then maintaining that first-order responsibility still applies to self-understandings that have not been chosen and cannot be discarded is no more objectionable than mainstream compatibilist accounts of responsibility. Of course, this is unlikely to persuade someone like Pereboom, who does not accept compatibilist accounts of responsibility, but I would suggest that the Heideggerian view's attribution of responsibility even in cases of unchosen self-understandings is not prima facie a fatal flaw.

As we will see in the following discussion of second-order responsibility, there is a deeper Heideggerian response to this problem as well. There, I will make the argument that, for Heidegger, part of being an authentic agent and achieving second-order responsibility is precisely confronting the issue that we have all been thrown into various self-understandings that we did not choose and cannot opt out of, but nonetheless, we must find a way to deal with them.

Problem of Immoral Self-Understandings

Another question that could emerge for this account of responsibility stems from the consideration of self-understandings that are morally wrong. This concern goes back to Tugendhat's worry that was discussed in chapter 3. If the Heideggerian account of agency provides no room for deliberation or practical reason, it seems that it would provide no resources for arguing that a particular self-understanding is immoral. In chapter 3, I argued that it is possible for agents to deliberate while acting on the Heideggerian view and to be held to rational, evaluative standards for acting well or acting poorly, but there, I only went as far as to consider deliberation from within the context of a particular self-understanding. And this is again what I focused on when discussing first-order responsibility in this chapter. It is possible to say that someone is responsive to the right solicitations for action in light of a particular self-understanding, but so far, I have not said anything about whether someone can be responsible in projecting toward a particular self-understanding in the first place. For example, suppose that someone is a serial killer. As we discussed above, this need not be a reflectively chosen self-understanding. On my account, it is sufficient that it is a self-understanding that is operative as the orienting component of someone's actions, that is, if this self-understanding allows certain actions to stand out as meaningful for the agent. For someone to be a serial killer, there are certain solicitations for action to which they must be responsive, such as looking for victims, avoiding police detection, etc. It seems at the very least to be counterintuitive to talk about a responsible serial killer who is responsive to the pull to perform the actions that are required to enact this self-understanding. In the previous examples involving being a responsible professor or responsible child, the judgment that one is responsible has a positive moral connotation. And given Heidegger's biography, the issue of Nazism is always present in the background. On my Heideggerian view, can one talk of a responsible serial killer or Nazi who is responsive to the "right" actions for enacting that way of being?

In a way, I think this question is just beyond the scope of Heidegger's thought. As we will see in the upcoming section of second-order responsibility, I do think Heidegger provides some resources for developing evaluative standards concerning which self-understandings one explicitly adopts, but largely, I take Heidegger at his word when he says that he is not interested in providing any sort of substantive ethical principles, which would be required to definitively rule out being a serial killer or a Nazi. At best, his thought provides the framework for understanding the structure of agency and responsibility that could serve as a prolegomena to a substantive ethical theory. With that in mind, then, I would suggest that there is nothing wrong with saying that a serial killer or a Nazi is responsible in this sense of first-order responsiveness. Again, there is a certain parallel here with the mainstream debate on responsibility that speaks in Heidegger's favor. When, for example, Frankfurt considers examples involving addicts and whether or not they can be responsible for their actions, no one takes him to be condoning drug use or drug addiction by talking about willing addicts. Instead, scholars read Frankfurt as trying to establish the internal structure of the process of action that must be in place for us to judge an agent responsible for their actions, whatever the content of those actions might be. That same standard should be applied to Heidegger's views of agency and responsibility as well. I think the problem is that Heidegger's personal moral failings make it so that scholars want something out of his work that is not quite fair to expect.

SECOND-ORDER RESPONSIBILITY

Now we have arrived at what I think is the culminating section of this book. This is not only because it is one of the last sections before the concluding chapter but also because this is the place where I will attempt to develop an account of what authentic agency means for Heidegger, and this account will bring together many of the ideas from the preceding chapters. I will make the case that authentic agency is characterized by the agent exhibiting second-order responsibility, or what Heidegger would consider true responsibility. As mentioned above, anyone familiar with *Being and Time* will notice that first-order responsibility as I have characterized it here seems very much like a description of inauthentic existence for Heidegger, and as such it cannot really provide a plausible account of Heideggerian responsibility. In fact, Heidegger says, "because the 'they' presents every judgment and decision as its own, it deprives the particular Dasein of its responsibility" (SZ, 127). Later in *Being and Time*, he addresses the exact sort of everyday responsiveness I discuss here, as he states that the "common sense of the 'they' knows only the satisfying of manipulable rules and public norms and the failure to satisfy them" (SZ, 288). This leads him to claim that in "Dasein's everydayness the agency through which most things come about is one of which we must say that 'it was no one'" (SZ, 127). Putting these passages together makes it clear that Heidegger thinks that action merely exhibiting this sort of responsiveness to the actions that are required to satisfactorily enact our operative norm-defined self-understandings lacks the required characteristics for responsibility.

The key reason for Heidegger's denial of responsibility in everyday agency seems to be that when acting in this way, we merely act as anyone else who holds the same self-understanding would in that situation. We act as the generic *das Man*, and there is no sense of an individual agent performing the action. Indeed, some Heidegger scholars have made the case that authentic agency for Heidegger is characterized by adopting a first-person stance in one's actions as opposed to a third-person stance.[2] As has been discussed throughout, the self-understandings that serve as the orienting aspect of our agency are defined by social norms or biological factors that apply in the same way to any other member of one's culture (in the case of social norms) or one's species (in the case of biologically defined self-understandings). So, in my daily actions when I enact my self-understanding of being a professor, I act more or less as anyone else employed in American academia in the twenty-first century would. I respond to student emails; I construct syllabi; I commute to my university, etc. This is what Heidegger means when he says we are all "representable" in our everyday activities—anyone else who shares my self-understanding would be able to stand in for me and do more or less what I do. That is why this everyday agency is sometimes described as being characterized by a third-person stance. My actions are not individualized, are not my own, but rather are merely what any generic person who shared my self-understandings would do. And this problem is not necessarily solved by the suggestion that I could own my actions by stepping back and reflecting more about what I am doing, since, as we saw in chapter 3, practical deliberation too takes place within the framework of some particular self-understanding. If I distanced myself from my everyday actions and explicitly deliberated about what I should do, I am still deliberating as anyone who shares my self-understanding would. Authentic agency, then, is concerned with actually coming to own my actions as an individual and being truly able to say that it is *I* who am the agent, making my actions not merely the generic, third-person enactment of particular self-understandings.

I mostly agree with this general approach to understanding authentic agency. I might tweak it a little to maintain that authentic agency is characterized by establishing a firm sense of myself as the agent performing rather than describing this as establishing a first-person stance, but I think the main thrust of my interpretation is the same. My specific task in this section is to show how this general understanding of authentic agency as agency with a true sense of self can be understood in terms of the same basic structure as agency generally, that is, as having a conative component and an orienting component, and how it is a form of responsiveness, in a way that parallels first-order responsibility.

Conative Component of Authentic Agency

When considering our actions generally, I have argued that the Heideggerian view posits a conative component that accounts for our being drawn toward performing certain courses of action. In our everyday actions, this conative component, when operating in an environment structured by the orienting component so that certain actions matter us, pulls us out toward possible actions available in our given situation. In chapter 1, I attempted to show how Heidegger develops the conative component of action from his early lectures on Aristotle's account of life, movement, and desire, and this way of thinking about agency very much arises from that paradigm of a living creature moving through the world, being called to pursue various actions that present themselves.

What would it look like, then, to have a conative component of agency that pulls us toward the authentic mode of existence, not some particular possibility of action encountered in the environment? It seems clear that Heidegger locates this pull toward existing authentically in the call of conscience. It might be worthwhile to point out that this idea has some prima facie plausibility generally. Conscience, even as thought of in the normal, everyday way, calls us not necessarily to take a particular action but rather calls to take up a different, morally better mode of existing. If we think of desire as what pulls us out toward performing various possible courses of action, we often think of and talk about conscience as that which exerts an internal pull on us, calling us to be better people. In Heidegger's terms, the call of conscience has the "momentum of a push—of an abrupt arousal" (SZ, 271). Furthermore, the "call of conscience has the character of an *appeal* to Dasein by calling it to its ownmost potentiality-for-Being-its-Self" (SZ, 269). We will get to considering what he means by "ownmost potentiality-for-Being-its-Self" in what follows, but from these passages early in his discussion of conscience, it is clear that Heidegger sees the call of conscience as having the conative force to move us toward an authentic mode of existing. He varies his language here—in the first passage quoted referring to the call as a "push," while in the second referring to it as an "appeal"—but to use the language that I have throughout, the call of conscience is what pulls us toward authentic existence.

The pull that the call of conscience exerts is a bit different from what occurs in everyday actions. Remember that I have been maintaining that the orienting component structures the situation that we find ourselves in such a way that various courses of action can stand out as meaningful and exert a pull on us. The conative component of everyday action is the being pulled that arises through the interaction of the agent with the surrounding world, and I have claimed that disposedness (*Befindlichkeit*) is Heidegger's formulation of this conative component in *Being and Time*. However, Heidegger repeatedly claims that the pull we experience from the call of conscience is not a form of disposedness but instead is a form of discourse. Heidegger makes it clear that the discourse of the call of conscience is not deliberative or adjudicative, as he states that "there is no corresponding counter-discourse [to the call] in which, let us say, one talks about what the conscience has said, and pleads one's cause" (SZ, 296). Instead, the call of conscience is a "summons" to take up authentic existence that does not lend itself to normal back-and-forth discussion (SZ, 273).

There are two features of this description of the call of conscience that I want to highlight. Since Heidegger focuses on the call of conscience and its character as a summons, he says that "to the call of conscience there corresponds a possible hearing" (SZ, 269–270). We have to be open to hearing the summons to be authentic, or in the terms I have been using in this chapter, we must be responsive to the call of conscience in order to act authentically. This is why I suggest that authentic agency and second-order responsibility are, like everyday agency and first-order responsibility, characterized by a particular responsiveness—a responsiveness to the summons of conscience. Thinking of Tugendhat's criticism as discussed in chapter 3, this in turn leads to another standard by which agents can be judged. In chapter 3, in the context of discussing the role of deliberation and practical reasoning in the Heideggerian account of agency, I suggested that there is an evaluative standard for judging actions on the Heideggerian view of agency insofar as productive actions can be judged on their suitability for actually making the end products, and other actions can be judged in terms of whether or not they successfully allow the agent to enact their operative self-understandings. In the first section of this chapter, I suggested that the language of first-order responsibility can be used as the evaluative description of the latter types of actions. Again, if an agent is responsive to the pull to perform the actions required to enact their operative self-understandings, then they are "responsible" in the first-order sense of the term. Now, we can say that an agent fails to act well, fails to be responsible in the second-order sense, when they fail to respond to the summons of conscience. Of course, at this point, I have not defined what the call of conscience is exactly calling us to do, but I do want to establish, to keep pushing back against Tugendhat's criticism bit by bit, that this does provide another evaluative standard for action from the Heideggerian point of view.

It has long been debated whether Heidegger thinks that there is some sort of obligation to act authentically, as I suggest in the above paragraph. I do recognize that it is not completely implausible to read him as denying such an obligation, but I want to go in the other direction here. The idea that there is an obligation to act authentically is reinforced by some of Heidegger's remarks in *The Essence of Human Freedom*. This idea of feeling pulled toward taking up a different way of existing is not confined to *Being and Time*. Heidegger says something similar in his analysis of Kant's categorical imperative in this later lecture course. There is always some difficulty in the interpretation of Heidegger's lecture courses in which he primarily seems to be explicating the thought of another philosopher (in this case, Kant), as there is always some question as to whether Heidegger himself endorses what he says in these lectures or whether he is merely doing his best to explain someone with whom he himself might not agree. With regard to *The Essence of Human Freedom* course, I would contend that in at least the last major section of the course, we find some of Heidegger's own thoughts and not merely his attempt to explain Kant's thought in Kant's own terms.

Heidegger is fairly dismissive of Kant's first formulation of the categorical imperative, maintaining that this specific formulation is a relic of the overly cognitive and rationalistic conception of human existence characteristic of the Enlightenment era. He states:

> If we observe ourselves in a completely unprejudiced way, without any assistance from philosophy, do we discover the categorical imperative as a fact within us? Do we discover as fact the demand: "So act that the maxim of your will could always hold at the same time as the principle of a universal legislation". We discover nothing of the sort. Instead, we find that this principle has its origin in philosophical thought, indeed in a specific philosophical system. . . . The categorical imperative of pure practical reason belongs to the Age of Enlightenment, to the time of the Prussia of Frederick the Great. Expressed in contemporary terms: the categorical imperative is a specific sociologically determined philosophico-ethico ideology, i.e. by no means is it the most general law of action for all rational beings as maintained by Kant. (GA 31, 286–287/196–197)

In effect, Heidegger is making a standard phenomenologist's move here—requiring that we bracket any historical or theoretical assumptions and constrain ourselves to what actually manifests itself in our experience of the world. Indeed, he goes on to claim that we do find something like the categorical imperative manifesting itself in the course of our actions. In his words: "The condition of the possibility of the experience of the law as fact is that we betake ourselves into the specific region of such facts, i.e. that we actually will. . . . Willing what? Everyone who actually wills knows: *to actually will is to will nothing else but the ought of one's existence"* (GA 31, 289/198). He is saying that we do experience the moral law in acting itself. More specifically, when acting, we experience the "ought of one's existence." As in his discussion of the call of conscience, here again he is saying that there is something experienced, at least at times, in our actions that calls us toward a specific mode of existence. Though he does not go into any detail, he even slips in a reference to conscience here, saying, "To be sure, one might say, this fact of an unconditional obligation may well exist, and if so is obviously connected with what we call 'conscience'" (GA 31, 291/199). There is this deep-seated experience of being summoned or feeling that one ought to take up a different mode of agency that appears both in *Being and Time* and *The Essence of Human Freedom*. So, I, again, want to suggest that just as first-order responsibility provides an evaluative standard for our actions, so does second-order responsibility insofar as we fail to achieve this latter sense of responsibility when we fail to be responsive to this summons to take up a different mode of agency.

Orienting Component of Authentic Agency

So far, we have only seen how Heidegger describes the pull we feel toward enacting a different mode of existence without saying anything about what this mode of existence would be like. When considering everyday agency, we have been using examples like being pulled toward grading papers in light of a self-understanding of being a professor or being pulled toward eating vegetables in light of understanding oneself as a healthy eater. Is there a self-understanding operative in authentic agency as well that allows us to hear and be responsive to the call of conscience or the pull of the "ought of existence"?

I want to suggest that Heidegger gives two different ways of thinking about the self-understanding operative in authentic agency, though, as we will see, both amount to the same thing. We find one of these ways, put in more Kantian terms, in *The Essence of Human Freedom*. As already mentioned above, Heidegger dismisses the universal law formulation of Kant's categorical imperative but maintains that there still is something right about Kant's idea that there is an experience of an "ought" present in agency. So, Heidegger sets out to reinterpret the second formulation of the categorical imperative in terms that he prefers. Recall that the second formulation of the categorical imperative states: "Act so that you treat humanity, whether in your own person or in that of another, always as an end and never as a means only."[3] The first step in Heidegger's reinterpretation of the categorical imperative is the consideration of what is meant by Kant's admonition to "treat humanity as an end [*Zweck*]." Heidegger states that an "end is what is represented in advance as the determining ground for the actualization of an object" (GA 31, 293/200). This sounds quite similar to his language in earlier works regarding projecting toward a for-the-sake-of-which that is to be enacted through our actions. The categorical imperative, then for Heidegger, is commanding us to enact humanity in our actions and have this understanding of ourselves as human be the guiding self-understanding of our action. The next question, then, is what is meant by "humanity" here. For Heidegger, humanity is to be understood as whatever is essential to being human (GA 31, 260/182). He proceeds to identify personhood (*Persönlichkeit*) as the essence of being human (GA 31, 260/182). Putting these pieces together, I take him to be saying that when we understand ourselves in terms of the essence of being human, we understand ourselves as persons. When this is the operative self-understanding in our action, then we are open to respond to the "ought of existence," as he puts it in this lecture course.

Saying that we should project ourselves toward being a person, though, still does not tell us much about the self-understanding operative in authentic agency. In *Being and Time*, Heidegger maintains explicitly that the projective element associated with being responsive to the call of conscience is a "projection of oneself upon one's ownmost Being-guilty" (SZ, 296). This makes some sense at the everyday level—to be responsive to the call of conscience, I must understand myself as guilty. From this starting point, Heidegger proceeds to analyze what is really at the core of our normal understanding of guilt. He isolates two main ways in which we (or at least German speakers) understand being guilty. The first common meaning of being guilty is captured by "owing something" or "having debts" (SZ, 281).[4] The second common meaning is "being responsible for something," in the sense of causing something to happen or bringing something about (SZ, 282). Together these two common meanings give us the general idea of "coming to owe something to Others," whether this be by breaking a law, coming to be indebted to other people, or being responsible for something done to other people (SZ, 282). It is easy enough to find experiential corroboration for this idea. We often feel guilty when we realize that we have done something that violates some norm or law or when we realize that we are responsible for doing something that harmed someone else. Heidegger does not stop here. He attempts to abstract from these normal ideas of being guilty to reach what he takes to be the underlying, unifying essence of what it means to be guilty. His first pass at a more formal conception of what it means to be guilty is: "*Being-the-basis* for a lack of something in the Dasein of an Other. . . . This kind of lacking is a failure to satisfy some requirement which applies to one's existent Being with Others" (SZ, 282). The idea is that when we feel ourselves to be guilty, there is a sense of a debt that has not been fully repaid or a rule that has not been followed. When we are addressed as guilty by our conscience, we are brought to an awareness of a certain lack in the way we are acting with respect to other people.

Heidegger wants to further push his conception of guilt past the common ways of conceiving it in order to bring out what is essential to the experience of guilt at the ontological level. He makes this clear by stating that the "idea of guilt must not only be raised above the domain of that concern in which we reckon things up, but it must also be detached from any relationship to any law" (SZ, 283). Bearing in mind the prior understanding of being guilty as showing some lack in one's actions, Heidegger defines the existential idea of guilt as "Being-the-ground [*Grundsein*] for a Being which has been defined by a 'not'"—that is to say, as "*Being-the-ground of a nullity* [*Nichtigkeit*]" (SZ, 283, translation modified). Here talk of violation of laws or norms or incurring debts with others is dropped, and Heidegger strips the concept of guilt down to what he sees as the essential core of being guilty—being the ground of a nullity. Ultimately, then, when Heidegger maintains that we are to understand ourselves as guilty, this is what he means—we understand ourselves as being the ground of a nullity.

At this point, Heidegger attempts to show how something like this existential conception of guilt is able to reveal the basic structural components of our being. He does this by examining the features of the main aspects of our existence discussed in Division I of *Being and Time*—thrownness (*Geworfenheit*), connected with disposedness, and projection (*Entwurf*), connected with understanding—and finding in each an essential nullity. With regard to thrownness, Heidegger says: "As being, Dasein is something that has been thrown; it has been brought into its 'there', but *not* of its own accord" (SZ, 284). By this Heidegger is emphasizing the fact that we come into a world that is not of our own making, and we do so through no choice of our own. Furthermore, "as being, it [Dasein] has taken the definite form of a potentiality-for-Being which has heard itself and has devoted itself to itself, but *not* as itself" (SZ, 284). Not only are we thrown into a world without our choice, but we are also always already existing in a certain way before we can actively choose how we want to exist. Heidegger makes it clear that we can never go back behind this initial thrownness and appropriate it in such a way that the nullity inherent in it is removed. The socio-historical situation into which we have been thrown is the basis for our being. No matter how we decide to move forward, anything that we do will have been done on the basis of the situation in which we find ourselves. This leads Heidegger to conclude that, "'Being-a-ground' means *never* to have power over one's ownmost Being from the ground up," and furthermore, this "'*not*' belongs to the existential meaning of 'thrownness'" (SZ, 284).

Heidegger then turns to the consideration of the nullity essentially involved in the projective aspect of our existence, which, as we discussed in chapter 1, he refers to as understanding, and I refer to as the orienting component of action. Connecting this idea to the nullity revealed by the experience of conscience, Heidegger says, "In having a potentiality-for-Being it [Dasein] always stands in one possibility or another: it constantly is *not* other possibilities, and it has waived these in its existentiell projection" (SZ, 285). What Heidegger is saying here is that in any given situation, when we project ourselves towards a particular self-understanding, we do so by foregoing other possible self-understandings. At every given moment there are possible ways of being that we are not taking up. To successfully enact any particular self-understanding is to simultaneously reject other self-understandings. This is the nullity contained in the very essence of the projective aspect of our existence and the orienting component of agency.

This is why he says that our existence generally is constituted by a nullity. Our essential ontological structures are defined in terms of nullity. I will provide further explanation of this in what follows, but I want to suggest now that understanding oneself as a person in *The Essence of Human Freedom* is equivalent to understanding oneself as being guilty, as being the basis of nullity in *Being and Time*. If understanding oneself as a person is understanding oneself in terms of the essence of being human as Heidegger would have it in *The Essence of Human Freedom*, and he maintains in *Being and Time* that the essential structures of human existence are defined by nullity, then understanding oneself as a person should be the same as understanding oneself as guilty. It might seem odd to insist on this convoluted equivalency at this point, but I am doing so to set up the following section. I ultimately want to get to what exactly it is that the call of conscience calls us to do. If it is right that we must understand ourselves as guilty (the orienting component) in order to be responsive to the call (the conative component), that still does not tell us much about the substance of acting authentically. This is where I find the language in *The Essence of Human Freedom* helpful. If the call of conscience is calling us to act in such a way so as to enact the self-understanding of being a person, that is getting closer to clear, intelligible directive.

The Directive of the Call of Conscience

Now we are at the point where we can consider what exactly the call of conscience calls us to do, or better put, what mode of agency it calls us to take up. This is not an easy task. As we discussed earlier in this chapter, Heidegger maintains that the call of conscience is a mode of discourse, but it is not the sort of deliberation about specific actions that one might expect. He goes as far as claiming that the call of conscience says "taken strictly, nothing. The call asserts nothing, gives no information about world-events, has nothing to tell" (SZ, 273). Nevertheless, he claims that "what the call discloses is unequivocal," and the "*direction it takes* is a sure one" (SZ, 274). This is why I think we can still say that, for Heidegger, conscience gives us a directive, pulls us in the direction of a certain mode of agency, though we still must work out how this is consistent with Heidegger's claim that conscience "asserts nothing."

As a first pass at articulating the directive given to us by the call of conscience, we can consider Heidegger's claim that we must take over the ground of our existence. In Heidegger's words, the "Self, which as such *has to* lay the ground for itself, can *never* get this ground into its power; and yet, as existing, it *has to* take over Being-a-ground" (SZ 284, translation modified, my emphasis on "has to"). Several lines down, he uses similar phrasing, claiming that this "ground is never anything but the ground for an entity whose Being *has to* take over Being-a-ground" (SZ 285, translation modified, my emphasis). In both places, we see the "has to" (*haben zu*) construction used to indicate the existence of a command, an imperative, dictating how we must act. We had assumed in chapters 2 and 4 that being the ground of one's actions was relatively unproblematic—this was just what was required for action to be possible at all. However, in his discussion of authenticity here, Heidegger does problematize the issue. In our normal everyday actions, it is really through our participation in the norms of the *das Man* that we are the ground for our actions. We are not the ground as individuals. The authentic agent is responsive to the call to "take over" the ground of their action as an individual. I do want to maintain my position in the earlier chapters that we are all the ground for our actions insofar as some individual commitment, even if only implicit, to some self-understandings is required for an individual agent to be pulled to perform any actions at all. There might be some slight difference in the way that Heidegger talks about this concept of "ground" in "The Essence of Ground" and *Being and Time*, though I am not sure how much hangs on this. As we saw in chapter 2, Heidegger claims that *Bodennehmen* is one of the two fundamental aspects of grounding. I interpreted *Bodennehmen* as more or less equivalent to disposedness (*Befindlichkeit*)—that aspect of our existence that allows us to feel the pull of certain actions, which provides "grounds" for acting. On my reading, every agent, even when acting inauthentically, must be "grounding" their actions in this sense. However, in *Being and Time*, Heidegger uses the noun *Grundsein*, "being a ground," in connection with the verb, *übernehmen*, "to take over" (SZ, 284–285). I take the implication to be that we are always the ground of actions in some sense, but since the self-understandings that orient our everyday actions are constituted by impersonal norms and biological constraints, there is also a sense in which we are not the ground of our actions as individuals, and acting authentically is a matter of taking over being a ground for one's own actions as an individual agent.

The crucial determination, then, is what to make of this command to take over the ground of our actions as individuals. I want to consider three different, plausible ways of interpreting this claim that I will argue ultimately prove to be unsatisfactory. First, there can be a tendency here to interpret Heidegger as promoting a sort of decisionism, according to which the way to be authentic, the way to take over being a ground, is to recognize that no external standards can be of use in making one's decisions and that the authentic individual takes the full weight of making decisions on themselves. Sartre's famous example of the student in World War II–era France, torn between staying in France to help his mother and going to Britain to join the resistance, is perhaps the paradigm of this view of authenticity.[5] If, as we have discussed, anxiety is a state in which the agent ceases to at all identify with any of their usual self-understandings, then perhaps authentic agency is a matter of making a committed choice with regard to which self-understandings one will take up going forward. Since the only evaluative standards available for making decisions are provided by the framework of some self-understanding or other, the choice to commit to a self-understanding at all exists outside of any evaluative standards. As we saw in chapter 3, this is Tugendhat's reading of Heidegger. If this reading is correct, then Heidegger's second-order responsibility might be similar to Kane's understanding of responsibility. There are certain moments, for Kane, when all external causal influences on our actions absolutely balance out, and it is completely up to the agent themselves to choose a course of action. These actions chosen by the agent shape their experiences and character going forward, so Kane can say that agents do have responsibility for their actions following these indeterminate, torn-decision moments. Heidegger himself encourages this interpretation when he says things like: "But on what basis does Dasein disclose itself in resoluteness? On what is it to resolve? *Only* the resolution itself can give the answer" (SZ, 298).

There are, of course, more nuanced interpretations of the directive to take over the ground of one's existence found in recent scholarship. Guignon develops a Frankfurtian reading, maintaining that being authentic is a matter of making a second-order decision, choosing to choose which self-understanding will be definitive for who one is an individual, which can be summarized in the following passage:

> If being caught up in average everydayness makes our doings unfree (or, more precisely, puts them outside the free/unfree distinction altogether), then being authentic should be a condition for our actions being characterizable as "free." In authenticity, we do indeed stand behind our actions: we own them and can own up to them. The actions are *ours*, where that means we can more or less wholeheartedly identify with them. Heidegger says that, in authenticity, we are fully "responsible" (*verantwortlich*) and not merely susceptible to being *held* responsible.[6]

Guignon, in this section of his paper, is primarily trying to explain what I have referred to in chapter 4 as existential freedom. The main idea here is that in our everyday actions, our actions are not our own—we merely act as anyone would in the given situation in which we find ourselves. It is really *das Man* that is the agent in these cases, not any one of us as individuals. These actions, on Guignon's view, are outside the free/unfree distinction. Truly free actions are, by contrast, ones that we can "own" and "wholeheartedly identify" with. I take Guignon to be saying here that we can own our actions by fully identifying with the self-understanding that provides the norms that guide our actions. Instead of unreflectively performing the actions that any professor would perform, I could instead wholeheartedly commit to my identity as a professor and take the norms definitive of this self-understanding as truly definitive of myself as a whole. This second-order choice would make my actions my own, and thus free, even though the specific actions I perform might be identical to the ones I performed before making this commitment. Guignon, then, more or less identifies this sort of freedom with true responsibility in Heidegger's sense. Though Guignon does not quote the specific passage from *Being and Time* here, I think it is fair to say that this is essentially his understanding of what it means to take over being the ground for one's actions. There is a choice to identify with a particular for-the-sake-of-which, and this also makes it so that the particular actions toward which we feel pulled are now "ours," even if the self-understandings that structure the situation of action are constituted by impersonal norms that are beyond the control of the individual agent. I see a small, but important, distinction between Guignon's view and the simpler, classic existentialist reading. Guignon's view allows for the possibility of being thrown into certain self-understandings that one cannot opt out of. Like the Frankfurtian compatibilist, Guignon's view makes it clear that we can be locked into certain self-understandings, while still maintaining that we can achieve true responsibility by choosing to fully identify with these self-understandings.

Finally, as discussed in chapter 3, Crowell, more than other commentators working in the Dreyfusian tradition, emphasizes the role of deliberation in action for Heidegger and proposes an account of Heideggerian responsibility as answerability—giving reasons for one's actions. Crowell criticizes those accounts of authentic agency that focus solely on the idea of wholehearted commitment, as he states, "this notion of commitment does not tell the whole story, for it does not reflect the specifically discursive aspect that, for Heidegger, belongs to taking over being-a-ground."[7] In this passage, Crowell points out, as I have done in this chapter, that Heidegger very clearly and repeatedly refers to the call of conscience as a mode of discourse, so scholars who construe authentic agency, taking over being a ground, solely in terms of commitment are missing something. This is why Crowell emphasizes, again as I do in this chapter as well, the etymology of "responsibility," or *verantwortlichkeit*, which contains the root word, *antworten*, "to answer." In his words, "To be responsible (*verantwortlich*) is to be *answerable*, and to be answerable for something is to be accountable for it, that is, to be prepared to *give* an *account* of oneself."[8] If we recognize the basic point about the call of conscience being a mode of discourse, then it could very well make sense to see "responsibility" as providing answers or reasons for one's actions. Indeed, throughout his work, Crowell plays on the dual meaning of *Grund* as reason and ground, which is why Crowell claims "to take over the ground into which I am thrown is to see my inclinations in a *normative* light, that is, as 'possible' rather than inevitable grounds of my behavior; it is to see them as potentially *justifying* reasons."[9] We considered this idea from Crowell in chapter 4 in the context of understanding Heideggerian freedom. Here, in this passage, Crowell makes it clear that he sees taking over being a ground as transforming those inclinations and normative commitments into which we have been thrown into grounds rather causes of actions by using them as justifying reasons. The idea seems to be that, for example, I might unreflectively be pulled to get in my car and drive to campus during any normal weekday in the middle of the semester. If someone asks why I am performing this action, I could give an answer, a reason, and say something like, "I understand myself as a professor, and being a professor requires that I go to campus on weekdays during the semester." In this sort of statement, I explicitly spell out which self-understanding orients my actions and which specific normative commitments are entailed by that self-understanding, thereby making it my own, in Crowell's view, and making myself answerable.

This is certainly one of those places where Heidegger's language is ambiguous enough to allow multiple different, plausible, and fruitful readings of his ideas, so I do not want to argue that any of the above are definitively misguided. I will, though, put forward and argue for my preferred interpretation of this directive to take over the ground of our existence. To put it succinctly, I take it as a command to embrace the finitude of our existence. This is not the sort of jejune, carpe diem interpretation sometimes elicited by Heidegger's analysis of being-towards-death, or a nihilistic interpretation claiming nothing matters, but rather it is the idea that we must act with the full recognition of the nullity inherent in all of the fundamental aspects of our existence, a nullity which is revealed by the call of conscience. Interpreting taking over being a ground in this way allows us to make sense of Heidegger's claim that the call of conscience says nothing but still pulls us in a definite direction. When he states that conscience says nothing, he means that the call of conscience is pulling us toward the recognition and embrace of the nullity or nothingness at the core of our existence. This is why Heidegger can claim that "though the call gives no information, it is not merely critical; it is *positive*" (SZ, 288).

In pulling us to embrace the nullity or finitude of our existence, the call of conscience is giving us some specific, that is, positive, directive to take up.

Obviously, this requires quite a bit of unpacking. As laid out above, the orienting component of authentic agency is the self-understanding of being guilty. Recall that being guilty, for Heidegger, means "*Being-the-ground of a nullity*" (SZ, 283, translation modified). So, taking over being a ground means embracing the nullity that is essentially constitutive for both disposedness and understanding. With regard to disposedness, the idea is that we come into the world as thrown into various self-understandings that we cannot opt out of. The self-understandings that make up our identity are always at least partially out of our control. I take the directive to take over the ground of our existence, or embrace the finitude of our existence, as I put it here, mean that we must own up to this fact of our existence, recognizing that we have, without ever making a choice, been thrown into various self-understandings that we cannot discard. So, we must find a way to enact these self-understandings with full recognition that we have *not* chosen them and can*not* opt out. What are the examples of ways of existing that pre-exist any voluntary choice on the part of the agent and cannot be completely discarded? For all of us, there are various aspects of our identity over which we have no control—being a native citizen of a certain nation, being someone's child, living in a certain historical era, being a creature who needs food, etc. It can be argued that, say, someone can always leave the nation one was born in, cut off all contact with one's parents, or shun all modern technology, but in each of these cases, distancing oneself from the circumstances in which one initially finds oneself still means that one has been thrust into a self-understanding that one did not choose, but that one nevertheless must enact it in some way, even if that enactment is trying to minimize the extent to which one identifies with that self-understanding. I take Heidegger to mean something like this when he states, "'Being-a-ground' means *never* to have power over one's ownmost Being from the ground up" (SZ, 284, translation modified).

I suggest too that this is a key component of being a person. Being a person requires the recognition that one must enact these sorts of self-understandings in some way and cannot just ignore them. For instance, I must understand myself at least partially as an American living in the twenty-first century and enact that self-understanding in some way. In my view, I would fail to properly be a person if I did not grapple with the fact that I have been thrown into this self-understanding and find it binding for myself in some sense. I would have to reflectively take up this way of existing for the sake of being a person, not for any more concrete, particular reason. In other words, I would try to enact a way of being an American not out of some sense of patriotism or, say, social pressure, but rather solely because this is one of the ways of existing that I have been thrown into, and I must take up in some way if I am to properly enact the self-understanding of being a person. In my view, second-order responsibility does not dictate how one must enact this self-understanding, but rather it dictates that one must reflectively let oneself be bound by this self-understanding and enact it in some way *for the sake of being a person*.

Taking over being a ground is not just embracing the finitude of existence with regard to thrownness and disposedness. Recall that understanding and projection toward a for-the-sake-of-which are also essentially constituted by nullity for Heidegger. Here, the idea is that the successful enactment of some finite number of self-understandings is only possible when we do *not* take on other self-understandings. We are often tempted to think that we can do all sorts of things, be all sorts of people, failing to grapple with the limitations placed upon us by the amount of time and energy we have. Trying to take on too many self-understandings at once leads to a failure to adequately enact any of them. I recognize, for instance, that committing to being, say, a competitive tennis player in my prime athletic years means that I am foregoing the possibility of being a competitive soccer player. Similarly, with scholarly pursuits, one might be able to attain a high level of competency in several academic disciplines, but there is a limit, and committing, say, to being a philosopher and a physicist probably means accepting that one cannot also be an economist. This is, I suggest, a key part of being a person—recognizing that one's choice to be a certain type of person means not being able to take up other self-understandings and not falling prey to the inclination to quickly bounce from one self-understanding to another without fully inhabiting and enacting any of them. Again, the important characteristic of the agent who achieves second-order responsibility is that they act for the sake of being a person. They do not drop or forego certain self-understandings because they no longer find them interesting, or it is no longer popular to play a certain sport. Rather, they discard or forego certain self-understandings with the awareness that this is what is required to successfully enact the self-understanding of being a person.

Now that I have sketched out my reading of the directive to take over being a ground, we can consider why I prefer this reading over the others mentioned above. This, again, is done not just for the sake of arguing against competing scholarly interpretations but rather to highlight what I take to be some important benefits of my interpretation. Starting the classic existentialist, decisionist reading of taking over being a ground, I would suggest that my interpretation is more substantive in that it is able to make sense of and incorporate more aspects of Heidegger's account of authenticity, not just a few select passages from Division II of *Being and Time* but, more importantly, if my reading is correct, then there are some fairly robust evaluative standards built into Heideggerian authentic agency. I will lay out what I take these standards to be in the next section, but I just want to point out here that I take this to be key advantage of my reading over the decisionist reading.

Turning to Guignon's reading, we might say that it works well enough for certain obviously socially defined self-understandings such as being a professor. If being a professor is something that I had just drifted into, unreflectively being pulled to perform actions that align with the norms that define this role, it makes sense to say that I can take over being the ground for my actions by reflectively making the second-order choice to fully embrace the identity of being a professor. Even though he does not necessarily highlight this, I also think this sort of account could work reasonably well with my suggested focus on the nullity inherent in the capacity for projecting upon and taking on various self-understandings. Making this sort of second-order choice to wholeheartedly identify with one or a small handful of possible self-understandings to the exclusion of others can be a way of acting that embraces the nullity and finitude inherent in our existence. I do, though, have some worries about reducing the idea of taking over the ground of one's existence to this idea of ownership through the second-order choice to wholeheartedly identify with a certain self-understanding. One issue is that some of Heidegger's comments in his analysis of being-towards-death suggest that it is fundamentally part of our existence that we cannot wholeheartedly identify with any specific self-understanding. For instance, he claims that death "gives Dasein nothing to be 'actualized,' nothing which Dasein, as actual, could itself *be*" (SZ, 262), while still maintaining that "death is Dasein's *ownmost* possibility" (SZ, 263). I take this to mean that in confronting the fact of our mortality, we realize that even when all everyday self-understandings drop away, we still exist as possibility. This is why death is our "ownmost" possibility. In being-towards-death, we realize that our existence is such that it can never be fully actualized in any particular everyday self-understanding. It is not possible to achieve the sort of total identification with any self-understanding, as Guignon seems to advocate. This might seem like a minor point, but I do think remembering the impossibility of this sort of total identification does illuminate an important aspect of being a person. We recognize that we do as a matter of fact operate with an understanding of ourselves as certain types of people, and it is this projection toward particular self-understandings that makes it possible for actions to exert a pull on us, but simultaneously, we have to face up to the fact that we can never completely identify with any particular self-understanding or even cluster of self-understandings. Our existence always extends beyond that. This is one of the challenges of being a person—recognizing that one must act with a commitment to the norms and constraints that define one's self-understanding while being aware that one can never totally make those norms and constraints one's own. There is always a gap, a nothingness, between ourselves and the self-understandings that we take on. As I suggest in chapter 1, this gap can explain weakness of the will, and as I suggest in chapter 4, this gap can explain Heidegger's understanding of freedom as letting ourselves be bound. Freedom is letting this gap collapse enough that we do feel bound by the constraints of some particular self-understandings so that we gain grounds for action and are able to act at all.

A second issue with Guignon's reading is that it might not work as well with different types of for-the-sake-of-whichs. Suppose we have a biological self-understanding such as being a creature who needs to eat. This is, of course, something that all of us, at least for the early years of our lives, take on unreflectively. We eat when we are hungry, and we eat what is provided to us by our caregivers without much thought. It strikes me as odd to say that one can become an authentic eater by wholeheartedly identifying oneself with this self-understanding. It is certainly true that many people become more reflective about how they should enact this self-understanding as they mature, considering, for example, whether it is ethical to eat meat or produce picked by exploited workers, or whether it is healthy to eat lots of foods high in sugars. But would we want to say that this more reflective enactment of this self-understanding boils down to wholehearted identification? I would suggest not. Instead, I would say we have in the case of the more reflective eater a recognition that they have been into a certain way of existing that is partially definitive for who they are, and now they are called to make something of that, that is, respond to the call to enact that way of existing in some particular way. I might feel that I should eat foods with less processed sugar and more organic fruits and vegetables. By doing so, I am not wholeheartedly identifying myself as a healthy eater; indeed, I might not even like abiding by these guidelines, but I feel that this is the best way to deal with this possible way of existing into which I have been thrown and whose defining power over my existence I cannot override. This need not occur only with biological self-understandings, either. As discussed above, there are other ways that we are thrown into self-understandings that are beyond our control—being an American, being someone's child, etc.—and I argue that being a person involves finding some way to successfully enact these self-understandings and reflectively letting oneself be bound by them.

This contrast with Guignon's view highlights the advantage of the Kantian reading of an experience of an "ought" at the core of our existence, according to which we need not wholeheartedly identify with the for-the-sake-of-whichs into which we have been thrown but rather can have a more grudging acceptance of a duty to enact them. I would suggest that we successfully take over being a ground for our existence when we reflectively and explicitly let ourselves be bound by the self-understandings into which we have been thrown from a responsiveness to the call to be persons. The wholehearted identification, if there is one here, is with the formal understanding of oneself as a person, not any specific socially or biologically defined self-understanding. I let myself be bound by, for instance, the self-understanding of being a creature who needs food, not because I find something especially important about that particular self-understanding and choose to fully identify with it but rather because I recognize that to properly enact the self-understanding of being a person, I will need to let myself be bound by the self-understandings into which I have been thrown and cannot discard. Following a Kantian formulation, we can say that a responsible agent in the second-order sense is one who acts for the sake of being a person.

Finally, we can turn to the consideration of Crowell's view. In chapter 3, I explained why I am sympathetic to Crowell's claim that deliberation is more a part of everyday Heideggerian agency than Dreyfus acknowledges, while still having some differences of opinion over what exactly Heideggerian deliberation in everyday agency looked like. Here I will explain why I am less sympathetic to Crowell's understanding of responsibility as answerability or reason-giving. I maintain, as laid out above, that there is a form of discourse in authentic agency for Heidegger, but it is fairly clear that Heidegger does not take this discourse to be nearly as concrete and specific as the formulation of explicit statements to justify actions. Again, as discussed in chapter 3, I think Crowell is motivated to put forward this conception of responsibility as giving reasons in large part due to his desire to defend the Heideggerian view from criticisms such as Tugendhat's that Heidegger's account of authenticity leaves us with no rational, evaluative standards by which to decide how we should evaluate or judge the actions of others. I have tried to show in the previous sections how the call of conscience, even while saying nothing, does give a positive directive to us. Now, in the following section, I will show how my view of conscience and second-order responsibility still involves some robust evaluative standards, perhaps allaying Crowell's worries.

The Evaluative Standards of Second-Order Responsibility

If I am right in maintaining that first-order responsibility provides some rational, evaluative standard for judging actions but does not necessarily condemn the enactment of clearly immoral self-understandings (e.g., being a Nazi), is there a properly moral normativity to be found in second-order responsiveness, which, on my reconstruction, involves a responsiveness to a deeply felt experience of the "ought of existence"? As with first-order responsiveness, I do think there is a rational, evaluative standard here, but I do not think it is necessarily a morally normative standard. As I suggested with regard to first-order responsibility, an agent can fail to be responsible in two ways: not being at all responsive to the pull to perform the actions required by their operative self-understandings or failing to properly judge which actions are required to enact their operative self-understandings.

The same two modes of failure hold for second-order responsibility. Just as one can fail to be properly responsive in the first-order sense by failing to be pulled at all toward the actions required to enact specific self-understandings, one can fail to be properly responsive in the second-order sense by failing to be at all responsive to the call of conscience. And indeed, Heidegger calls this failure to be open to the call of conscience inauthenticity, and as we saw earlier, he maintains that there is no true responsibility in this mode of agency. The other form of failure possible with regard to second-order responsibility is to fail to properly enact the operative self-understanding of being a person. This failure is a bit more complicated to explain. As I laid out above, I understand the directive to take over the null ground of one's existence as a directive to let oneself be bound by the self-understandings into which one has been thrown and cannot opt out of and make the choice to forego possible understandings that one could not successfully enact, embracing the finitude inherent in both disposedness and understanding. Understood this way, the directive of the call of conscience does give us some evaluative standards for which self-understandings one should adopt. With regard to our disposedness, second-order responsibility requires that we correctly understand which self-understandings we have been thrown into and cannot opt out of. One of the examples I have given of such an understanding is being someone's child. All of us are thrown into this self-understanding and cannot opt of it, even if one can enact this self-understanding in different ways, and in the extreme, enact it by disowning one's parents and cutting off contact with them. The standard of second-order responsibility does not dictate how one must enact this self-understanding, but rather it dictates that one must reflectively let oneself be bound by the self-understanding and enact it some way for the sake of being a person. There are a host of biological self-understandings that belong in this category of self-understandings that we are thrown into and cannot opt out of, but there are self-understandings purely defined by social norms that apply here too. Everyone is thrown into being the citizen of a certain country at birth. Again, one can enact this self-understanding in different ways, even the extreme one of renouncing one's birth citizenship and becoming a citizen of a different country, but second-order responsibility requires that everyone reflectively let themselves be bound by some variation of this self-understanding. Again, this evaluative standard of second-order responsibility would not definitively rule out enacting clearly immoral self-understandings, but it would provide a standard for judging agents who fail to reflectively bind themselves to certain self-understanding into which they have been thrown.

There is also a rational, evaluative standard pertaining to the other fundamental component of human existence: understanding. With regard to understanding, I suggested that embracing one's finitude here amounts to recognizing that one cannot project oneself toward too many self-understandings, as doing so would make it impossible to successfully enact any of them. Being responsible in the second-order sense is recognizing the limits of one's time, energy, physical abilities, etc. and reflectively foregoing or discarding certain possible self-understandings so that one can successfully enact others for the sake of being a person. It is, as discussed above, not enough to drop certain self-understanding because one is bored of it, socially pressured to drop it, etc. Responsibility here involves a reflective paring down of self-understandings for the sake of being a person. Again, there is no prohibition on adopting specific self-understandings, but there is still an evaluative standard that allows to judge that someone fails to properly be a person when they have too many operative self-understandings and do not pare them down.

All of these considerations are unlikely to be fully satisfactory to a critic of Heidegger who faults him for not including in his thought some principle that could be used to clearly rule out adopting immoral self-understandings. I am not engaging in full-blown Heidegger apologetics here, arguing that if one understands and configures things just so, then one can fashion a standard for criticizing, say, enacting the self-understanding of being a Nazi. I do, though, want to argue that there are more robust rational, evaluative standards built into the Heideggerian conceptions of agency and responsibility than his critics typically recognize. There is something correct in the decisionism accusation of Heidegger's notion of authenticity leveled by critics like Tugendhat in that second-order responsibility, even on my account, provides neither prohibitions of specific self-understandings nor prohibitions of specific enactments of various self-understandings nor prescriptions to adopt specific self-understandings or specific ways of enacting those self-understandings. Those specifics still are dependent on the situation into which the individual agent has been thrown. My view, however, does provide some evaluative standard by which one can judge an agent to have failed to successfully enact the self-understanding of being a person. So, I would suggest that second-order responsibility, like first-order responsibility, does not include a truly moral normative standard but includes a fairly robust nonmoral evaluative standard. As I also maintained with first-order responsibility, it seems in some ways unfair to fault the Heideggerian account of responsibility for not including built-in moral principles that could be used to condemn certain immoral actions when mainstream accounts of responsibility do not do this either.

Some might be tempted by another route of finding some substantive moral standard imbedded in this conception of second-order responsibility. Almost since the first publication of Heidegger's account of authenticity, the criticism has been lodged against him that he does not provide a satisfactory account of how relations with other people factor into being authentic, perhaps most famously by Emmanuel Levinas.[10] To be sure, he includes cryptic references to authentic engagement with others in his discussion of authenticity, such as the claims that "when Dasein is resolute, it can become the 'conscience' of Others," and, "only by authentically Being-their-Selves in resoluteness can people authentically be with one another—not by ambiguous and jealous stipulations and talkative fraternizing in the 'they'" (SZ, 298). However, he fails to give any systematic or more concrete explanation of what this would look like. Now, one might think that given my focus here on the connection between responsibility and responsiveness, there might be a possibility for filling in the gaps left by Heidegger and attempting to provide some account of how responsiveness also means being responsive to the existence and needs of other people. I will not take up this possibility, as I tend to side more with the critics in this case. In my account of first-order responsiveness developed here, the responsive agent is pulled to perform the actions that align with the norms of their operative self-understandings, and frequently this could mean being responsive to the needs of others around them. If I understand myself as a professor, my being properly responsive would involve showing some concern for the needs of my students. But I think this is a sort of indirect responsiveness to others, insofar as the real basis of judging me to be appropriately responsive is whether I am properly enacting the self-understanding that is operative *for me*. It just so happens that sometimes being responsive to the actions that align with my self-understanding means that I will be concerned about the needs of others.

Similarly, one might think that Heidegger's invocation of Kant's categorical imperative in *The Essence of Human Freedom* could provide a way to connect my account of second-order responsiveness to an authentic responsiveness to others. After all, Kant says that we treat humanity, whether in our selves *or others*, as an end in itself and never merely as a means. Again, though, I think this stretches the textual evidence Heidegger leaves us farther than I am comfortable with. As I have laid out in this chapter, he emphasizes the respect for personhood (*Persönlichkeit*) demanded by the categorical imperative and then equates personhood with *self*-responsibility, which I have argued means a second-order responsiveness to the call to take over the ground of one's existence. This second-order responsiveness again might very well indirectly mean being concerned with others at the practical level. For instance, I have been using the example of being someone's child as a self-understanding by which the responsible agent must reflectively let themselves be bound. One might think that this provides a moral directive to, for example, take care of one's parents as they age. However, I have maintained that a responsible agent should let themselves be bound by this self-understanding for the sake of being a person, not because of a direct responsiveness to others, even if a side-effect of achieving second-order responsibility is in fact taking care of one's parents as they age. I would not, therefore, characterize this as a brute, direct concern for the other of the sort that a critic like Levinas would want.

Locating the Self in Second-Order Responsibility

As mentioned at the outset of this section, I do agree with the general thrust of those scholars who see the establishment of a true first-person perspective as a key component of authentic agency for Heidegger. We are now in a position to see how my account of second-order responsibility also involves a self-directed component in a way that everyday agency does not. Remember that in our everyday actions, that to which we are responding are actions available to us in our situation of action. We are drawn out to perform certain actions through our interaction with the world around us. If one wants to maintain, as I have, that this pull toward courses of action available in our situation is still made possible by our individual commitment to various self-understandings that structure the way the situation shows up to us, it can still be pointed out that these various self-understandings are shaped by social norms that transcend the individual agent and make it so that our being pulled to perform certain actions is more or less what it would be for any generic agent with our self-understandings in that situation. In other words, in our everyday actions, we are pulled to act by a surrounding world that transcends us, and this world is structured by social norms that transcend any of us as individual agents. First-order responsibility, then, is always a matter of being responsive to something external to the individual agent. I want to claim that second-order responsibility is differentiated by virtue of the internality of that to which the agent is responsive. As we have been discussing, second-order responsibility is achieved when the agent is responsive to the pull of the call of conscience or the "ought of existence," both of which are purely internal phenomena. This is why Heidegger restates of the categorical imperative in *The Essence of Human Freedom* as follows:

> Thus the categorical imperative says: before anything else, in all your actions, always act in your essence. The essence of person is this self-responsibility: to bind oneself to oneself, but not egotistically, i.e. not in relation to the accidental "I". To be in the mode of self-responsibility, to answer only to the essence of one's self. To give this priority in everything, to will the ought of pure willing. (GA 31, 293/200–201)

Second-order responsibility is self-responsibility in that it is a responsiveness to something internal to the self—the pull to enact the self-understanding of personhood. There is an internal directionality to this responsiveness, or perhaps better, a self-directed responsiveness. Heidegger expresses the same idea in *Being and Time*, though perhaps in slightly more difficult language. He says things like, "*In conscience Dasein calls itself*" (SZ, 275). Statements such as this imply that responsiveness to the call of conscience is again a self-responsiveness or self-responsibility.

The sense of self developed in authentic agency, though, goes further than that. There is something similar to Frankfurt's hierarchical model of responsibility here, as Guignon points out. In responding to the call to understand ourselves as persons, we take a reflective stance on all of the self-understandings that normally structure the world of our everyday existence and orient our actions. These everyday self-understandings are seen in light of the self-understanding of being a person, and it is this second-order stance toward our self-understandings that constitutes selfhood. When we act in such a way as to take over the null ground of our existence, we are constituting selfhood in that mode of agency. This is why Heidegger repeatedly says things like, "in understanding the call, Dasein lets its ownmost Self *take action in itself* in terms of that potentiality-for-Being which it has chosen" (SZ, 288). When properly responsive to the call of conscience and acting so as to take over being a ground, we actually constitute ourselves as selves in our actions.

Second-Order Responsibility and Ontological Freedom

In order to tie off the last thread, we can consider, as we did for first-responsiveness, the connection between freedom and second-order responsiveness. When we think of freedom as ontological freedom, again, freedom is a matter of opening up a space in which objects can manifest themselves and certain courses of action can appear as meaningful. Again, ontological freedom is equivalent to grounding—that interaction of the conative and orienting components of action that opens up a space in which possible actions can appear as salient to us as agents. Ontological freedom is a necessary condition for second-order responsibility too—it is the full description of the state of openness required to hear the call of conscience. In his words, "When Dasein understandingly lets itself be called forth to this possibility, this includes its becoming free for the call—its readiness for the potentiality of getting appealed to" (SZ, 287). Heidegger refers to this state of openness as "wanting to have a conscience [*Gewissenhabenwollen*]" (SZ, 270). He also calls this "wanting to have a conscience" resoluteness (*Entschlossenheit*) (SZ 270, 296–297). As has often been pointed out by Heidegger scholars, "resoluteness" has a very willful connotation in English, but the German *Entschlossenheit* has a more ambiguous meaning. It can mean being opened up, coming from the negative prefix, *ent-* that precedes the past participle of the verb, *schliessen*, meaning "to close," and being resolved, coming from the verb, *entschliessen*, meaning "to firmly decide or resolve." As a special type of ontological freedom, resoluteness is constituted by the projection toward a particular self-understanding, which we have already seen is being guilty, and a special form of disposedness, which we have not yet touched upon. Heidegger makes it clear that anxiety is the form of disposedness operative in resoluteness, since it is in anxiety that all of our everyday self-understandings drop out along with all of the solicitations to perform various salient actions in the world around (SZ, 296). When this world of everyday significance drops away, and our attention is no longer directed purely outward into the swirl of our daily activities, we are left open to hear the internal call of conscience. In this way, ontological freedom, albeit a special instance thereof, is also the necessary condition for the achievement of second-order responsibility.

NOTES

1. Francois Raffoul also takes this approach of working out a Heideggerian conception of responsibility as responsiveness in his work *The Origins of Responsibility* (Bloomington, IN: Indiana University Press, 2010), especially in chapter 7. He, too, makes it clear that Heideggerian responsibility cannot be understood in causal terms, and being responsible is not a matter of being the cause of one's actions in the right way. My approach differs from Raffoul's in that he seems to view Heidegger's discussions of responsiveness in *Being and Time* as the precursors of Heidegger's abandonment of any strong focus on individual self-identity and agency as his thought matures. In other words, Raffoul reads the responsiveness built into authenticity in *Being and Time* as the beginning of Heidegger's dismantling of the notion of the autonomous individual agent as he transitions to thinking of a non-subjective responsiveness to being as such. As I remark in the Introduction to this work, I do not disagree with those scholars whose work traces Heidegger's early thought into his later thought, with its shift away from a focus on individual agency, but following Heidegger down the path of such a shift is not helpful for my project here.

2. Taylor Carman's *Heidegger's Analytic: Interpretation, Discourse, and Authenticity in* Being and Time (Cambridge: Cambridge University Press, 2003) is perhaps the most prominent example of this. See especially chapter 6 of that volume, "Authenticity and Asymmetry."

3. Immanuel Kant, *Groundwork of the Metaphysics of Morals*, eds. Mary Gregor and Jens Timmerman (Cambridge: Cambridge University Press, 2012), 4:429

4. This works better in German. The adjective *schüldig* means "guilty," and *Schulden* means "debts."

5. Jean-Paul Sartre, "The Humanism of Existentialism," in *Existentialism: Basic Writings*, eds. Charles Guignon and Derk Pereboom (Indianapolis, IN: Hackett, 2001), 296–297.

6. Charles Guignon, "Heidegger's Concept of Freedom, 1927–1930," in *Interpreting Heidegger: Critical Essays*, ed. Daniel Dahlstrom (Cambridge: Cambridge University Press, 2011), 87.

7. Steven Crowell, *Normativity and Phenomenology in Husserl and Heidegger* (Cambridge: Cambridge University Press, 2013), 211.

8. Crowell, *Normativity and Phenomenology in Husserl and Heidegger*, 211.

9. Crowell, *Normativity and Phenomenology in Husserl and Heidegger*, 299.

10. See his *Totality and Infinity*, trans. Alphonso Lingis (Pittsburgh: Duquesne University Press, 1969).

Chapter 6

Concluding Thoughts

After doing the heavy lifting of putting together what I hope are coherent and plausible Heideggerian accounts of agency, freedom, and responsibility and their interconnections, I want to conclude by thinking a bit about how this volume fits into the larger philosophical context. Despite having thought and written about these issues for the better part of a decade, this work still feels to some extent preparatory—the basis upon which more work can be done and further questions can be asked. It seems a bit audacious and presumptuous if I were to think that, say, one single chapter on freedom can definitively develop a Heideggerian conception of freedom and conclusively establish how this Heideggerian conception connects to and deviates from the mainstream free will debate. It is from this perspective of humility and acknowledgment of the insufficiency of what has come prior to this that I want to lay out my concluding thoughts on the work I am presenting here.

POTENTIAL WEAKNESSES OF MY ACCOUNT

As I mention in the Introduction, I am not aiming to give an exhaustive interpretation of Heidegger's early texts with regard to his analysis of agency, freedom, and responsibility. I readily admit that I focus on those works of Heidegger that are conducive to making the case I want to make and the passages within those works that do the same. There are certainly other works and other passages that might present problems for my interpretation of Heidegger on one point or another, but I hope that everything I have put forward here is based on his work and texts and has some level of internal consistency. So, I am not as worried about these potential exegetical weaknesses. One broader question that comes to mind, though, is whether, if I set aside my predilections as a Heidegger scholar, what I have presented is a truly compelling philosophical account of these topics or merely as close as one is likely to get if one is limited to working with aspects of Heidegger's thought. As a colleague asked me, "Do you actually believe what you are saying here?" I will not pretend to give anything like a full, decisive answer to that question, as it begins to feel like a whole separate project, but I would like to briefly consider some thoughts on this question.

I do feel as though there are some potential philosophical weak spots in the account I have put forward (and readers, no doubt, will have others to add). Perhaps the biggest potential weakness for me is the Heideggerian critique of causality that I lay out in chapter 2. Recall that Heidegger bluntly states that natural/efficient causality simply is temporal succession. One event precedes another, and we call the prior event the cause, and the latter, the effect. I argue then, from the Heideggerian position, that natural causality does not align with the fundamentally nonsuccessive temporality of human existence, so natural causality cannot be used to understand human agency at the fundamental level. Instead, we should see the interaction of the conative and orienting component of action and the process through which they bring actions about as fundamentally noncausal. My worry is that Heidegger is criticizing a very simplistic notion of causality and treats that notion of causality as the main (only?) version of the concept in modern philosophy and, presumably, among his contemporaries in the early twentieth century. At least as far back as Hume, there was the thought that causality is constituted not only by temporal succession but also by the constant conjunction of two events. So, it is not enough to say that one event preceded the other to establish a causal relation, but rather these two events must happen in the same order with regularity for there to be a causal relation between them.[1] Moreover, the understanding of causality in terms of constant conjunction could perhaps evolve in such a way so as to make the focus on temporal succession lessen and let the law-like regularity of the connection between the cause and the effect come to the fore. If this were the case, then could one see the operation of Heidegger's conative and orienting components as causal insofar as projecting toward a particular self-understanding will reliably allow the same actions to stand out as meaningful to the agent, even while still accepting that this operation is temporally nonsuccessive? Heidegger's description of everyday actions in terms of *das Man* and doing what anyone would do in a particular situation given a particular self-understanding might very well suggest this very constant conjunction understanding of causality, as might his emphasis on the binding character of freedom. Similarly, there have been influential counterfactual theories of causation.[2] The idea is that one event, C, is the cause of another event, E, when the "counterfactual 'if not C, then not E' is true."[3] So, if it is true that my television would not turn on without pressing the power button on the remote control, then we can say that pressing the power button on the remote control causes the television to turn on. Again, here, it is not immediately clear that temporal succession is essential to this theory of causality. In various examples throughout this work, I found myself using counterfactual language to describe the way that the adoption of various different self-understandings would result in different courses of action. For example, in some of my professor-related examples, I might claim that if I did not understand myself as a professor, the action of submitting an abstract to conference would not exert a pull on me. That seems like a counterfactual statement of dependence between the conative and orienting components of action, which would imply that their interaction is causal, again, even if it is not temporally successive.

And of course, if the argument against causal theories of action from chapter 2 is seriously weakened, then that will have implications for the Heideggerian account of freedom that I develop in chapter 4. If it turns out that Heidegger's account of grounding is more in line with a causal understanding of action than he thinks, that would imply that his conception of freedom might not depart as much as I suggest from the normal framework of the free will debate, and there might be more serious concerns about causal determinism for Heideggerian freedom. If Heidegger's account of freedom is brought closer to the mainstream free will debate, then it also stands to reason that the Heideggerian account of responsibility I put forward in chapter 5 would be as well. If grounding is actually to be understood in causal terms, then my notion of second-order responsibility as being responsive to the call to make oneself authentic by taking over the ground of one's actions starts to seem like it is merely saying that responsibility is about the agent being the cause of their own actions, in much the same way that responsibility is thought of in the mainstream responsibility scholarship. So, there is a great deal of weight placed on the anticausal argument in chapter 2, and if that argument falls, the arguments that follow it will at least wobble as well.

I do not want to attempt a full-fledged defense of the Heideggerian position here. Again, I do think the issue of Heidegger's critique of causality is a serious potential weakness that deserves more substantive and in-depth consideration than I will provide here. I do, however, want to point toward potential ways to shore up Heidegger's position. Both the theories of causality that focus on the law-like conjunction of events and the counterfactual theories do still claim that temporal succession is necessary for causality. Stathis Psillos, in his "Regularity Theories," maintains that there are three claims that make up the essential "kernel" at the heart of all regularity theories of causality:

c causes e iff

    i. c is spatiotemporally contiguous to e;
    ii. e succeeds c in time; and
    iii. all events of type C (i.e., events that are like c) are regularly followed by (or are constantly conjoined with) events of type F (i.e., events like e).[4]

Even while highlighting constant conjunction as the defining feature of these theories of causality, Psillos does claim that this conjunction must have a specific temporal ordering—the effect temporally succeeding the cause. Similarly, in her "Counterfactual Theories," L. A. Paul states that these theories "focus on counterfactuals concerning temporally successive, suitably distinct events C and E that describe cases where, if C had not occurred, E would not have occurred."[5] Again, even if the idea of counterfactual dependence claims are made the focus of these theories, they still rely on thinking about the effect as temporally succeeding the cause. These considerations leave me thinking that Heidegger might indeed have been too quick and too simplistic in his reduction of causality to temporal succession, but it might still be that temporal succession is a necessary, but not sufficient, condition for currently influential theories of causality. The other thing to notice in both of these general characterizations of regularity theories and counterfactual theories is that they think of causality as a relationship holding between two events. On the Heideggerian account of agency, the orienting and conative aspects of agency are not at all events. Enacting a self-understanding is a continual projecting toward a specific for-the-sake-of-which that is a fundamental aspect of our being, not some discrete event. Similarly, experiencing the world in such a way so as to be immediately drawn toward actions that matter to us is, again, a fundamental feature of our existence. Again, I do not take this to be a complete defense of Heidegger's position, but I do think there is room for more work to be done here to sort through how serious the threat to my Heideggerian argument against causal theories of action is from these more sophisticated theories of causality, such as regularity or counterfactual theories.

I would also suggest that even if the Heideggerian critique of causal theories of action largely fails, it might not be devastating for the Heideggerian accounts of freedom and responsibility that I develop in chapters 4 and 5. If grounding is indeed a causal interaction, it would make the resulting notions of freedom and responsibility less different from those found in the mainstream debate, but the Heideggerian conceptions of freedom and responsibility might still be seen as interesting views within the compatibilist cluster of theories. I argued that Heideggerian ontological freedom does provide an account of how we can be the origin of our actions without requiring the existence of alternative possibilities. I do not think that those fundamental features of ontological freedom change if one wants to argue that grounding is causal rather than noncausal. If grounding is causal, then perhaps the Heideggerian view of freedom would be seen as a compatibilist one insofar as we could still be said to be the origin of our actions because our actions have a certain causal structure that makes them free actions, and this would hold even if it is not possible to pursue alternative courses of action. Furthermore, my Heideggerian account of responsibility could still work as a compatibilist account of responsibility as it can be agnostic about the truth of causal determinism while still providing an account of the circumstances in which agents are responsible either in the first-order or in the second-order sense. This is not to say that I am ready to give up on the Heideggerian argument against causal theories of action, but if one were not persuaded by the arguments in chapter 2, I do think such a reader could still find chapters 4 and 5 interesting and plausible.

Another worry connected to Heidegger's argument against causal theories of action is that, as I laid out in chapter 2, he relies on his account of the nonlinear structure of human existence to do so. I have tried to make the best case that I can for the Heideggerian view in that chapter, but I must confess that sometimes I have a hard time completely buying into it myself. I think much of my discomfort is due to the stubborn phenomenological experience of much of our existence as a sequence of "nows" that proceed one upon another. This is not so much a philosophical worry as it is perhaps one of failing to mesh philosophical commitment with lived commitment. By this I mean that I do think Heidegger makes a strong argument that we should not understand the temporal structure of our existence in terms of successive "nows" at the fundamental level, and I understand this argument intellectually, but the concrete experience of temporality as straightforwardly successive is very difficult to shake. One point to make in Heidegger's favor here is that there is now a venerable tradition in modern physics and the philosophy of time to raise doubts about our phenomenological experience of the passage of time, albeit for different reasons from the ones that motivate Heidegger. So, one could ask if it really is so bold of Heidegger to ask us to believe that our normal, everyday experience of time is in fact not indicative of the fundamental nature of our existence. And if that is the case, are we so sure that it is farfetched to claim that the fundamental temporal structure of our existence is nonlinear?

POTENTIAL STRENGTHS OF MY ACCOUNT

Moving on, then, past the points that stick out to me as potential weaknesses, I want to consider the reasons why I find, as I finish this work, the Heideggerian accounts of agency, freedom, and responsibility developed here interesting and compelling, even if I might not be able to say that I am fully convinced. As I lay out in the Introduction, I had the hope that my Heideggerian accounts of agency, freedom, and responsibility could at least serve as interesting and somewhat plausible contrasts to some of the dominant views in those areas in the mainstream, Analytic tradition, and I do think that modest hope has been fulfilled. Even if I am not convinced by my own Heideggerian account, it still seems fruitful to explore these potentially overlooked ways of understanding these issues and working out rough ways that we can have meaningful conceptions of freedom and responsibility that do not get bogged down in the traditional debate over free will and determinism. Another claim I make in the Introduction that I hope has been borne out is that my account here would be a more unified Heideggerian account of agency, freedom, and responsibility than otherwise found in Heidegger scholarship. Again, even if I have concerns about specific aspects of the views I have developed here, and there are certainly parts that are underdeveloped, I do think the big picture hangs together fairly well. By that I mean that it is clear how the later concepts of freedom and responsibility are built upon the earlier work on a general conception of agency, and the connections between these concepts make sense (more or less).

Aside from just being reasonably satisfied that I paid off some claims made in the Introduction, I do think my work here establishes a rough framework for Heideggerian accounts of the three main concepts that can be built upon and extended in interesting ways. Throughout this work, I have used brief sketches of prominent positions in the mainstream scholarship to serve as contrasts to the Heideggerian positions that I develop. There is the possibility for a much more thorough engagement with contrasting mainstream views in future work, as I already suggested with the specific issue of causality. Also, as I mention in various endnotes scattered through the text, there is scholarship in the mainstream of philosophy of action that might align with and bolster the Heideggerian account that I put forward here. For example, I have already mentioned Michael Thompson's *Life and Action* as an example of a nonpsychologistic, somewhat Aristotelian account of action that has been influential in the philosophical mainstream. Also, Scott Sehon develops a noncausal, teleological account of action and a corresponding position on the free will debate in his *Free Will and Action Explanation*.[6] There were moments in the process of writing this book that I found myself going further into the weeds of mainstream scholarship than I intended and would pull myself back a bit when I caught myself doing this, as I very much intended this work to be primarily a work of Heidegger scholarship that put forward the most plausible Heideggerian view rather than a general work in the philosophy of action. However, I do think it would be very interesting and fruitful in future work to perhaps slacken the commitment to fidelity to Heidegger's texts and see if more loosely Heideggerian accounts of the central concepts considered here could be developed in closer dialogue with the mainstream debate—venturing further into providing arguments against opposing views and perhaps borrowing from those mainstream accounts more similar to mine to bolster the Heideggerian position.

Finally, I think it would be a very good idea to address recent empirical research pertaining to the topics discussed here. I feel that there is a tendency among Heidegger scholars to dismiss any empirical research on human existence and behavior as "merely ontic," that is, already locked into understanding humans as essentially present-at-hand things whose being can be measured and quantified, and thus fundamentally flawed and unworthy of serious engagement. I have two main objections to this tendency. First, Heidegger, especially in his early, most explicitly phenomenological work, is quite interested in describing concrete, everyday experience and is on the lookout for "phenomenological attestation" of his more abstract ontological analysis. While some empirical studies might contain philosophically questionable assumptions, social scientists often provide careful, detailed descriptions of how people act and experience the world in their everyday lives. It seems that there might very well be a missed opportunity for Heidegger scholars to support Heidegger's ontological analysis with some recent, rigorously obtained phenomenological attestation instead of just relying on their own or Heidegger's "armchair" accounts of what our concrete experience of the world is like.

For instance, in his seminal 1979 work, *The Ecological Approach to Visual Perception*, the psychologist J. J. Gibson introduced the concept of affordances. Gibson's claim is that animals (humans included) perceive the world around them in terms of how it affords them with various action possibilities. In his words, the "*affordances* of the environment are what it *offers* the animal, what it *provides* or *furnishes*, either for good or ill."[7] He provides multiple examples of affordances. Perhaps the most basic is the way that an animal sees a flat, horizontal, fairly rigid surface as something that affords support for it to walk.[8] However, he thinks this idea extends to all of the sorts of objects we are likely to encounter in our everyday activities. A longer rigid object might afford the possibility of clubbing or hammering something. A round object might afford the possibility of throwing or using it as a missile.[9] Gibson recognizes that "this is a radical hypothesis, for it implies that the 'values' and 'meanings' of things in the environment can be directly perceived."[10] What is important for Gibson is that in contrast to the dominant psychological views of the day that worked under the presumption that perception was a matter of the eyes and the mind constructing meaning from purely physical, meaningless visual stimulation, Gibson proposed that we (and other animals) directly perceive meanings in our environment in the course of our daily activities. As he states, "What we perceive when we look at objects are their affordances, not their qualities. . . . Phenomenal objects are not built up of qualities; it is the other way around. . . . The meaning is observed before the substance and surface, the color and form, are seen as such."[11] A chair, for instance, is immediately perceived as something that allows us to sit. We do not first have to perceive all of the individual qualities of the chair and then conclude that it would be adequate for sitting. Gibson is aware that someone might very well question whether he is proposing a subjectivist position that renders all properties of perceived objects relative to the particular observer. He responds by saying that an "affordance is neither an objective property nor a subjective property; or it is both if you like. An affordance cuts across the dichotomy of subjective and objective and helps us to understand its inadequacy. It is equally a fact of the environment and a fact of behavior. It is both physical and psychical, yet neither. An affordance points both ways, to the environment and to the observer."[12]

It is not novel to suggest that there are parallels between Gibson's account of our perceptual experience of the world and Heidegger's account of our existence as being-in-the-world.[13] Scholars I have mentioned here like Dreyfus, Kelly, and Wrathall all at times use Gibson's language of affordances to describe the Heideggerian view of agency. Of course, Gibson's work is clearly focused on explaining perception, and he uses the concept of affordances as a key part of that explanation. He is not yet providing a theory of motivation. It seems, though, that the implication is obvious. We experience the world around us as affording us with various possibilities for action, and these affordances are not merely in our heads but rather exist in the reciprocal relation between agent and environment. These affordances then solicit us or pull us to perform certain actions. Of course, this is only one example of a supporting connection that can be made between Heidegger's thought and recent empirical research in the social sciences, but I would hope that a more thorough exploration of recent research of this sort would lead to more interesting connections like that with Gibson. Finding such empirical support can only help the Heideggerian view.

The other general problem that I find with the tendency of Heidegger scholars to dismiss empirical research as merely "ontic" is that when there are experimental results that conflict with the Heideggerian views of agency and human existence generally, Heideggerians should still clearly explain why exactly they feel entitled to reject these results. Claiming that the scientific experimental approach is ontic is unlikely to persuade non-Heideggerian philosophers and almost certainly will not persuade the scientists actually doing the research. Here, again, I will not do a thorough review of relevant recent research, but I will point to another single example to show how I think this sort of more detailed Heideggerian criticism of empirical research could go.

Benjamin Libet conducted a now famous series of experiments purporting to show that there is an unconscious, neurological initiation of our actions that precedes any conscious intention to act.[14] Knowing that the performance of actions that we normally consider to be voluntary was preceded by an electrical change ("readiness potential") that could be recorded on the scalp of the agent, Libet developed an experiment designed to test whether an agent performing certain simple actions formed a conscious intention to act before or after the recording of this readiness potential. To do this, he asked test subjects to flick their wrists and report the time at which they became aware of the "wish or urge" to act. After repeated trials, Libet found that the readiness potential began approximately 400 milliseconds before the test subject reported being conscious of the intention to flick her wrist. He defines free will in a way that aligns with traditional philosophical views by saying that free actions must meet two conditions:

1) "There should be no external control or cues to affect the occurrence or emergence of the voluntary act under study," and
2) The "subject should feel that he or she wanted to do it, on her or his own initiative, and feel he or she could control what is being done, when to do it or not to do it."[15]

According to his experimental results and his interpretation of these results, the test subjects fail to meet the second condition, since the readiness potential begins to appear before the subject is conscious of her intentions, thereby implying that the agent cannot have conscious control of when their actions actually take place. From these results, Libet concludes that we do not have free will as traditionally conceived.[16]

It is certainly true that the presuppositions of Libet's experiment belie a "merely ontic" view of human existence and human agency that reduces the explanation of our actions to empirically observable physiological phenomena like electric charges traveling through nerves. However, the Heideggerian who is critical of these presuppositions can and should go further. Libet assumes that people can and do perform actions (like flicking their wrist) outside of any context and indeed seems to take these actions to be paradigmatic of agency as such. Based on the Heideggerian account of motivation that I develop in chapter 1, I would suggest that we ask what self-understanding the test subjects are enacting when performing the actions asked of them in these experiments. I think the likely candidate here is that of "test subject"; that is, participants in the study understand themselves as test subjects in this situation and will be pulled to take the actions that they think will allow them to successfully enact such a self-understanding. This might mean that they are concerned with following the instructions given by the researcher, doing "well" in the experiment, etc. On the account developed here, that self-understanding would allow for certain actions, such as a random flick of the wrist, to stand out as meaningful to the agent/test subject and pull them toward performing these actions. If my account is right, then it would be quite expected that the test subject is already engaged in the action of flicking their wrist before registering some explicit "urge" or "wish." Both the orienting component of action (the enacted self-understanding) and the conative component of action (the pull toward performing an action) do not essentially manifest themselves as discrete mental states available to internal inspection. The "urge" to act is the slightly retroactive attempt to name and reify the phenomenological experience of being pulled to perform a certain action.

Moreover, given the Heideggerian account of freedom developed here, we can say that the test subject's actions are still free. Libet presupposes that the subject must feel that they can "control what is being done, when to do it or not to do it," but I have attempted to show that there can be a meaningful sense of freedom that does not rely on the subject feeling like they "control" if and when they act. On the Heideggerian view, the agent can still very well be the ground of their actions by projecting toward a particular self-understanding that allows certain actions to appear as meaningful or even necessary, but being a ground need not mean having control, and indeed, as I argued in chapter 4, Heideggerian freedom is characterized by being bound in one's actions. Control, if it is important at all on the Heideggerian view, might only come up in the sense of letting ourselves be bound to perform certain actions. More would have to be said, obviously, to develop a thorough criticism of Libet's experiment and his conclusions drawn from it, but this is, again, a brief example of the sort of work that I think Heideggerians should be engaged in.

In sum, then, while I acknowledge that this work is undeveloped in areas and open to legitimate criticism and questioning, I do think that it also has served to sketch rough accounts of agency, freedom, and responsibility that can serve as the platform for future work in these areas.

NOTES

1. See Stathis Psillos's "Regularity Theories," in *The Oxford Handbook of Causation*, eds. Helen Beebee, Christopher Hitchcock, and Peter Menzies (Oxford: Oxford University Press, 2009), 131–157, for an overview of what Psillos calls "regularity theories" of causation.
2. See L. A. Paul's "Counterfactual Theories," in *The Oxford Handbook of Causation*, eds. Helen Beebee, Christopher Hitchcock, and Peter Menzies (Oxford: Oxford University Press, 2009), 158–184, for an overview of this approach to understanding causality.
3. L. A. Paul, "Counterfactual Theories," 158.
4. Stathis Psillos, "Regularity Theories," 131.
5. L. A. Paul, "Counterfactual Theories," 158–159.
6. Scott Sehon, *Free Will and Action Explanation: A Non-Causal Compatibilist Account* (Oxford: Oxford University Press, 2016).
7. James J. Gibson, *The Ecological Approach to Visual Perception* (New York: Taylor and Francis, 2015), 119.

8. Gibson, *The Ecological Approach to Visual Perception*, 119
9. Gibson, *The Ecological Approach to Visual Perception*, 125.
10. Gibson, *The Ecological Approach to Visual Perception*, 125.
11. Gibson, *The Ecological Approach to Visual Perception*, 125.
12. Gibson, *The Ecological Approach to Visual Perception*, 121.

13. Aside from the Heidegger scholars already mentioned, see also Vincent Blok, "Being-in-the-World as Being-in-Nature: An Ecological Perspective on Being and Time," *Studia Phaenomenologica* XIV (2014); Judith Effken Endre Kadar, "Heideggerian Meditations on an Alternative Ontology for Ecological Psychology: A Response to Turvey's (1992) Proposal," *Ecological Psychology* 6 (1994).

14. Here I am relying on his description of his work in "Do We Have Free Will?," in *The Oxford Handbook of Free Will*, ed. Robert Kane (Oxford: Oxford University Press, 2002), 551–564.

15. Libet, "Do We Have Free Will?," 552.

16. He does, however, allow for the ability to veto actions by choosing to stop the impulse to act in a way similar to that suggested by Sean Kelly, whose position we briefly discussed in chapter 4.

Bibliography

Aho, Kevin. "Logos and the Poverty of Animals: Rethinking Heidegger's Humanism." *The New Yearbook for Phenomenology and Phenomenological Philosophy* VII (2007): 1–18.
Aristotle. *De Anima*. Translated by Terence Irwin and Gail Fine. In *Readings in Ancient Greek Philosophy*, edited by Patricia Curd, S. Marc Cohen, and C. D. C. Reeve. Indianapolis, IN: Hackett, 2011.
———. *De Motu Animalium*. Translated by Martha Nussbaum. In *Aristotle's* De Motu Animalium, edited by Martha Nussbaum. Princeton, NJ: Princeton University Press, 1978.
———. *Nichomachean Ethics*. Translated by Terence Irwin. Indianapolis, IN: Hackett, 1985.
———. *Physics*. Translated by Terence Irwin and Gail Fine. In *Readings in Ancient Greek Philosophy: From Thales to Aristotle*, 4th edition, edited by Patricia Curd, S. Marc Cohen, and C. D. C. Reeve. Indianapolis, IN: Hackett, 2011.
Audi, Robert. "Intending." *The Journal of Philosophy* 73, no. 13 (1973): 387–403.
Bailey, Christiane. "The Genesis of Existentials in Animal Life: Heidegger's Appropriation of Aristotle's Ontology of Life." *Heidegger Circle Proceedings* 1, no. 1 (2011): 199–212.
Blattner, William. *Heidegger's Temporal Idealism*. Cambridge: Cambridge University Press, 1999.
Blok, Vincent. "Being-in-the-World as Being-in-Nature: An Ecological Perspective on Being and Time." *Studia Phaenomenologica* XIV (2014): 215–35.
Breivik, Gunnar. "Skillful Coping in Everyday Life and Sport: A Critical Examination of the Views of Heidegger and Dreyfus." *Journal of the Philosophy of Sport*, 34, no. 2 (2007): 116–34.
Carman, Taylor. "Was Heidegger a Linguistic Idealist?" *Inquiry* 45, no. 2 (2002): 205–15.
———. *Heidegger's Analytic: Interpretation, Discourse, and Authenticity in* Being and Time. Cambridge: Cambridge University Press, 2003.

Chisholm, Roderick. "Human Freedom and the Self," Lindley Lecture Series (University of Kansas Department of Philosophy, 1964), accessed on January 10, 2020, https://kuscholarworks.ku.edu/bitstream/handle/1808/12380/Human%20Freedom%20and%20the%20Self-1964.pdf.

Crowell, Steven. *Normativity and Phenomenology in Husserl and Heidegger*. Cambridge: Cambridge University Press, 2013.

Dancy, Jonathan. *Practical Reality*. Oxford: Oxford University Press, 2000.

Danto, Arthur. *Analytical Philosophy of Human Action*. Cambridge: Cambridge University, 1973.

Davidson, Donald. "Actions, Reasons, and Causes." In *Essays on Actions and Events*, 3–19. Oxford: Oxford University Press, 2001.

Davis, Bret W. *Heidegger and the Will: On the Way to Gelassenheit*. Evanston, IL: Northwestern University Press, 2007.

D'Oro, Giuseppina and Constantine Sandis. "From Anti-Causalism to Causalism and Back: A History of the Reasons/Causes Debate." In *Reasons and Causes: Causalism and Anti-Causalism in the Philosophy of Action*, edited by Giuseppina D'Oro and Constantine Sandis, 7–48. New York: Palgrave Macmillan, 2013.

Dreyfus, Hubert. *Being-in-the-World: A Commentary on Heidegger's* Being and Time, *Division 1*. Cambridge, MA: MIT Press, 1991.

———. "Could Anything Be More Intelligible Than Everyday Intelligibility?: Reinterpreting Division I of *Being and Time* in the Light of Division II." *Bulletin of Science and Technology*, 24, no. 3 (June 2004): 265–74.

———. "The Return of the Myth of the Mental." *Inquiry* 50, no. 4 (2007): 355.

Endre, Kadar and Judith Effken. "Heideggerian Meditations on an Alternative Ontology for Ecological Psychology: A Response to Turvey's (1992) Proposal." *Ecological Psychology* 6 (1994): 297–341.

Fine, Kit. "Guide to Ground." In *Metaphysical Grounding*, edited by Fabrice Correia and Benjamin Schneider, 37–80. Cambridge: Cambridge University Press, 2012.

Fischer, John Martin. "Compatibilism." In *Four Views on Free Will*, by John Martin Fischer, Robert Kane, Derk Pereboom, and Manuel Vargas, 44–84. Oxford: Blackwell, 2007.

Frankfurt, Harry. "The Problem of Action." *American Philosophical Quarterly* 15, no. 2 (Apr. 1978): 157–162.

———. "Alternate Possibilities and Moral Responsibility." In *The Importance of What We Care About*, 1–10. Cambridge: Cambridge University Press, 1988.

———. "Freedom of the Will and the Concept of a Person." In *The Importance of What We Care About*, 11–25. Cambridge: Cambridge University Press, 1988.

Gibson, James J. *The Ecological Approach to Visual Perception*. New York: Taylor and Francis, 2015.

Goldman, Alvin. *A Theory of Human Action*. Princeton, NJ: Princeton University Press, 1970.

Golob, Sacha. *Heidegger on Concepts, Freedom and Normativity*. Cambridge: Cambridge University Press, 2014.

Guignon, Charles. "Heidegger's Concept of Freedom: 1927–1930." In *Interpreting Heidegger: Critical Essays*, edited by Daniel Dahlstrom, 79–105. Cambridge: Cambridge University Press, 2011.

Han-Pile, Beatrice. "Freedom and the Choice to Choose Oneself in *Being and Time*." In *The Cambridge Companion to Being and Time*, edited by Mark Wrathall, 291–319. Cambridge: Cambridge University Press, 2013.

Hatab, Lawrence. *Ethics and Finitude: Heideggerian Contributions to Moral Philosophy*. Oxford: Rowman and Littlefield, 2000.

Haugeland, John. "Truth and Rule-Following." In *Having Thought: Essays in the Metaphysics of Mind*, edited by John Haugeland. Cambridge, MA: Harvard University Press, 1998.

Hume, David. *A Treatise of Human Nature*. Oxford: Clarendon Press, 1978.

Kane, Robert. "Introduction: The Contours of the Contemporary Free Will Debates." In *The Oxford Handbook of Free Will*, edited by Robert Kane, 3–41. Oxford: Oxford University Press, 2002.

——— *A Contemporary Introduction to Free Will*. Oxford: Oxford University Press, 2005.

——— "Libertarianism." In *Four Views on Free Will*, by John Martin Fischer, Robert Kane, Derk Pereboom, and Manuel Vargas, 5–43. Oxford: Blackwell, 2007.

Kant, Immanuel. *Groundwork of the Metaphysics of Morals*, edited by Mary Gregor and Jens Timmerman. Cambridge: Cambridge University Press, 2012.

Kelly, Sean. "Perceptual Normativity and Human Freedom." Philpapers Archive. Accessed January 8, 2020. https://philpapers.org/archive/KELPNA.pdf.

Kenny, Anthony. *Action, Emotion and Will*. London: Routledge, 1963.

Korsgaard, Christine. *Self-Constitution: Agency, Identity, and Integrity*. Oxford: Oxford University Press, 2009.

Lafont, Cristina. *Heidegger, Language, and World Disclosure*. Cambridge: Cambridge University Press, 2000.

Libet, Benjamin. "Do We Have Free Will?" In *The Oxford Handbook of Free Will*, edited by Robert Kane, 551–64. Oxford: Oxford University Press, 2002.

Liddel, Henry George and Robert Scott. *A Greek-English Lexicon*, revised and augmented by Sir Henry Stuart Jones. accessed January 4, 2020, http://www.perseus.tufts.edu/hopper/text.

Melden, A. I. *Free Action*. London: Routledge, 1961.

Mele, Alfred. *Springs of Action: Understanding Intentional Behavior*. Oxford: Oxford University Press, 1992.

Montero, Barbara Gail. *Thought in Action: Expertise and the Conscious Mind*. Oxford: Oxford University Press, 2016.

Nussbaum, Martha. "The Role of Phantasia in Aristotle's Explanation of Action." In *Aristotle's* De Motu Animalium, edited by Martha Nussbaum, 221–69. Princeton, NJ: Princeton University Press, 1978.

Okrent, Mark. "Equipment, World, and Language." *Inquiry* 45, no. 2 (2002): 195–204.

Paul, L. A. "Counterfactual Theories." In *The Oxford Handbook of Causation*, edited by Helen Beebee, Christopher Hitchcock, and Peter Menzies, 158–84. Oxford: Oxford University Press, 2009.

Pereboom, Derk. "Determinism al Dente." *Nous* 29, no. 1 (March 1995): 21–45.

Peters, R. S. *The Concept of Motivation*. London: Routledge, 1958.

Polt, Richard. "A Heideggerian Critique of Cyberbeing." In *Horizons of Authenticity in Phenomenology, Existentialism, and Moral Psychology*, edited by Hans Pedersen and Megan Altman, 181–99. Dordrecht: Springer, 2015.

Psillos, Stathos. "Regularity Theories." In *The Oxford Handbook of Causation*, edited by Helen Beebee, Christopher Hitchcock, and Peter Menzies, 131–57. Oxford: Oxford University Press, 2009.

Raffoul, Francois. *The Origins of Responsibility*. Bloomington, IN: Indiana University Press, 2010.

Ratcliffe, Matthew. *Experiences of Depression: A Study in Phenomenology*. Oxford: Oxford University Press, 2015.

Sartre, Jean-Paul. "The Humanism of Existentialism." In *Existentialism: Basic Writings*, edited by Charles Guignon and Derk Pereboom, 290–308. Indianapolis, IN: Hackett, 2001.

Schürmann, Reiner. *Heidegger on Being and Acting: From Principles to Anarchy*. Bloomington, IN: Indiana University Press, 1987.

Searle, John. *Intentionality: An Essay in the Philosophy of Mind*. Cambridge: Cambridge University Press, 1983.

Sehon, Scott. *Free Will and Action Explanation: A Non-Causal Compatibilist Account*. Oxford: Oxford University Press, 2016.

Sinhababu, Neil. "The Desire-Belief Account of Intention Explains Everything." *Nous* 47, no. 4 (2013): 680–96.

———. *Humean Nature: How Desire Explains Action, Thought, and Feeling*. Oxford: Oxford University Press, 2017

———. "The Humean Theory of Motivation Reformulated and Defended." *The Philosophical Review* 118, no. 4 (2009): 465–500.

Smith, Michael. "The Humean Theory of Motivation." *Mind* 96, no. 381 (January 1987): 36–61.

Taylor, Charles. *The Explanation of Behaviour*. London: Routledge, 1964.

Thompson, Michael. *Life and Action*. Cambridge, MA: Harvard University Press, 2008.

Tugendhat, Ernst. "Wir sind nicht fest verdrahtat: Heidegger's 'Man' und die Tiefendimensionen der Gründe." In *Aufsätze: 1992–2000*, 138–62. Frankfurt am Main: Suhrkamp, 2001.

Vogler, Candace. *Reasonably Vicious*. Cambridge, MA: Harvard University Press, 2002.

Winch, Peter. *The Idea of a Social Science*. London: Routledge, 1958.

Wrathall, Mark. "Autonomy, Authenticity, and the Self." In *Heidegger, Authenticity, and the Self: Themes from Division Two of Being and Time*, edited by Denis McManus, 193–214. New York: Routledge, 2015.

Index

anxiety (*Angst*), 18–19, 79, 89, 131, 144
Aristotle, xix, 1–9, 13, 27, 38, 43, 45, 61, 64, 68
authenticity, as authentic agency, xxi–xxiii, 17–19, 60–63, 71–72, 74, 77–80, 88–90, 92–93, 110–11, 114–16, 120–35, 137–43, 149

behavior (*Benehmen*), 92, 100–102, 105
being-toward-death (*Sein-zum-Tode*), 18–19, 89, 102, 133, 136
belief: as *dōxa*, 65–66, 68, 116; place in ontology of action, xiii, xix–xx, 1, 2, 4, 14, 20–21, 23–27, 31, 34–35, 42, 46, 48–51, 65–66, 68, 70–71, 77
bindingness (*Verbindlichkeit*), xxii, 101–7, 134, 148

Carman, Taylor, 67
categorical imperative, 125–27, 141–42
causality, xx, xxii, 32–34, 37–38, 41–44, 46–48, 54–55, 84, 88, 95–96, 98–99, 108–9, 113, 148–50
Chisholm, Roderick, 84, 94, 108, 113–14
compatibilism, xiv–xvi, xxi–xxii, 32, 84–87, 108–9, 113–14, 119, 132, 150

comportment (*Verhalthung*), 92, 100–102, 105
conative component of action, xix–xx, 2, 5–6, 13, 20, 23, 25–26, 35–36, 38, 42, 44, 46, 48–49, 51–55, 65–66, 69, 88, 95–99, 115, 117, 123–24, 129, 143, 148–50, 155
conscience (*Gewissen*), 62, 111, 123–24, 126–27, 129–30, 132–34, 138–39, 141–44
Crowell, Steven, xix, 61, 74–77, 95, 97, 102, 106, 132–33, 138

das Man (the one), 9–10, 15, 122, 130, 132, 148
Davidson, Donald, 2, 14, 31–33, 43, 48–51, 54
Davis, Bret, xvii–xviii
desire: as *ōrexis*, 4–5, 64–65; place in ontology of action, xiii, xix, xx, 1, 2, 4, 5, 20–27, 31, 34–36, 42, 46, 48–52, 64, 77, 84–86, 94
determinism, xiv, 32, 83, 85–86, 94–98, 101, 108–9, 151
direction of fit, 20–22, 27, 34–35
discourse (*Rede*), 64–65, 67, 74, 76, 124, 129, 132–33, 138

disposedness (*Befindlichkeit*), xx, 6, 14, 21, 39–40, 64, 67, 124, 128, 130, 134–35, 139, 144
distinguishing (*krīnein*), 3, 5, 7, 9, 11, 92
Dreyfus, Hubert, xiv, xviii–xxi, 10, 12, 22–26, 32–34, 42, 47–49, 60, 61–64, 67–68, 72–74, 104, 106

existential freedom, xxii, 88–90, 92–95, 100, 106, 109–11, 132

finitude, 133–36, 139–40
first-order responsibility, xxiii, 113–21, 123–24, 126, 138–43, 151
Fischer, John Martin, 85–87, 108, 113–14
for-the-sake-of-which (*Worumwillen*), 8–9, 11–16, 22, 26, 39, 44, 50, 53–54, 67, 90–91, 102, 105–7, 127, 132, 135, 137, 150
Frankfurt, Harry, 84–87, 94, 108, 113–14, 121, 131–32, 143
free will, xiii–xiv, xvi–xviii, xxi–xxii, 32, 37, 83–88, 93–97, 100, 107–11, 113, 117, 149, 152, 155

Gibson, J.J., 153–54
Golob, Sacha, 33–34, 42, 47, 51–55, 88, 90, 92, 94–98, 103–4, 110
ground (*Grund*), xxi–xxii, 34, 42–48, 50–52, 54–55, 96–100, 108, 110–11, 117, 128, 130–37, 139, 141, 143, 149–50, 156
Guignon, Charles, 88, 90, 93–95, 97, 110, 131–32, 136–37, 143
guilt (*Schuld*), 127–29, 134, 144

Han-Pile, Beatrice, 88, 90, 110
Humean theory of motivation, xix–xx, 1–2, 4, 15, 20–24, 26, 35–36, 42, 48

Kane, Robert, 83–85, 87, 94, 108, 113–14, 131

Kant, Immanuel, xvii–xviii, 33–34, 37–38, 45, 83, 103–4, 125–26, 137–38, 141
Kelly, Sean, 103–5, 154

Lafont, Cristina, 67
libertarianism, xiv, xvi, xxi, 32, 84, 86–87, 94, 107–8, 113–14
Libet, Benjamin, 154–56

mental states, place in ontology of action, xiii, 6, 20, 22–25, 31–35, 42, 46–49, 51, 55, 60, 62, 66, 73, 88, 96, 99, 109, 156
mood (*Stimmung*), 6, 39–41, 44, 89
movement (*Bewegung, kineīn*), 2–7, 26–27, 38, 45, 48, 52, 92, 123
movedness (*Bewegtheit*), 27

norms, 9–19, 51, 61, 80, 89, 91, 93, 103, 105–6, 116, 119, 121–22, 128, 130, 132, 136, 139, 141–42
nullity (*Nichtigkeit*), 128–29, 133–36

Okrent, Mark, 67
ontological freedom, xxii, 90–92, 95–97, 100–101, 104, 106–11, 117, 143–44, 150
orienting component of action, xx–xxi, 2–3, 5–7, 9, 13–14, 20–21, 23–25, 27, 35–36, 38, 42–44, 46, 48–49, 51–55, 63, 65, 68–69, 77–78, 95–99, 111, 116–17, 120, 122–24, 129, 134, 148–50, 155

passivity, 26–27, 34–35, 90
perception (*aīsthesis*), 3, 5, 7, 9, 153–54
Pereboom, Derk, 86–87, 113, 119
personhood (*Persönlichkeit*), 127, 129, 134–43
phrōnesis, 7, 61, 68, 70–71, 78
poīesis, 7–9, 71, 75–76
prāxis, 7, 64, 71, 75–76, 92

projection (*Entwurf*), 9, 14, 39–41, 44, 46, 50–51, 53, 66–68, 72, 74, 91–92, 102, 105–6, 117, 128–29, 135, 144

Ratcliffe, Matthew, 109
resoluteness (*Entschlossenheit*), xxii, 63, 79, 94, 106, 131, 141, 143–44

Schürmann, Reiner, xvii
second-order responsibility, xxiii, 113–16, 119–21, 124, 126, 131, 135, 138–44, 149, 151

tēchne, 7–8, 68, 70–71, 78
temporality, xx, 34, 37–42, 44, 47–48, 54, 95–96, 148–51
thrownness (*Geworfenheit*), 6, 12, 21, 128, 135
Tugendhat, Ernst, 63, 77–79, 120, 124, 131, 138, 140

understanding (*Verstehen*), xx, 7–15, 39–41, 64, 66–68, 74, 92, 128–29, 134–35, 139–40

weakness of the will, 17–19, 137
Wrathall, Mark, 61–62, 154

www.ingramcontent.com/pod-product-compliance
Lightning Source LLC
Chambersburg PA
CBHW051525230426
43668CB00012B/1742